Crime and the Internet

Is the Internet ⋯ d boy to
become the bigg ⋯ e all now
susceptible to c⋯ ⋯having to
leave the comfo ⋯ ⋯ave been
articulated since⋯ ⋯inologists
have been slow t⋯ ⋯at cybercrimes are, what ⋯ ⋯n remain
largely unanswer⋯

Organised int⋯ ⋯ crimino-
logical debates th⋯ ⋯ks at the
general problem ⋯ currently
understood by th⋯ ⋯hallenges
that are presente⋯ different
types of cybercri⋯ contemplates some of t⋯ criminal
justice system.

David S. Wall is⋯ ⋯Department
of Law, Universit⋯

Crime and the Internet

Edited by David S. Wall

London and New York

First published 2001
by Routledge
11 New Fetter Lane, London EC4P 4EE

Simultaneously published in the USA and Canada
by Routledge
29 West 35th Street, New York, NY 10001

Routledge is an imprint of the Taylor & Francis Group

Typeset in Goudy by Taylor and Francis Books Ltd
Printed and bound in Great Britain by The Cromwell Press, Trowbridge,
Wiltshire

British Library Cataloguing in Publication Data
A catalogue record for this book is available from the British Library

Library of Congress Cataloging-in-Publication Data
Crime and the internet/edited by David S. Wall.
p. cm
Includes bibliographical references and index
1. Computer crimes. 2. Internet. I. Wall, David, 1956 -
HV6773 .C75 2001

ISBN hbk - 0-415-24428-5
       pbk - 0-415-24429-3

Contents

Contributors

Yaman Akdeniz is a Lecturer in Cyberlaw at the University of Leeds where he teaches and writes about Internet related legal and policy issues. Yaman is also the founder and director of Cyber-Rights & Cyber-Liberties (UK), a non-profit civil liberties organization (http://www.cyber-rights.org/yamancv.htm) (Checked 29 June, 2001). He has given written and oral evidence on a number of occasions to governmental bodies which include committees of the European Union and the United Nations. His publications include *Sex on the Net? The Dilemma of Policing Cyberspace* (South Street Press, 1999) and *The Internet, Law and Society* (ed. with C. Walker and D. Wall, Longman, 2000).

Bela Chatterjee is a Lecturer in Law at the University of Lancaster. She completed her undergraduate degree at the University of Leicester before taking a Master's degree in Child Law and Policy at Brunel University. She subsequently conducted research into cyberpornography, cyberidentity and law for her doctoral thesis.

Louise Ellison is a Lecturer in Law at the University of Manchester and previously taught at the University of Reading. Her Ph.D., awarded in 1997 by the University of Leeds, was a comparative study of rape trials in England and Wales and the Netherlands. Her primary research and teaching interests are criminal law and evidence. Louise recently co-edited *Feminist Perspectives on Evidence* (with M. Childs, Cavendish, 2000) and is currently completing a monograph entitled *The Adversarial Process and the Vulnerable Witness* (Oxford University Press, forthcoming).

Peter Grabosky is a Professor in the Research School of Social Sciences at the Australian National University. He was formerly the Deputy Director of the Australian Institute of Criminology. In addition to his broad portfolio of criminological publications, Peter has published a number of books and articles that are specifically related to crime and new technologies. These publications include *Crime in the Digital Age: Controlling Telecommunications and Cyberspace Illegality* (with R. Smith, Federation Press, 1998) and *Electronic Theft: Crimes of Acquisition in the Digital Age* (with R. Smith and G. Dempsey, Cambridge University Press, 2001). In July 1998, Peter was elected President of the Australian and New Zealand Society of Criminology. In 1999 he was elected to the Board of Directors and became Deputy Secretary General of the International Society of Criminology.

Marjorie Heins is the Director of the Free Expression Policy Project at the National Coalition Against Censorship in New York City and was formerly director of the American Civil Liberties Union's Arts Censorship Project, where she was counsel in a number of major Supreme Court cases, including *Reno v. ACLU*. She is the author of *Not in Front of the Children: 'Indecency', Censorship, and the Innocence of Youth* (Hill & Wang, 2001), *Sex, Sin, and Blasphemy: A Guide to America's Censorship Wars* (New Press, 1993), and *Three Questions About Television Ratings*, in *The V-Chip Debate* (Lawrence Erlbaum, 1998). In 1998-2000, Marjorie was a fellow of the Open Society Institute, which supported much of the research for *Not in Front of the Children*.

Michael Levi is Professor of Criminology at Cardiff University. His major research contributions to criminology have been in the fields of white-collar crime and corruption, organized crime, money-laundering and violent crime, and his books include *The Phantom Capitalists* (Gower, 1981   originally Heinemann) and *Regulating Fraud* (Routledge, 1987). His new book, *White-Collar Crime and its Victims* (with A. Pithouse Oxford University Press, 2001), explores both the impact of fraud on individual and institutional victims and also their responses to it.

Paul Norman is the Director of International Programmes at the Institute of Criminal Justice Studies, University of Portsmouth. Paul is an interdisciplinary political scientist researching regional cooperation, international organizations and international police policy-making. His current research focuses upon regional cooperation in the southern African region. Paul leads for the Institute on an EU-funded collaborative degree programme which forms part of a major police reform programme in Mauritius. Paul's recent publications include 'European Union Police Policy-Making and Co-operation', in Carr, F. & Massey, A. (eds) *Public Policy in the New Europe* (Edward Elgar, 1999) and 'The Terrorist Finance Unit and the Joint Action Group on Organised Crime' (*Howard Journal of Criminal Justice*, 1998, Vol. 27, No. 4).

Ken Pease is a visiting Professor in the Jill Dando Institute at University College London. He was formerly the head of the Applied Criminology Group and Professor of Criminology in the School of Human and Health Sciences at the University of Huddersfield. He has worked on the issue of repeat victimisation for 12 years and on the British Crime Survey for 14 years. Ken's current work explores the anticipation of crime trends, and the results of all of his research have been published as Home Office Research Papers. Ken has acted as a consultant to the United Nations, the Council of Europe and the Customs

Cooperation Council. He is the only academic to sit on the Home Office National Crime Prevention Agency. A former Parole Board member and committed supporter of the Victim Support organisation, Ken was awarded the OBE for services to crime prevention in June 1997.

Russell Smith is the Deputy Director of Research at the Australian Institute of Criminology. Prior to becoming a Lecturer in Criminology at the University of Melbourne in 1990, Russell practised as a solicitor in Melbourne – he is a Barrister and Solicitor of the Supreme Court of Victoria and a Solicitor of the Supreme Court of England and Wales. Russell has written widely on various aspects of computer crime, fraud control, and professional regulation. His books include the following: *Medical Discipline* (Clarendon Press, 1994), *Crime in the Digital Age* (with P. Grabosky, Federation Press, 1998), *Health Care, Crime and Regulatory Control* (Hawkins Press, 1998), and *In Pursuit of Nursing Excellence* (Oxford University Press, 1999). He has just completed a new book entitled *Electronic Theft: Crimes of Acquisition in Cyberspace* (with P. Grabosky and G. Dempsey, Cambridge University Press, 2001).

Paul Taylor is Senior lecturer in the Sociology of Technology at the University of Salford. He is the author of *Hackers: Crime in the Digital Sublime* (Routledge, 1999) and he is currently conducting follow-up research with Tim Jordan of the Open University for a co-authored work that is provisionally entitled *Hacktivists: Rebels with a cause?* Paul's other main research interest relates to cyberpunk fiction and its potential contribution to social theories of new technologies.

Clive Walker is Professor of Criminal Justice at the University of Leeds. He has written extensively on criminal justice, civil liberties and media issues. His books include *Political Violence and the Law in Ireland* (Manchester University Press, 1989), *The Prevention of Terrorism in British Law* (2nd edition, Manchester University Press, 1992), *Justice in Error* (ed. with K. Starmer, Blackstone Press, 1993), *Miscarriages of Justice* (ed. with K. Starmer, Blackstone Press, 1999). In relation to the Internet, Clive was the editor of 'Crime, Criminal Justice and the Internet' (special edition, *Criminal Law Review*, Sweet & Maxwell, London, 1998), director of the UK Law Online project http://www.leeds.ac.uk/law/hamlyn/ and co-editor of *The Internet, Law and Society* (with Y. Akdeniz and D. Wall, Longmans, 2000).

David Wall (Editor) is the Director of the Centre for Criminal Justice Studies at the University of Leeds, where he conducts research and teaches in the fields of policing, criminal justice processes, crime and information technology. He recently developed a research unit which is dedicated to the study of cyberlaw and cybercrimes, and completed a short programme of research into information technology and crime for the DTI and the Home Office. He has also worked for the G8 Lyon group as a moderator on their

(Paris) initiative to develop government-industry dialogues with regard to cybercrimes. David has published a wide range of articles and books on issues related to criminal justice; the books include *Policy Networks in Criminal Justice* (ed. with M. Ryan and S. Savage, McMillan Press, 2001), *The British Police* (with M. Stallion, Police History Society, 1999), *The Chief Constables of England and Wales* (Ashgate/Dartmouth, 1998), *Access to Criminal Justice* (ed. with R. Young, Blackstone Press, 1996), *Policing in a Northern Force* (with K. Bottomley, C. Coleman, D. Dixon and M. Gill, Hull University, 1991). Within the specific area of cybercrime and cyberlaw David has edited *Cyberspace Crime* (Ashgate/ Dartmouth, 2002), and he co-edited *The Internet, Law and Society* (with Y. Akdeniz and C. Walker, Longman, 2000); he also edited two special issues of the *International Review of Law, Computers and Technology* on 'E-commerce' (Vol. 13/2, 1999) and 'Cybercrime vs. Cyberliberties' (Vol. 14/1, 2000).

Matthew Williams is a Lecturer in Criminology at Cardiff University. He was previously a Ph.D. student at Cardiff where he conducted research for his doctoral thesis into the aetiology of online deviance, with a specific focus upon derision and abusive speech. Matt has written and conducted research within the areas of cybercrime, crime reduction and new technologies, and methods of online research. He is currently on the board of directors for the Association of Internet Researchers (AoIR) and he is a member of the Criminology Research Centre within the School of Social Sciences at Cardiff University.

Preface

The Internet is one of the greatest sensations of recent times. It has become a symbol of our technological ingenuity and offers humankind an awesome array of benefits. However, the thrill of those prospects has been accompanied by public fears about the potential scale of criminal opportunities that can arise. Fears, which, in the absence of reliable information to the contrary, have been nurtured and sustained by media sensationalism. Yet, our practical experience of the Internet is that few of these fears have actually been realised. Furthermore, there is clearly emerging a body of evidence to show that the criminal reality of the Internet is not the all engulfing "cyber-tsunami", but, like the terrestrial world, a large range of frequently occurring small-impact crimes.

One could argue that criminologists have been slow to explore these emerging fears and new criminal behaviours, and engage in debate about them in order to develop useful bodies of knowledge that could enlighten the public and provide the basis for informed policy. In the criminologists' defence, however, it could be argued that there is wisdom in exercizing caution and in waiting for reliable trends of behaviour to emerge. But in the first years of the new millennium, the questions about what cybercrimes are, what their impact will be and how we should respond to them remain largely unanswered: the time for understanding is now.

The origins of this collection go back to two conferences. The first was the 14th Annual conference of the British and Irish Legal Education Technology Association, held in York, UK, in 1999. This conference successfully brought together an international group of academics, practitioners (mainly police and lawyers) policy-makers and cyber-libertarians. The second was the cybercrime stream at the British Society of Criminology Conference, held in Leicester in July 2000, whose seven panels acted as a focal point for criminologists interested in the impact of information technology. As the collection took shape, a number of further contributions were added.

My thanks go to the cast of contributors for their efforts: after all, it is their ideas, hard work and excellence which make this book possible. They are, in order of appearance: Ken Pease, Peter Grabosky and Russell Smith, Mike Levi, Paul Taylor, Bela Chatterjee, Marjorie Heins, Yaman Akdeniz, Louise Ellison, Matt Williams, Paul Norman and Clive Walker.

More specifically I would like to thank the following people for bringing the book to fruition. Geraldine Craven and Theakston assisted greatly in formatting the various chapters, and Zaiton Hamin and Sue Wellings assisted in organizing the York conference. Martyn Oliver loaned me his eagle eye as copy editor, and Mari Shullaw and James MacNally at Routledge provided great help and support in the conceptualization and preparation of the book.

Finally, I would like to acknowledge the support of colleagues who have tolerated me for years. At the University of Leeds are Clive Walker, Jackie Schneider (now at the University of Portsmouth), Zaiton Hamin, Adam Crawford and Yaman Akdeniz. Colleagues elsewhere include (in no particular order): Stuart Hyde, Philip Leith, Allan Castle, Bill Tafoya, Hedi Nasheri, Rachel O'Connell, Steve Savage, Robert Reiner, Les Johnston, Tim Newburn, Jim Sheptycki, Philip Stenning and many others.

Last – but not least – my special thanks go to Helen, Harrison, Sophie and James for simultaneously brightening up my life and ensuring that I got very little sleep during the process of compiling the book.

1 Cybercrimes and the Internet

David Wall

Introduction

The mid-to-late 1990s was a time of considerable opportunity for virtual innovators. The share prices of the dot.coms shot through the roof and attracted
"blue chip" investments, making the new virtual ventures seem all the more
viable. During this period, value became firmly attached to ideas, rather than
things, and for a few golden years the heightened market optimism confused
the "virtual" with the "real". A scenario emerged, reminiscent of Tulipmania in
Holland during the seventeenth century (Moggach, 1999) and the South Sea
Bubble in the early eighteenth. Widespread optimism over this ebullient
market drove investment in ventures that were not only non-viable, but were
not due to recoup for some considerable time. Furthermore, many of the
assumptions about market growth and technological development which
underpinned the stock valuations were themselves rather poorly founded. But
this same optimism also drove further technological developments, and looked
to make happen the original prophecy.

For years it seemed as though the virtual bubble could not – and would not
– burst. The media recounted each wonderful episode of the development of
the new technology, and each example of brave virtual entrepreneurship. But
the prevailing mentality was such that if one was not *on* the virtual juggernaut
then one was *off* it; and these times also generated great anxiety, because the
uncertainty of the "new" technology shattered the comfort and familiarity of
the "old". Sensing a split in their audience between the believers and the
agnostics, the media simultaneously ran cautionary tales of the future of
things to come alongside the tales of technological and entrepreneurial
heroism. In other words, the mid-to-late 1990s was also a great time for the
cyber-soothsayers, who informed the public that using the Internet would
make them vulnerable to new types of criminals; criminals who, rather ironically, were taking advantage of the very same qualities of the Internet that
attracted the entrepreneurs and consumers. The public were left in no doubt
that if the cyber-pornographers did not completely erode what was left of
their existing moral fibre, then they would fall victim to cyber-terrorists,
cyber-stalkers, cyber-fraudsters, etc. These fears were intensified by the global

concerns over the Y2K "Millennium Bug", a simple design fault in PC operating systems which, it was predicted, would cause the collapse of key installations within national infrastructures.

The turning point came upon the chime of the first stroke of the new millennium midnight. It became immediately apparent that the Four Horsemen of the Virtual Apocalypse were not riding that night; nor did they ride on any other night since, and neither the anticipated "Electronic Pearl Harbor" (Smith, 1998) nor the "cyber-tsunami" and its accompanying global meltdown occurred. The moment of silence was filled with the familiar crime SNAFU: property was still being stolen, individuals were still at personal risk from assault, motorists still drove too fast. From that time onwards the hot wind of change gradually transformed into the cool breeze of realism, and the dot.com bubble began to develop a slow puncture. However, this deflation should not be interpreted as a demonstration that the Internet fails to live up to expectations; rather, it illustrates that we are simply coming to terms with the phenomenon of cyberspace, and that we are acquiring a much more realistic understanding of its impact. Consequently we should not underestimate the potential harm of cybercrimes or play down the importance of the need to understand them, especially within their individual contexts.

As the virtual fog begins to lift, it is apparent that these are still early days in the lives and times of cyberspace. A growing body of literature about various aspects of cybercrime is emerging, and there are a number of books which use the rubric. Some of these are useful,[1] others are not. I hope that the present volume builds upon and further develops the foundations laid by the useful works. Not only does it seek to add to our understanding of cybercrimes, but it gives those understandings some perspective by further mapping out the terrain, and also by adding analytical depth and, where possible, a theoretical framework that will provide a basis for further study.

The first part of this introductory chapter briefly identifies the various harmful behaviours that we currently understand to be cybercrimes, at how they impact and in what ways and upon whom, in order to suggest a framework for understanding them. The second part identifies some of the problems and pitfalls that criminologists will encounter when they engage with the subject. The third part outlines the structure of the collection and locates the chapters within it.

Understanding the impact of cybercrimes

In a rather contradictory way, the term "cybercrime" does not actually do much more than signify the occurrence of a harmful behaviour that is somehow related to a computer. It has no specific referent in law, and it is a concept that has been largely invented by the media. Yet, despite the rather unsystematic attempts to define it, the term nevertheless regularly invokes a knee-jerk response from the media, policymakers, politicians, academics and the public alike. Like sticky paper on a shoe, it is a term that cannot be easily shaken off and dismissed as it has quickly become absorbed into popular parlance; and, whilst it has no specific meaning, it signifies a range of activities and has considerable currency. So it is our job as criminologists to understand the behaviours that it describes and to assist the understanding of others. But what *are* cybercrimes? Are they that important? And if they are important, then what qualities do they possess to generate such concern? Finally, how do we understand them? How can we put them into perspective? The following paragraphs suggest that we need to distinguish between the different levels of their impact, but also that it makes sense to look at cybercrimes in terms of the type(s) of behaviour and impacts that they represent.

Levels of impact

The Internet has impacted upon criminal and/or harmful activity in three main ways – this is after discounting the fact that many of the behaviours that have been identified as cybercrimes are not actually crimes as such but invoke civil remedies instead (Wall, 2000a). First, the Internet has become a vehicle for communications which sustain existing patterns of harmful activity, such as drug trafficking, and also hate speech, bomb-talk, stalking and so on. Newsgroups, for example, circulate information about how to bypass the security devices in mobile telephones or digital television decoders (Mann and Sutton, 1998; Wall, 2000b). Second, the Internet has created a transnational environment that provides new opportunities for harmful activities that are currently the subject of existing criminal or civil law. Examples would include paedophile activity, and also fraud. Third, the nature of the virtual environment, particularly with regard to the way that it distanciates time and space (Giddens, 1990: 6), has engendered entirely new forms of (unbounded) harmful activity such as the unauthorized appropriation of imagery, software tools and music products, etc. Indeed, at the far extreme of this third category, the trans-jurisdictional, contestable and private nature of some of the harms indicates a scenario where there exists new wine, but no bottles at all! It is important, therefore, to disaggregate these three levels of impact because they each invoke different policy responses and require quite different bodies of understanding. Cutting across these three levels, or depths, of impact lie four broad areas of harmful activity which are currently raising concerns (see Wall, 1999, 2000a).

Types of behaviour

Each of the following four areas of harmful activity illustrates a range of activities and behaviours rather than specific offences, reflecting not only bodies of law, but also specific courses of public debate.

"(Cyber)-trespass", or hacking/cracking, is the unauthorized crossing of the boundaries of computer systems into spaces where rights of ownership or title have already been established. Computer hackers played an important role in the early stages of the conceptual development of the Internet, combining high levels of specialized knowledge to test out and develop new ideas with a staunch ethical belief in freedom of access to all information. Initially they were applauded as a celebration of the genius of youth and the pioneering spirit of America (Chandler, 1996: 229), but they have subsequently become demonized (Chandler, 1996; Duff and Gardiner, 1996; Ross, 1990; Sterling, 1994; Taylor, 1999; Jordan and Taylor, 1998). Although a distinction is increasingly being made between the principled trespasser (the hacker) and the unprincipled trespasser (the cracker), their skills and beliefs are now commonly regarded as a major threat to the interests of those who are attempting to effect monopoly control over cyberspace: namely commerce and the state. It is because of this ideological baggage that the term "cyber-trespasser" is used here instead.

When the range of cyber-trespassers is examined it is found that they clearly represent a spectrum of qualitatively different types of behaviour. In its mildest form, cyber-trespass is little more than an intellectual challenge resulting in a harmless trespass; at its worst it is full-blown information warfare (Szafranski, 1995: 56). Four basic types of cyber-trespasser can be identified from the literature. Young (1995: 10) distinguishes between *utopians* who naively believe that they are contributing to society by demonstrating its vulnerabilities,[2] and *cyberpunks* who are aggressively anti-establishment, and who intentionally cause harm to targets which offend them. In addition, two further types of cyber-trespassers can be identified: the *cyber-spy* and the *cyber-terrorist*. The practical distinction between the groups is often blurred because cyber-spies and cyber-terrorists must by definition be expert crackers in order to be able to gain access to sites. Most acts of cyber-trespass probably fall between these extreme positions.

"(Cyber)-deceptions/thefts" describes the different types of acquisitive harm that can take place within cyberspace. At one level lie the more traditional patterns of theft, such as the fraudulent use of credit cards and (cyber)-cash, and a particular current concern is the increasing potential for the raiding of on-line bank accounts as e-banking becomes more popular.

Credit card frauds over the Internet arise from the fraudulent use of appropriated credit cards to buy goods over the Internet from the many virtual shopping malls and auction sites. In common with telephoned transactions, the cyber fraudster does not need to have the actual credit card in order to shop over the Internet; only the card number and expiry date, together with the name on the card and a delivery address, are required. All are details that can be obtained from, for example, a discarded credit card voucher.[3]

The cyber-cash concept is developing rapidly and, while its developers envisage the eventual establishment of a self-contained monetary system within cyberspace, current concepts of cyber-cash are linked to the use of smart cards which are loaded with electronic cash equivalents at specific banking points. Such points of access will eventually be available through the Internet. At the time of writing, six or more major banks in the UK had undertaken, or had been represented in, trials of cyber-cash facilities (AAP Newsfeed, 1998).[4] Whilst the security potential for cyber-cash is considerably greater than conventional cash, especially when transactions are accompanied by a personal identification number, it is highly likely that the illegal reproduction of cyber-cash credits will quickly become a challenge for offenders.

At another level is cyberpiracy, which is the appropriation of new forms of intellectual property that have been created or popularized within cyberspace.[5] It is the computer programme, expressed in the form of a digital code, that generates, through a computer system, "virtual products", such as images, music, office aides or interactive experiences – to name but a few. The appropriation of these "virtual products", or of the programme itself, does not "permanently deprive" the owner of their use (Smith and Hogan, 1999), which is one of the legal definitions of theft. Thus, piracy is becoming an increasingly challenging type of cybertheft as it is causing us to reconsider our understanding of property and also of the very act of theft itself.

It will be remembered that one of the distinguishing characteristics of cyberspace was the fact that monetary values are attached to ideas rather than to objects. In parallel to the growth of the Internet has been an increase in the number, complexity and application of intellectual property laws relating to trademarks, copyright, patents and – in the USA – privacy and publicity laws (Boyle, 1996; Madow, 1993; Wall, 1996; Vagg, 1995). When cyberspace and intellectual property laws intersect they become a powerful force, especially during a time when, as Baudrillard observes, economic activity has come to be the outcome rather than the cause of cultural values and norms (Vagg, 1995: 87; Baudrillard, 1988). Importantly, the fact that productive ideas can now be effected without the need for the modes of physical production means that the monetary value of those ideas is further increased. Therefore, these various forms of intellectual property, especially trademarks, domain names and character merchandise, are becoming, so to speak, its "real estate". So the terrain of cyberspace becomes pockmarked by the struggle for control over this "intellectual" real estate. This development raises concerns about the proliferation of legal activity involving intellectual property law and the potential emergence of unjust power imbalances (Boyle, 1996). More specifically, the establishment of monopoly control through law enables those in control to further determine where the boundaries between desirable and undesirable behaviours will lie.

There are two, related strands of this type of piracy. The first is the counterfeiting of products such as toiletries, designer labels and character merchandise, which is becoming a rapidly expanding business and which tends to exist on the peripheries of cyberspace, using the Internet as a distribution network. The second variant of cyber-piracy/theft (that of stealing intellectual properties) is quite different and finds the boundaries between criminal and civil law extremely blurred. It is where owners' interests in their properties – for example, in images, trademarks, texts, music[6] or general character merchandise – are threatened by theft or by their release into the public domain of the Internet. The main threat to the owner is the dilution of their control over their intellectual property. The term "dilution" is used in intellectual property law to describe the reduction in value caused by unrestricted use. The threat of dilution is therefore used to justify the continuation of legal control,[7] even though the appropriation of a property may not necessarily be motivated by the prospect of financial gain, but for artistic or moral reasons.[8]

"(Cyber)-pornography/obscenity", as the term suggests, is the publication or trading of sexually expressive materials within cyberspace. The cyberporn/obscenity debate is very complex because pornography is not necessarily illegal. The test in the UK and many other jurisdictions is whether or not the materials are obscene and deprave the viewer, but there are considerable legal and moral differences as to what are the criteria that enable law enforcers to establish obscenity and depravity. In Britain, for example, individuals daily consume images through the various facets of the mass media that might be classed as obscene in some Middle-Eastern countries.

The role of pornography in the Internet's career has been contradictory. On the one hand, it has probably scared many people, particularly concerned parents, from using it to its full potential. On the other hand, it was pornography that got people, mostly men, interested in the Internet; and though it was this interest which created a market for pornography, it also drove the development of the technology that was designed to deliver pornography in the form of an electronic service. Furthermore, and controversially, it is arguable that the virtual sex-trade not only pioneered the virtual transaction, but it also demonstrated the commercial potential of the Internet to the normally conservative business community. Finally, the virtual sex-trade has played an important role in the governance of the Internet. In seeking legitimacy, the "adult" sites which mainly peddle the kind of pornography that is the product of consensual acts between adults have not only coalesced in order to create economies of scale and to share trust relationships with the customers, but they have also sought actively to expose child-pornographers and eradicate them from the Internet. The organization called Adult Sites Against Child Pornography (ASACP) is one such arrangement.[9]

Perhaps the most alarming impact of Internet pornography was the moral panic that it gave rise to during the early-to-mid 1990s: a panic which – fuelled by prevailing feminist philosophies and the findings of the (subsequently discredited) Carnegie Mellon Survey, which stated that as much as half of all Internet use may be related to the consumption of pornography (Rimm, 1995) – drove/steered the debate which led to the passage of the Communications Decency Act 1996 (47 USC s.223) (CDA) in the USA. In 1997, the following year, this Act was partially overturned (*ACLU et al. v. Reno*, 1997). The whole episode promoted the cause of, and the need for, publicly informed policy.

"(Cyber)-violence" describes the violent impact of the cyberactivities of another upon an individual or a social or political grouping. Whilst such activities do not have to have a direct physical manifestation, the victim nevertheless feels the violence of the act and can bear long-term psychological scars as a consequence. The activities referred to here range from cyber-stalking to hate-speech to tech-talk.

Cyber-stalking includes the persistent tracking and harassment of an individual by another – for example, by the persistent sending of e-mails – and the sending of obscene messages or even death threats. The problem lies in deciding where to draw the line between the genuine threat and the nuisance (Ellison and Akdeniz, 1998; Chapter 9 of this volume). The flexibility of this borderline was apparent in the Jake Baker case (*United States of America v. Alkhabaz*, 1997). In the mid-1990s Baker was prosecuted after publishing fantasy rape-torture and snuff stories on the newsgroup called "alt.sex.stories". In one story, "Doe", Baker named the victim as one of his fellow students (Wallace and Mangan, 1996: 63). Baker had not stalked the girl in the real-time sense of surreptitiously following the victim; in fact, he had not even contacted her. Moreover it was later suggested that the girl's real name was only used because one of the syllables in it rhymed with the popular name for the penis. Yet he had caused her and others who had read the story considerable worry. Although it was initially about violence, the Baker case eventually became one in which the central issue became his right to freedom of speech.

If cyber-stalking violates the individual, then cyber-hate violates social or ethnic groupings. The Internet is the site of some very disturbing hate-speech. Perhaps one of the most dramatic examples of hate-speech on the World Wide Web is Holocaust denial, which, as the name implies, attempts to rewrite history by denying that the persecution of the Jewish people by the Nazis ever took place (*R. v. Zundel*, 1992; Greenberg, 1997: 673).

A worrying development of cyber-violence arises from the convergence of hate-speech and tech-talk. The latter circulates the technologies which can make the former a reality. At one end of the spectrum is the free circulation of sophisticated technologies which are designed to circumnavigate existing infras-tructural frameworks.[10] At the other end is bomb-talk, which ranges from the circulation of instructions that describe how to make a bomb or other weaponry to the deliberate targeting of groups with a view to committing an act (see Wallace and Mangan, 1996: 153). The policing of both of these latter examples of cyber-violence is frustrated by the fact that in some jurisdictions, for example the US and Canada, whilst the intent behind hate-speech might contravene some criminal codes, the fact that they are "speech" gives them protection under the US Constitution and Canadian Charter of Rights[11] which guarantee freedom of expression (see Becker *et al.*, 2000).

By breaking the analysis of cybercrimes down into different levels and types of impact, criminological debates can engage more clearly with the issues at hand. Furthermore, criminologists are then spared the frustration of comparing, for example, the "apples" of cyber-violence with, say, the "Tuesdays" of cyber-theft. But while this taxonomy might usefully assist criminologists to sing from the same song sheet, the following impediments frustrate their abilities to sing in tune and conduct research into cybercrimes.

Problems with researching cybercrimes

Lack of statistics

A hindrance to those seeking to study cybercrimes is the lack of any form of officially recorded statistics. There exist a number of reports which purport to estimate the extent of cybercrime, particularly with regard to hacking and commercial activities. However, most of these reports have been produced by commercial organizations which constitute the emerging cybercrime security industry, and they tend to lack not only standardized conceptualizations of the "crimes" but also systematic reporting or recording methodologies. Even if such standardized and systematically obtained statistics were readily available, it is arguable that the following factors would still obscure the visibility of the behaviour and its impacts.

Visibility of the victims and the under-reporting of offences

There is frequent confusion over who the victims of cybercrime are and how they are being victimized. Not only can victims vary from individuals to social groups, but the harm done to them can range from the actual to the perceived. In cases involving cyber-stalking or the theft of cybercash, the victimization is very much focused upon an individual. However, in other cases, such as cyber-piracy or cyber-spying/terrorism, the impact of victimization is usually directed towards the corporate entity. Moreover, as has been found with the reporting of white-collar crimes, it is likely that many victims of cybercrimes, be they primary or secondary victims, individuals or organizations, may be unwilling to acknowledge that they have been victimized, or it may take them some time to realize it. At a personal level, this could arise because of embarrassment, ignorance of what to do or just simply "putting it down to experience". Alternatively, where the victimization has been imputed by a third party upon the basis of an ideological, political, moral or commercial assessment of risk, the victim or victim group may simply be unaware that they have been victimized or may even believe that they have not, as we have seen is the case in some of the debates over Internet pornography.

At a corporate level the fear of the negative commercial impact of adverse publicity in terms of lost market share can greatly reduce willingness to report victimizations. Of importance here is the observation that the model of criminal justice which public law enforcement organizations offer to corporate victims is not generally conducive to their business interests (Wall, 2000b; Goodman, 1997). For these reasons, the corporate victim may simply favour civil, rather than criminal, remedies because of the lesser burden of proof or because they feel that they can stay in control of the justice process, or that they might find it easier to claim for losses through insurance, or simply pass on the costs of victimization directly to their customers.

Offender profiles

The little factual knowledge that does exist about cyber-offenders suggests that they are fairly atypical in terms of traditional criminological expectations, they tend not to be the burly folk-devils that the elaborate descriptions of their offences in the media would often have us believe. Hitherto, most debates over the criminology and policing of traditional crimes have tended to be mainly located within the analysis of working-class or underclass sub-cultures. Cyber-offenders, on the other hand, are more likely to share a broader range of social characteristics and the cases of hacking and other Internet-related offences that have been reported in the media would suggest they are likely to be young, clever and fairly lonely individuals who are of middle-class origin, often without prior criminal records, often possessing expert knowledge and often motivated by a variety of financial and non-financial goals. So, for example, we find that the hackers Pryce and Bevan, who were once described as "a greater threat to world peace than Adolf Hitler" (Gunner, 1998: 5; Wall, 2000a; Power, 2000: ch. 6), were not only very young, but Pryce was still at school (Ungoed-Thomas, 1998: 1). Similarly, the much reviled cyberstalker Jake Baker was a young introverted student (*United States of America v. Alkhabaz*, 1997; Wallace and Mangan, 1996). It is very likely that offender profiles will vary across each of the previously-mentioned groupings of cybercrimes. However, the most impor-tant point to emphasize here is that the special characteristics of the Internet enable individuals to commit crimes that would previously have been beyond their means. In the worst-case scenario, they can become the law enforcer's worst nightmare: the empowered single agent described by Ken Pease in Chapter 2 of this volume.

Trans-jurisdictionality

The trans-jurisdictional nature of cyber-crimes creates many problems for the enforcement of law. Typically, policing strategies are often reduced to deci-sions that are made at a very local level about the most efficient expenditure of finite resources. Such decisions become complicated where different juris-dictions cover the location of the offence committed, the offender, victim and impact of the offence. Furthermore, this trans-jurisdictional issue can be complicated by confusion over whether or not some of the harms fall under civil or criminal laws, which can vary across jurisdictions.

Yet there are also examples where such trans-jurisdictionality has provided policing bodies with a flexible tool by which to maximize the potential for gaining a conviction, particularly with regard to "forum-shopping", so that the prospect of achieving the most effective investigation and/or prosecution is achieved. A number of cases from both sides of the Atlantic demonstrate the enabling aspect of the trans-jurisdictionality of the Internet. In *United States of America v. Robert A. Thomas and Carleen Thomas* (1996) the prosecutors "forum-shopped" to seek a site where they felt a conviction would best be secured; consequently Tennessee, rather than California, was chosen because of the greater likelihood of conviction. In *R v. Arnold* and *R v. Fellows* (1996) the investigation was passed on from the US to the UK police because the former believed that the latter were more likely to gain a conviction.

Confusing risk assessment with reality: media sensitization shaping public knowledge

An important (shaping) factor in the public debate over cyber-crimes is the "media sensitization" of Internet-related issues, which has heightened their overall newsworthiness, especially with regard to the dark side of the Internet. Such sensitization is gradually moulding the legal and regulatory responses to harms by inflating public concerns and therefore providing the regulatory bodies with an (often implied) mandate for taking action; see, for example, the history of the Communications Decency Act in the USA (mentioned earlier in this chapter in the context of the Carnegie Mellon Survey, and also in Chapter 7). Moreover, public awareness is further heightened by the common failure of journalists, pressure groups, policymakers and others to discern between "potential" and "actual" harms, an act that is made easy by the virtual impossibility of making any systematic calculation of the extent of cybercrimes.

As we develop an understanding of the virtual environment of cyberspace, an interesting but paradoxical situation is emerging. On the one hand it is now quite clear that, in its various capacities, the Internet really does have the capability to transcend economic, political, geographical, social and even racial and gendered boundaries that the early commentators had predicted. On the other hand, although the mass media would have us believe otherwise, the anarchy and widespread criminality arising from those qualities, were predicted by those who favoured early regulation, have not yet materialized. By comparison, cyberspace is remarkably ordered, considering the large numbers of individuals who inhabit it and also the breadth of their involvement(s) with it (see Chapter 11). Commentators such as Johnson and Post (1996), Lessig (1999) and Greenleaf (1998) have also argued that the "digital realism" imposed by the architecture of the Internet results in a regulable environment. Although this environment is, as Grabosky and Smith (1998: 233) demonstrate, both subject to and the product of a series of regulatory dilemmas,[12] Wall has argued (2000a, also see Chapter 11 of this volume) that a perceivable multi-tiered structure of governance already exists in cyberspace to maintain various types of order. However, whilst the dark side of cyberspace is probably not as large as originally anticipated, it is nevertheless formidable and will continue to be explored for opportunities: consequently, the concerns over this dark side are driving the debate over regulation.

The political economy of cyberspace and the ongoing-power struggle for control over it

The final consideration in our understanding of cybercrimes is the definitional state of flux that still exists because of the "political" tensions that are still actively shaping definitions of (cyber-) behaviour. As the increasing political and commercial potential of the Internet gives rise to a new political economy of information capital, a new set of power relationships is forged. Consequently the definitions of acceptable and unacceptable cyber-behaviour are themselves shaped by this ongoing power play or "intellectual land-grab" that is currently taking place for (market) control (see Boyle, 1996, but also the discussion in Chapter 5 of this volume). Of concern is the increasing level of intolerance that is now being demonstrated by the new power players towards certain "risk groups" that they perceive as a threat to their interests. A very good example of this intolerance is the magnitude of the reaction by the music industry to the websites which distribute MP3 files (Carey and Wall, 2001). However, whilst such intolerance tends to mould broader definitions of deviance, the construction of deviance is not so simply one-sided, because definitions of crime and deviance arise not only from the social activity of elite or power groups, but also from that of common members of society and offenders themselves: "[T]he struggle around the definition of crime and deviance is located within the field of action that is constituted by plural and even conflicting efforts at producing control" (Melossi, 1994: 205).

In sum, criminologists who seek to understand cybercrimes will not only have to consider the varying degrees to which cybercrimes impact upon victims, they will also have to acknowledge the different and distinct groups of behaviours that also exist. However, criminological efforts will be further frustrated by the varying levels of visibility, victim awareness, media sensitization and overall definitional fluidity that characterizes this field of study.

Acknowledgement of these characteristics and impediments is crucial to future research design. In some cases a combination of traditional and white-collar criminologies will suffice to inform such designs. In other forms of enquiry, which involve the more abstract types of harmful behaviour on the Internet, new criminologies will have to draw upon a range of disciplines, such as socio-legal studies, geography or psychology. The general message, then, is that a criminological knowledge base relating to the Internet needs to be developed which brings together a range of criminologies that will sit side by side. The contributions within this collection do not claim to achieve this end, but they do bring together a range of criminologists, and through their individual efforts such a body of knowledge may begin to develop.

The structure of the book, its contributors and contributions

One of the exciting aspects of working in a fairly new area of research such as this is that it is a great leveller; everyone starts from more or less the same position and reputations have yet to be forged. Consequently the contributors vary from very senior research professors, to young academics, to practitioners, each distinguishing themselves in their own individual ways.

The book brings together under its cover a collection of research that has been drawn from various jurisdictions and from a range of disciplinary backgrounds. As a consequence the chapters vary in terms of the subjects covered and also the perspectives held. The organization of the book follows the structure described earlier in this introduction. The first part, comprising this chapter and Chapter 2, overview the issues. The contributions in the second part (Chapters 3–10), focus upon the four groups of behaviour that were identified earlier; deception, trespass, obscenity, violence. In part three (Chapters

11–13), the contributions explore the impact of cybercrimes upon the criminal justice processes, namely the police and the courts.

In Chapter 2, Ken Pease maps out the debate over crime futures, in the process making the distinction between "meatspace" (humans) and "cyberspace" (the Internet). He then describes the UK Government's "Foresight" initiative which generally seeks to address the challenge of crime in the information age. Ken observes that our "crime futures" actually hold no great surprises, but they will, nevertheless, challenge many of the conventional wisdoms that shape public policy.

In their chapter on cyber-deceptions/theft, Peter Grabosky and Russell Smith explore the telecommunications-based frauds that have emerged as the result of the convergence of technologies. Arguing against over-regulation, they poignantly observe that a balance has to be drawn which allows a tolerable degree of illegality in return for the creative exploitation of the technology.

Mike Levi follows by discussing the growing phenomenon of computer fraud and argues that computer-related frauds have gained considerable attention as the Internet has become an increasingly popular vehicle for commercial activity. Drawing upon his long experience of analysing white-collar crime, Mike compares the risks and realities that underpin the urban legends which surround the Internet and its users and abusers. He argues that not only do we need to know how the organization of digitized work affects the opportunities for fraud, but we also we need a more sophisticated understanding of the problematic relationship between the broader (theoretical) potential for cybercrime and the much smaller incidence and prevalence of computer crime for economic gain.

Fraudulent activities are not the only sources of urban legends; indeed most of the urban legends are linked to the exploits of the cyber-trespassers, the hackers and the crackers. The literature which describes these differences is plentiful. However, much of this literature tends to be retrospective and, although it does a sterling job in documenting hacker history, it rarely considers the future of the hacker. In his chapter, Paul Taylor explores the twentyfirst-century (re)incarnation of the ethical hacker in the shape of the "hacktivist" who has resurrected the original ethos of hacking in order to resist global capitalism. He concludes that the hacktivists' imaginative re-engineering of the technological code contained within the Internet actually enables them to engage more successfully with the more abstract capitalist code that has most effect upon the so-called "real" world.

The activities of hackers, crackers and fraudsters have not only generated public fears, they have also stimulated the public imagination by their virtual derring-do. But, it was the moral panic over pornography on the Internet during the mid-1990s which was largely responsible for bringing the Internet and its content to public attention. That moral panic subsided during the late 1990s, and much of the current literature and debate on Internet pornography has since tended to focus upon the issues of free speech and civil liberty. Marjorie Heins, one of the ACLU (American Civil Liberties Union) team which overturned part of the Communications Decency Act (CDA) of 1996, considers the criminalizing of online speech in order to protect the young. She revisits the debates that led to the CDA, arguing that criminalizing online speech, especially when it relates to sexual subjects, is frequently justified as necessary to protect minors from physical or psychological harm, but that in doing so it unconstitutionally reduces the adult population using the Internet to writing, publishing and reading "only what is fit for children".

Bela Chatterjee then takes the pornography debate to a new level as she follows the "last of the rainmacs" to peep on the virtual top shelf in order to consider the ways that virtual pornography is shaping – and has already shaped – our understanding of sexuality and its social mores. Bela observes that cyber-pornography facilitates the expression of a series of plural identities and sexualities that challenge a body of law based upon much narrower concepts of sexuality.

In his chapter, Yaman Akdeniz places the debates about the impact of pornography within the context of the general discussion over illegal and harmful content on the Internet. He analyses recent developments in the regulation of Internet content and concludes that there is far too much anxiety about what is and what is not available on the Internet. He then opines that the specific technical solutions that have been created to prevent illegal and harmful content can be problematic, in that they can also restrict netizens' rights to freedom of expression. Yaman deprecates the current emphasis upon the protection of children from harmful content, and, instead, believes that there should be a greater emphasis on promoting the Internet as a positive and beneficial medium. Furthermore, he argues that self-regulation is an effective method of moderating the impacts of harmful Internet content, as long as Internet users and industry are involved in setting the policies.

Yaman's chapter on harmful content provides a useful segué from the debates over pornography into the vexed issue of cyberviolence, which can take various forms. At one end of the spectrum of cyberviolence lies hate speech, which tends to impact upon specific social, political or religious groups. Much has been written about hate speech, following cases such as *R. v Zundel* (1992), and in the main, it is well serviced by the literature.[13] As Yaman observes in his chapter, some jurisdictions make hate speech illegal, as they also do with pornography/obscenity, whereas others protect it as a form of free speech – a disparity which causes some serious dilemmas for the policing of cyberviolence.

At the other end of the cyberviolence spectrum lies cyber-stalking, about which there is considerable public concern but little knowledge. It is particularly menacing because individuals can fall prey to "invisible" tormentors. In her chapter, Louise Ellison looks at the problems, particularly the legal aspects, of tackling harassment on the Internet. On the one hand, she observes that the Internet is a faceless medium which makes it an ideal tool for the would-be cyber-stalker. On the other hand, however, she opposes hard legal measures against the stalkers because such sanctions could whittle away fundamental freedoms, whilst not necessarily achieving their stated objective. Louise favours a more educated use of the Internet, so that individuals are aware of issues such as stalking and can adopt tactics to avoid them.

Of course, one of the main problems for members of the public, law enforcement and the judicial process is where you draw the line between aggression and violent language, because the tools of Internet violence are words. To illuminate this matter, Matt Williams looks at the language of cybercrime in order to explore the many different types of language and their impacts upon the individual. He argues that "real" and "virtual" phenomena are inextricably connected, particularly as the reliance upon online text to sustain their identity makes individuals vulnerable to such attacks. As a consequence, online abusive acts affect "actual" lives.

The final part of this book looks at the impact of cybercrimes upon the various criminal justice processes, and in particular the police and the courts. The main problems are those of identifying harms, catching the perpetrators and prosecuting them. David Wall looks at the maintenance of order and law on the internet and observes that, hitherto, much of the debate over policing the internet has focused upon crime control through law enforcement. He argues that not only is the Internet a regulable medium, but there currently exists a multi-tiered structure of governance which, at different levels, performs the dual task of maintaining order and also enforcing law.

Paul Norman then looks at the policing of hi-tech crimes within a global context through transnational policy networks. He explores the nature of governance within the EU's third pillar, and examines how this has changed since the Treaty on European Union (TEU) formalized the EU's Justice and Home Affairs (JHA) policy process. He argues that a transnational power elite is acting relatively autonomously on a broad range of criminal justice issues, in the name of action, in order to counter transnational organized crime.

But what happens when cybercriminals and their terrestrial counterparts are brought to court? In the final chapter in this volume, Clive Walker considers the impact of the Internet, not just upon the criminal courts, but also on the criminal justice processes. Clive argues that the language of new managerialism within the courts is the language of Arthur Anderson, not Thomas Paine, and he believes that the Internet could radically counter-balance some of the exclusivity that results from the technocratization of the criminal justice process by encouraging more public engagement in it.

Conclusion

The main certainty that we have about the Internet is that it is here to stay and will continue to have an increasing influence upon our lives during the coming decades. As it continues to impact upon human behaviour, it will therefore continue to impact upon criminal behaviours. Some of those behaviours are entirely predictable, and we can draw upon existing criminological knowledge, but others are not so predictable and they require new bodies of knowledge and understanding. Hopefully this collection will encourage and facilitate the development of this knowledge and understanding.

Notes

1 An exceptionally useful book is Grabosky and Smith (1998). Although this book was published in 1998 it has only recently become widely available in the UK and was therefore not available to many of the contributors at the time of writing.
2 See Paul Taylor's chapter on Hacktivists in this collection (Chapter 5).
3 See "Is shopping on the Web safe?" at www.internetflowers.com/aif_secure.html (checked, 5 June 2001).
4 The concept of cyber-cash is differentiated here from the company called CyberCash, which offers web and electronic credit card, cheque and cash products.
5 The topic of cyber-piracy is not discussed within this collection other than in this introductory chapter.
6 See the debates on MP3 in Carey and Wall (2001).
7 The dilution argument is highly contested (see Madow, 1993).
8 For example, in the UK the authors of the Jet report, in direct contrast to those who had commissioned it, felt that its publication was in the public interest, which puts a slightly different spin on this argument. See Akdeniz (1997).
9 See the Association's website, www.asacp.org (checked, 5 June 2001). They provide a facility to report offensive web pages at www.asacp.org/reportsite.html (checked, 5 June 2001).
10 See Mann and Sutton (1998) for a very comprehensive description of the use of newsgroups to distribute information about the technologies used for committing offences.
11 In the USA by the First Amendment to the US Constitution, and in Canada by the Canadian Charter of Rights s. 2.
12 These include: (a) privacy v. accountability; (b) national sovereignty v. globalism; (c) user-friendliness v. security; (d) trust v. efficiency in law enforcement; (e) security v. creativity; (f) individual v. state interests.
13 See, for example, the listings at the Cyber-Rights site, www.cyber-rights.org (checked, 5 June 2001).

References

Cases

ACLU et al. v. Reno (1997), 117 S. Ct. 2329.

R v. Fellows and *R v. Arnold* (1996) (Court of Appeal, Criminal Division), *The Times*, 3 October.

R. v. Zundel (1992) 95 D.L.R. (4th) 202 (1992) and (Can. Sup. Ct. Aug. 27, 1992, unreported).

United States of America v. Alkhabaz (1997); U.S. App. Lexis 9060; (1996) 104 F.3d 1492; (1995) 48 F.3d 1220 and U.S. App. Lexis 11244.

United States of America v. Robert A. Thomas and Carleen Thomas (1996) 74 F.3d 701; 1996 U.S. App. Lexis 1069; 1996 Fed. App. 0032P (6th Cir).

Texts

AAP Newsfeed (1998) "Nationwide General News; Finance Wire", *AAP Newsfeed*, 18 March.

Akdeniz, Y. (1997) "Copyright and the Internet", *New Law Journal*, 147: 965–6.

Baudrillard, J. (1988) "Consumer Society", in M. Poster, *Jean Baudrillard: Selected Writings*, Oxford: Blackwell.

Becker, P.J., Byers, B. and Jipson, A. (2000) "The Contentious American Debate: The First Amendment and Internet-based Hate Speech", *International Review of Law Computers and Technology*, 14, 1: 33–42.

Boyle, J. (1996) *Shamans, Software and Spleens: Law and the Construction of the Information Society*, Cambridge, MA: Harvard University Press.

Carey, M. and Wall, D.S. (2001) "MP3: more beats to the byte", *International Review of Law, Computers and Technology*, 15, 1: 35–58.

Chandler, A. (1996) "The changing definition and image of hackers in popular discourse", *International Journal of the Sociology of Law*, 24, 2: 229–51.

Duff, L. and Gardiner, S. (1996) "Computer crime in the global village: strategies for control and regulation – in defence of the hacker", *International Journal of the Sociology of Law*, 24, 2: 211–28.

Ellison, L. and Akdeniz, Y. (1998) "Cyberstalking: The Regulation of Harassment on the Internet", in C. Walker (ed.) "Crime, Criminal Justice and the Internet", Special edition, *Criminal Law Review*.

Giddens, A. (1990) *The consequences of modernity*, Cambridge: Polity Press.

Goodman, M. (1997) "Why the police don't care about computer crime", *Harvard Journal of Law and Technology*, 10, Summer: 465–94.

Grabosky, P.N. and Smith, R.G. (1998) *Crime in the Digital Age: Controlling communications and cyberspace illegalities*, New Brunswick, NJ: Transaction Publishers.

Greenberg, S. (1997) "Threats, harassment and hate on-line: recent developments", *The Boston Public Interest Law Journal*, 6, Spring: 673.

Greenleaf, G. (1998) "An endnote on regulating cyberspace: architecture vs law?". *University of New South Wales Law Journal*, 21, 2; available at www.austlii.edu.au/au/other/unswlj/thematic/1998/vol21no2/greenleaf.html (checked, 5 June 2001).

Gunner, E. (1998) "Rogue hacker turned legit code-cracker", *Computer Weekly*, 7 May: 5.

Johnson, D.R. and Post, D. (1996) "Law and Borders: The Rise of Law in Cyberspace", *Stanford Law Review*, 48, May: 1367.

Jordan, T. and Taylor, P. (1998) "A sociology of hackers", *Sociological Review*, November: 757–80.

Lessig, L. (1999) "The Law Of The Horse: What Cyberlaw Might Teach", *Harvard Law Review*, 113, December: 501.

Madow, M. (1993) "Private Ownership of Public Image: Popular Culture and Publicity Rights", *California Law Review*, 81, January: 125–240.

Mann, D. and Sutton, M. (1998) "Netcrime: more change in the organisation of thieving", *British Journal of Criminology*, 38, 2: 210–29.

Melossi, D. (1994) "Normal Crimes, elites and social control", in D. Nelken (ed.), *The Futures of Criminology*, London: Sage.

Moggach, D. (1999) *Tulip Fever*, London: Heinemann.

Power, R. (2000) *Tangled Web: Tales of Digital Crime from the Shadows of Cyberspace*, www.usatoday.com/life/cyber/tech/review/crh625.htm (checked, 5 June 2001).

Rimm, M. (1995) "Marketing pornography on the information super-highway", *Georgetown Law Journal*, 83, 5: 1849–934.

Ross, A. (1990), "Hacking away at the counter-culture", *Postmodern Culture*, 1, 1 (online subscription journal at muse.jhu.edu/journals/postmodern_culture/v001/1.1ross.html).

Smith, G. (1998) "Electronic Pearl Harbor", *Issues in Science and Technology Online*, Fall, (online journal at www.nap.edu/issues/15.1/smith.htm) (checked, 5 June 2001).

Smith, J. and Hogan, B. (1999) *Criminal Law*, 9th edn, London/Edinburgh/Dublin: Butterworths.

Sterling, B. (1994) *The Hacker Crackdown*, London: Penguin.

Szafranski, R. (1995) "A Theory of Information Warfare: Preparing for 2020", *Airpower Journal*, 9, Spring: 56–65.

Taylor, P. (1999) *Hackers: Crime in the Digital Sublime*, Routledge: London.

Ungoed-Thomas, J. (1998) "The Schoolboy Spy", *Sunday Times*, 29 March, 5: 1–2.

Vagg, J. (1995) "The policing of signs: trademark infringement and law enforcement", *European Journal on Criminal Policy and Research*, 3, 2: 75–92.

Wall, D.S. (1996), "Reconstructing the soul of Elvis: the social development and legal maintenance of Elvis Presley as intellectual property", *International Journal of the Sociology of Law*, 24, 2: 117–43.

—— (1998) "Policing and the Regulation of Cyberspace", in C. Walker (ed.) "Crime, Criminal Justice and the Internet", Special edition, *Criminal Law Review*.

—— (1999) "Cybercrimes: New wine, no bottles?", in P. Davies, P. Francis and V. Jupp (eds), *Invisible Crimes: Their Victims and their Regulation*, London: Macmillan.

—— (2000a) "Policing the Internet: maintaining order and law on the cyber-beat", in Y. Akdeniz, C.P. Walker and D.S. Wall (eds), *The Internet, Law and Society*, London: Longman.

—— (2000b) "The Theft of Electronic Services: Telecommunications and Teleservices", annex to *Turning the Corner*, London: Office of Science and Technology.

Wallace, J. and Mangan, M. (1996) *Sex, Laws and Cyberspace*, New York: Henry Holt.

Young, L.F. (1995), "United States computer crime laws, criminals and deterrence", *International Yearbook of Law, Computers and Technology*, 9, 1: 1–16.

2 Crime futures and foresight

Challenging criminal behaviour in the information age

Ken Pease

Introduction

As the information age progresses, so new forms of criminal behaviour emerge and our crime futures rapidly become the present. These futures demand new forms of criminological understanding, and this chapter explores the ways in which such understanding is being fostered. The first part will look briefly at the relationship between innovation and crime, the second will consider the role of criminology in regard to emerging crime types and profiles. The final part contemplates the findings of the UK Government's aptly named "Foresight" initiative.

Innovation and crime

There is an illusion of constancy about crime, fostered by the annual publication of the Criminal Statistics, the levels of crime known to the British police. The numbers of thefts, assaults and the like move (mostly) upwards or (more recently) downwards in apparently lawful progression. The same is true of successive British Crime Surveys, where the same closed-ended questions and analysis yield trend lines but miss out on the more subtle shifts in the events covered. Both Criminal Statistics and British Crime Surveys give the impression that some "thing" is being measured, of which we get more or less as time passes. In a crude sense this is true, if the measured thing is taken to be the product of crime opportunities and criminal inclination. In another sense it is not, in that the means whereby people gain advantage over others by force or fraud themselves change dramatically.

Innovation changes crime. The constancy of crime trends achieved by the shoe-horning of crime facts into legal categories blinds us to those changes. For example, poisoning all but disappeared as a method of murder, as a result of improvements in forensic pharmacology and the control of poisons (Walsh, 1994). Change is hidden most completely in respect of what used to be called white-collar crime, because there we lack real data about even the basic trajectory of offending afforded by Criminal Statistics. At least they, with the right cast of mind, may evoke curiosity about what lies behind the categories. Lacking even that, we must rely on ethnographies of white-collar crime to offer the beginnings of insight.

Crime statistics provide only one of the means by which the fluidity of crime phenomena is hidden. Experience suggests that, while people live together, some of the strong will continue to abuse those unfortunate enough to live with them. Some paedophiles will continue to befriend single women to gain (sexual) access to their children, some children will continue to assault and threaten each other, some men will continue to rape. Where there are things to be damaged, some will continue to damage them. Further, the physical plant of society – homes, businesses, transport systems – change only slowly. There will still be recognizable platforms, trains with limited communications and surveillance equipment and paper-based ticketing systems, and the crime which they spawn, for some time to come.

The debate about whether crime changes or remains the same (not that such a debate has featured in criminology) would be pointless, with echoes of the nature–nurture controversy in social science. Asking how much of the flavour of a cake is attributable to its ingredients (nature) and how much to its baking (nurture) is hopelessly naive. Likewise, one cannot sensibly conduct a debate without considering new crimes and new means of committing old crimes. People in pubs glass each other. People in Elizabethan alehouses did not "pewter" each other, the availability of knives being much greater and the effect of pewter on the victim's face being much less dramatic than that of broken glass. Cordless drills made illegal entry to property of various kinds easier. What did the chronically violent use before baseball was invented, and its bats became widespread among the firearm-less robber, even in countries where the game of baseball was seldom played? How do changes in European differentials in duty on tobacco, combined with the lowering of borders, drive patterns of smuggling? How does the sheer volume of cross-border traffic drive rates of importation of people and drugs? As with nature–nurture, crime is 100 per cent stable and 100 per cent volatile, depending on the aspects of the criminal event in focus. Whatever remains invariant, we cannot treat crime as *nothing but* constant, else we lose prevention opportunities.

Criminology is a discipline with a long past, a short history and no future. Thinkers have always seemed fascinated by deviance, a fascination which has only recently been translated into systematic empirical research. That research has lacked a future orientation. The fact that David Farrington and Roger Tarling (1986) could have titled their excellent book *Prediction in Criminology* and not excited comment is remarkable. The book was exclusively about the prediction of the future criminality of individual people, not the future characteristics of crime. It is as though criminology has nothing to say about the future of crime. Crime trends, looked at in terms of specifically who does what to whom (rather than in terms of its legal categorization) are both fascinating and potentially useful in clarifying who will probably do what to whom in the future.

How can criminology get itself a future?

First we need a construct system which acknowledges the future. As a young psychologist, I published in a journal which boasted to its contributors that the paper on which it was printed would last 5,000 years. Since no-one would read such a journal more than twenty years later, other than to ridicule its contents, this struck me as inviting excessive authorial self-regard. Struggling after construct systems for the future will quickly appear ridiculous. Even the genius Arthur C. Clarke didn't get everything right. This means that developing construct systems for the future should be the responsibility of those of us close to the end of our careers, who will be safely dead or demented by the time the inadequacy of those systems becomes manifest.

Ridiculous does not mean useless. Almost any speculation will be of use, since the aim is to elaborate future thinking rather than to be right. The Department of Trade and Industry's Foresight panel concerned with crime (see Foresight, 2000a; 2000b) will be useful in this regard. There are some signs that criminologists are thinking in future-enabling ways. For example, the classification of stealable things in terms of VIVA (low Volume, low Inertia, high Value and moderate Access) and its successor acronyms CRAVED (Concealable, Removable, Available, Valuable, Enjoyable and Disposable) (Felson, 1998; Clarke, 1999) and EVADED (Enduring, Valuable, Available, Distributable, Easy to use and Desirable) (Foresight, 2000b; Wall, 2000) allow speculation about the crime consequences of products and services which do not yet exist.

Second, we need a context of change into which to place the future. Crime anticipation will always be contingent on the specifics of history. Seed adulteration was taken seriously only when wartime made the amateur vegetable grower nationally important (Flood, 1998). Cigarette and alcohol smuggling seems be approaching the threshold of tax loss where serious enforcement begins. Marketing philosophies for cars and computer peripherals, where the initial purchase is less important than the opening of a revenue stream of parts and supplies, change the pattern of theft. As a consequence, theft of external vehicle parts grew enormously at a time when other vehicle crime types fell (Sallybanks and Thomas, 2000).

Third, we need a way of thinking about crime-reductive tactics. The usual model for this is taken to be the environmental movement, whereby design and operation of industry and the public sector is pressed towards sustainability. This model looks a little threadbare in the wake of the failure at The Hague in late 2000 to reach agreement building on the Kyoto accord, and in the UK the ending of the fuel tax escalator and other actions which are distinctly environmentally unfriendly. None the less, the movement towards environmental sustainability has affected attitudes throughout the Western world, in Western Europe substantially and in North America cosmetically. It still seems the best model we have.

Foresight on crime

For all its shortcomings, the Foresight Crime Panel represents an important milestone in UK thinking about crime futures. It may be criticized as un-heroic in focusing on the UK and the middle term, excessively concerned with changes rather than the constants of the abuse of power, both globally and domestically (in both senses). However, even in recognizing its deficiencies, a more elaborated construct system to apply to crime futures emerges.

It is impossible to say whether recent increases in future thinking about crime are parallel consequences of the same *zeitgeist* which led to the formation of the Foresight panel, or whether the panel advanced or even set in train some of those changes. The latter *feels* true. Either way, the result is cautiously heartening in that the first two of the three issues identified as necessary for criminology to get itself a future are beginning to be addressed.

Perhaps the origins of Foresight should be described. A few people, Paul Ekblom of the Home Office (see Ekblom 1997, 1999), Nick Ross the journalist, and my colleague at Huddersfield Michelle Rogerson, were all involved. Trawling through reports of the first phase of the Foresight programme (see Rogerson *et al.*, 2000), two things became evident:

- Developments in crime were rarely considered, and then only superficially.
- Technological developments set out in the reports of sectoral panels had unacknowledged crime implications.

The absence of crime chimed with a more general criticism of the enterprise, namely that the first phase of the programme emphasized economic well-being at the expense of quality-of-life considerations. Crime victimization or its anticipation is a major factor in diminishing quality of life. Incorporating a crime element in the second phase was thus not only justified in its own right but also constituted an attempt to remedy the quality-of-life deficit.

Other specific changes of recent years (whether by *zeitgeist* or mediated by the agency of Foresight) have been:

- The involvement of the Royal Society of Arts, the Design Council and Central St Martins College of Art and Design (in the inspirational person of Dr Lorraine Gamman) in attempts to shape futures by designing out crime (see Learmount *et al.*, 2000 for a relevant report to the Design Council). So far, bags and chairs have been looked at by the Gamman team, and student residences and bicycles by the Royal Society of Arts through its student design competition.
- The establishment of the Jill Dando Institute of Crime Science at University College London (for which the journalist Nick Ross deserves enormous credit), headed by Gloria Laycock, to coordinate the contributions of science to crime reduction. The research ideas emerging from that range from ways of parsing free text fields in crime reports to maximize the information they yield, to the operation of the National DNA Database in ways which maximize the rate of detection of prolific offenders.

As for the Foresight Crime Panel itself, the belief context was set out as follows (Foresight, 2000a):

1   New technology will allow individuals to commit crimes previously beyond their means (the "empowered small agent").

2   The speed and globalization of criminal innovation may leave institutional responses, mainly nationally based, in a frantic attempt to keep up.

3   Proof of identity needs to become more sophisticated and general, since identity theft will proliferate as a means of self-enrichment and a cloak for violent and sexual crimes.

4   Crime will exploit the new electronic world. As the writer of a letter to *Wired* magazine opined, "A fool and his money are soon parted. The Internet just makes it quicker and easier."

5   Location-aware and microchipped valuables will, in time, shrink the universe of stealable things.

6   In the wake of item 5, people may become increasingly the target of offenders thwarted in their pursuit of goods.

It really does not matter much for the value of the Foresight programme whether or not these things come to pass, although the commissioned papers appended to the Foresight report make them plausible as working assumptions. What matters instead is developing a repertoire of anticipations, a fleet-footed-ness in the light of emerging crime trends. Perhaps the central belief is the second, which involves the re-conceptualization of crime and its reduction as a process of co-evolution, or an arms race. It is difficult to overstate how profound are the implications of such a change in thinking. It requires a flip from seeing crime as static to seeing it as dynamic.

The Panel's recommendations are as follows. Each will be discussed in turn.

Recommendation 1: That a dedicated funding stream be established to focus science and technology attention on crime reduction   Science and engineering attention is given to crime and its reduction, but this is limited to circumstances where immediate commercial opportunities are perceived. The problem of identity theft was taken by the Panel to be a major threat, one which was reflected in recent rises in the fraudulent use of credit cards. The use of biometric identification procedures is clearly central to this. How can we prove who we are (and no-one else is who we are)? At the level of police investigation, we need to de-couple the notion of name from that of personal identification. The existence of the national DNA database, and the trend whereby ever smaller amounts of material from crime scenes can be analysed, taken together mean that we should be thinking in terms of DNA and fingerprint identity, rather than name identity. DNA is taken from the scenes of crimes (crime scene samples) and from those charged with offences (criminal justice samples). The Forensic Science Service supplies to police forces details of matches which it identifies. These may be matches between crime scenes, or between crime scene samples and criminal justice samples. Matches between crime scene samples and crim-inal justice samples almost conclusively place a named putative offender at a crime scene. Because they are supported by name identity, the information conveyed by such matches is easily accessed within current ways of thinking. However, substantial information is also conveyed by scene-to-scene matches: for example, which are the prolific unknown offenders, with whom and across what range do they co-offend, are they "recruiters" who initiate a number of neophytes into crime, and how versatile are they across crime types? Having identified name-unknown prolific offenders, DNA analysis can clarify attributes like hair colour, dentition, myopia and the like which would limit the number of possible offenders to a manageably small group. Progress towards DNA-based offender profiling require advances in genetics (and those advances must be cast in ways which are recognized to have operational policing relevance), and a parallel change in police perceptions of information conveyed by scene-to-scene matches, and their operational implications. The police hate what they call Klingon, i.e. scientific work not moulded to address their daily concerns. Such a programme requires hard cross-discipline work which currently lacks a "focus to attract, identify, direct and fund research" (Foresight, 2000b: 14).

Recommendation 2: That a national e-crime strategy is established, for all levels of e-crime In his essay appended to the Foresight report, David Wall anticipates a profound change in what should be policed and how it should be policed. He writes:

> A major challenge for the future will be to establish appropriate policies for policing offending behaviours that relate to electronic services. Given the tensions that exist between private and public interests, it is likely that a joined-up policing approach will/should be adopted to allow corporations to resolve their own victimization, but in collaboration with the police service, even if this collaboration is reduced to the forwarding to the latter of criminal intelligence.
>
> (Wall, 2000)

That the web generates disintermediation is a commonplace, with those mediating between people and services (travel agents, record companies, book-shops and the like) being squeezed out. Wall takes the logic one stage further to argue, in effect, that the police may be one of the intermediaries who will be thus squeezed. This fits with what we know, and has profound implications.

People now live in both "meatspace" and "cyberspace". Routine activity theory suggests that crime will occur when a motivated offender and suitable victim coincide in the absence of a capable guardian (see, e.g., Felson, 1998). In meatspace, the number of such coincidences is limited by the speed at which people can traverse their spatial environment. In cyberspace, this is not the case. Very large numbers of people can be defrauded at once, by that product of the information age the empowered small agent. The possibilities for deception are almost unlimited, since the e-identities are legion behind which an offender can hide. In the Dickens novel *Great Expectations*, the character Wemmick makes his home into a complete refuge from the world outside. These days,

Wemmick's defences would be bypassed, as he could be cyberstalked via his home and office PCs. The Internet ends the age of the home-as-refuge just as artillery ended the age of the castle-as-fortress. Nor is the image overblown, as the empowered small agent blurs the distinction between crime and terrorism to the point of meaninglessness.

Apart from its direct effects, the Internet is voracious of meatspace – or obscene cyberspace – raw material. In a recently reported case, some quarter-of-a-million images of child pornography were accessed in one police investigation. One indiscreet, perhaps obscene, e-mail from a young woman, intended only for her boyfriend, ended up with an audience of millions. Edited cartoons of cartoon characters in obscene poses are now commonplace (including Bart and Lisa Simpson. Do these constitute paedophilic images?) Nowhere is the proper view of crime as constant flux so appropriate as it is for e-crime, and legislation and enforcement aimed at its control. Glick (2001) notes a report suggesting that of fifty-two countries surveyed, only the Philippines has adequately updated its statute book to deal with cybercrime. This was a direct consequence of its inability to prosecute the student responsible for the "LoveBug" virus. This Foresight Panel recommendation was not the most difficult to arrive at.

Recommendation 3: That the wider impact of new technology on the criminal justice system is reviewed – including training, equipment, funding, coordination and consistency – and action taken to address the issues identified   The history of policing and justice is local, with police forces and magistrates court areas being proudly independent. Despite "cross-border crime" still being in common currency as the way of referring to crime across force boundaries, such boundaries form no part of the offender psyche, particularly those offenders operating on a national or global scale. The nonsense of a local perspective was thrown into relief when the Crime Panel's secretary reported that an officer of one force had carried out a survey of Internet crime in his area (finding there to be little). Many further issues arise with digital photography, where editing is easy, and there is no analogue image of the world such as is involved in photosensitive paper developed in a chemical soup.

One issue with which the Panel dealt only superficially was the virtual impossibility of restricting information whenever one wishes to protect the innocent. In recent weeks, the name of a soccer player hounded by a very disturbed young woman was withheld in the print media yet was readily available on the Internet.

Recommendation 4: That thinking on crime reduction is incorporated into the mainstream of central government decision-making   This is certainly the most radical of the Panel's recommendations. It takes its line from S17 of the Crime and Disorder Act 1998, which requires local authorities to consider the crime consequences of all the authority's decision-making (see Moss and Pease, 1999; Moss, 2001). Implicit in S17 is the notion that crime may be the unintended consequence of the ways in which people do business in the public sector, and that attending to such consequences would ensure that cost-free or cost-limited decisions, which would generate less crime, were at least considered. For example, there is now good evidence that building homes to "Secure by Design" standards yields less crime (Armitage, 2000). Not considering crime consequences when approving plans for development, particularly in high crime areas, would be in breach of S17. This attempt to be pre-emptive is limited, however, to local authorities. We thus have the absurd situation that appeals against refusals of planning permission are heard by a tribunal which is part of central government, and which is thus not bound by S17. Thus planning permission can be properly refused locally, in adherence to S17, and an appeal against the refusal properly allowed centrally, since no S17 obligation exists. That all of this charade happens at public expense simply adds insult to injury. The Foresight Crime Panel thus advocates extension of S17 in some form to the decisions of central government. There was much discussion in the Panel about whether S17 obligations should be further provided. This writer believes that it could properly be extended at least to transport providers.

In its agreed thinking concerning the private sector, the Panel was intrigued by the Turnbull recommendations of the Institute of Chartered Accountants in England and Wales (see Foresight, 2000b: 20). These require inclusion of arrangements for managing corporate risks in company annual reports. The Panel emphasized that this should include assessments of risks associated with crime. Of course, by itself this would not be enough, since it would include only risks to the profitability of the company concerned. Thus a company could make flagrantly criminogenic products and still adhere to Turnbull recommendations. Ideally, the Turnbull recommendations should be extended, as good corporate citizenship, to establish a standard for corporate behaviour in relation to crime committed against, or using, its products. One could perhaps rewrite the history of the mobile phone in relation to crime, had manufacturers and service providers been minded to operate in ways which minimized the crime burden imposed through its products, and maximized their crime reductive use.

Recommendation 5: That a programme is developed to address crime at all stages of a product's life cycle   This recommendation has clear links with Recommendation 4. In essence, it aspires to create a culture of attack testing into product design and operation. The elements, verbatim, were:

- Identifying the roles of manufacturers, retailers and consumers in developing secure products.
- A voluntary standards system within manufacturing which would show that the "criminogenic capacity" of a product had been addressed to diminish criminal misuse and "stealability".
- The contribution of the retailer, particularly the impact of e-commerce and home delivery on crime.

- How to encourage a climate of demand for secure products among consumers.
- An annual award for new products which have been designed with crime reduction in mind.

The third of these elements may perhaps be used to illustrate the thinking. In so far as e-commerce develops, many vans will bring many parcels to many doors. What do they do when they get there? Will the goods just be left outside, left with a neighbour, returned to the depot? What will be the occupancy cues gleaned by van-drivers, unscrupulous neighbours or passers-by? The issue can be thought of in terms of community development or a technological quick fix (or both). In the former, streets might have designated delivery houses, different ones for each day of the week, where occupancy is guaranteed. This would require neighbours to talk to each other, agree arrangements, chat when they collect their parcels. They would even discover each others' names! In the latter, the e-commerce version of the cat flap or old-style coal delivery would be created. (Coal used to be delivered in sacks which were emptied down a chute sloping into a coal bunker, from which the householder would extract coal as needed. The coal merchant would have no access to the inside of the home, and people could not easily steal the coal without risking imprisonment in the bunker because the chute sloped downwards.) The e-commerce equivalent of such delivery mechanisms should be subject to attack testing by those simulating a burglar's or fraudster's cast of mind.

Foresight's future

The Panel is now at its halfway mark. It will progress through a number of Task Forces. Task Forces identified at this point are:

- Science and Technology: to identify cross-cutting technologies.
- Business and Crime: to explore how crime risks can inform business decision-making.
- Connected Society: to explore the role of technology in strengthening communities.
- Products and Crime: to develop crime reduction through design.

The frustrating part of the Panel's work is that its major impact is likely to be through osmosis rather than by direct influence, and hence never be properly attributable to the Panel itself. A further frustration is the mixture of science and Realpolitik which the process entails. For the process to advance, there must be a critical mass of people for whom Foresight thinking comes naturally. For this reason, Recommendation 4 is arguably the most important, since it integrates such thinking into people's working worlds.

There is a case for saying that, even if Foresight thinking becomes widespread, it will enjoy only transient influence, because the notions of crime and blame are so intertwined. A crime is solved when someone to blame is found (see Wilkins, 1997). A crime is understood when the offender's motivation is revealed. Foresight thinking requires a focus on the crime event, and the adjustment of the world to limit the translation of criminal inclination into criminal action. A half-remembered study by the ethologist Niko Tinbergen comes to mind (see Tinbergen, 1989, for an overview of work in this tradition). Spotted fly-catchers (as their name suggests) pluck flies out of the air. Feeding them by hand eliminates their need to pluck things out of the air. After a while, hand-fed birds begin to move as if plucking flies out of the air. This is known as a vacuum response. To labour finally to the point, most offenders are unlike the spotted flycatcher. They will do things which gain most satisfaction at least effort. When non-criminal alternatives present themselves which are as profitable for as little effort (an admittedly difficult threshold to reach for, among others, successful drug-dealers) the non-criminal alternative will be accepted. While flycatchers pluck imaginary flies out of empty air, burglars do not pluck imaginary videos out of empty houses. Crime, while regrettable, is largely sensible in its choice of target and execution. Foresight thinking requires the problem of crime to be separated from the problem of the criminal, and crime reduction to be recognized as very imperfectly associated with changes in the criminal. Yet designing a society which resists crime may continue to be seen as beside the point, with wickedness and its control retaining their mantle as the proper road to crime control. The road leads nowhere but to fruitless polemics, but this observation does not guarantee that it will not be taken.

References

Armitage, R. (2000) *An Evaluation of Secured by Design Housing within West Yorkshire*, Briefing Note 7/00, London: Home Office.

Clarke, R.V. (1999) *Hot Products: Understanding, Anticipating and Reducing Demand for Stolen Goods*, Police Research Series, Paper 112, London: Home Office.

Ekblom, P. (1997) "Gearing up against crime: A dynamic framework to help designers keep up with the adaptive criminal in a changing world", *International Journal of Risk, Security and Crime Prevention*, 2, 4: 249–65.

—— (1999) "The Conjunction of Criminal Opportunity: A Tool for Clear, Joined-Up Thinking about Community Safety and Crime Reduction", in S. Ballintyne, V. McLaren and K. Pease (eds), *Key issues in crime prevention, crime reduction and community safety*, London: IPPR.

Farrington, D.P. and Tarling, R. (1986) *Prediction in Criminology*, London: HMSO.

Felson, M. (1998) *Crime and Everyday Life*, Thousand Oaks, Ca: Pine Forge Press.

Flood, R. (1998) "Seed Quality and Seeds Legislation – The Story So Far", *Seed News*, Ryton: HDRA; pp. 3–8.

Foresight (2000a) *Just Around the Corner*, Report of the Crime Prevention Panel, London: Department of Trade and Industry.

—— (2000b) *Turning the Corner*, Report of the Crime Prevention Panel, London: Department of Trade and Industry.

Glick, B. (2001) "Cyber criminals mock the archaic", *Computing*, 4 January, p. 32.

Learmount, S., Cooper, R. and Press, M. (2000) *Design Against Crime: a report to the Design Council, the Home Office and Department of Trade and Industry*, Cambridge: Cambridge University Publications Centre.

Moss, K. (2001) "Crime Prevention vs Planning. Is S.17 a Material Consideration?", *Crime Prevention and Community Safety: An International Journal*, 3, 1: 3–8.

Moss, K. and Pease, K. (1999) "S.17 Crime and Disorder Act 1998: A Wolf in Sheep's Clothing?", *Crime Prevention and Community Safety: An International Journal*, 1, 4: 15–19.

Rogerson, M., Ekblom, P. and Pease K. (2000) "Crime reduction and the benefit of foresight", in S. Ballintyne, V. McLaren and K. Pease (eds), *Secure Foundations*, London: IPPR.

Sallybanks, J. and Thomas, N. (2000) "Theft of External Vehicle Parts: An Emerging Problem", *Crime Prevention and Community Safety: An International Journal*, 2, 1: 17–22.

Tinbergen, N. (1989) *The Study of Instinct*, Oxford: Clarendon Press.

Wall, D.S. (2000) "The Theft of Electronic Services: Telecommunications and Teleservices", attached to Foresight Crime Prevention Panel, *Turning the Corner*, Report of the Crime Prevention Panel, London: Department of Trade and Industry.

Walsh, D.P. (1994) "On the Obsolescence of Crime Forms", in R.V. Clarke (ed.), *Crime Prevention Studies 2*, Monsey, NY: Willow Tree Press.

Wilkins, L.T. (1997) "Wartime Operational Research in Britain and Situational Crime Prevention", in G. Newman, R.V. Clarke and S.G. Shoham (eds), *Rational Choice and Situational Crime Prevention*, Aldershot: Avebury.

3 Telecommunication fraud in the digital age

The convergence of technologies

Peter Grabosky and Russell Smith[1]

Introduction

At the beginning of the twenty-first century, the convergence of computing and communications technologies has altered considerably the way in which industrialized communities function. It has created untold benefits for education, delivery of health services, recreation and commerce, and changed considerably the nature of modern workplaces and patterns of employment. Unfortunately, it has also created unprecedented opportunities for crime (see Grabosky and Smith, 1998; Grabosky, Smith and Dempsey, 2001). Identifying these vulnerabilities, and mobilizing appropriate countermeasures, will be one of the great challenges facing us as the new millennium unfolds.

This chapter will suggest that much computer-related illegality lies beyond the capacity of contemporary law enforcement and regulatory agencies alone to control, and that security in cyberspace will depend on the efforts of a wide range of institutions, as well as on a degree of self-help by potential victims of digital crime. The ideal configuration may be expected to differ, depending upon the activity in question, but is likely to entail a mix of law enforcement, technological and market solutions. Given the fact that cyberspace knows no boundaries, and that computer crime often transcends national frontiers, effective countermeasures will also require a substantial degree of international cooperation.

We begin by discussing ten of the latest forms of digital crime – that is, crime that involves information systems as instruments or as targets of illegality. By "digital", we refer to the fact that information systems simply operate by reducing data to streams of zeros and ones. Almost every type of information is thus able to be transmitted across telecommunication networks connected either by wires or by means of radio communication.

Varieties of digital crime

The varieties of criminal activity that can be committed with or against information systems are surprisingly diverse. Some of these are not really new in substance – only the medium is new. Others represent entirely new forms of illegality altogether. These forms of crime are not necessarily mutually exclusive, nor is the following list exhaustive.

Theft of telecommunications services

The "phone phreakers" of three decades ago set a precedent for what has become a major criminal industry. The market for stolen communications services is now large. There are those who simply seek to avoid or to obtain a discount on the cost of a telephone call, whilst there are others, such as illegal immigrants, who are unable to acquire legitimate information services without disclosing their identity and their status. There are others still who appropriate information services to conduct illicit business with less risk of detection. All pose a significant challenge to carriers and service providers – and to the general public, who often bear the financial burden of fraud.

The means of stealing telecommunications services are diverse, and include the "cloning" of cellular phones and the counterfeiting of telephone cards. It may also entail gaining unauthorized access to an organization's telephone switchboard (PBX). By gaining access to a PBX, individuals or criminal organizations can obtain access to dial-in/dial-out circuits and then make their own calls or sell call time to third parties (Gold, 1999). Offenders may gain access to the switchboard by impersonating a technician, by fraudulently obtaining an employee's access code, or by using software available on the Internet. Some sophisticated offenders loop between PBX systems to evade detection. Additional forms of service theft include capturing "calling card" details and on-selling calls charged to the calling card account, and counterfeiting or illicitly reprogramming stored-value telephone cards.

It has been suggested that up to 5 per cent of total industry turnover has been lost to fraud (Schieck, 1995: 2–5; Newman, 1998). Costs to individual subscribers can also be significant. In one case, computer hackers in the United States illegally obtained access to Scotland Yard's telephone network and made £620,000-worth of international calls for which Scotland Yard was responsible (Tendler and Nuttall, 1996).

Communications in furtherance of criminal conspiracies

Just as legitimate organizations in the private and public sectors rely upon information systems for communications and record-keeping, so too are the activities of criminal organizations enhanced by technology.

There is evidence of telecommunications equipment being used to facilitate organized drug trafficking, gambling, prostitution, money laundering, child pornography and trade in weapons (in those jurisdictions where such activities are illegal). The use of encryption technology may also place criminal communications beyond the reach of law enforcement.

Information piracy/counterfeiting/forgery

Digital technology permits perfect reproduction and easy dissemination of print, graphics, sound and multimedia combinations. It is now possible, for example, to download from the Internet music from the latest CDs and feature films. The temptation to reproduce copyright material for personal use, for sale at a lower price, or, indeed, for free distribution, has proven irresistible to many. According to the *Straits Times* (8 November 1999), a copy of the most recent James Bond film *The World is Not Enough* was available free on the Internet before its official release. This, and similar incidents, have caused considerable concern to owners of copyright material. When creators of a work, in whatever medium, are unable to profit from their creations, there can be a chilling effect on creative effort generally, in addition to financial loss.

It has been estimated that losses of between fifteen and seventeen billion US dollars are sustained each year by industry through copyright infringement (United States Information Infrastructure Task Force, 1995: 131). The Software Publishers Association has estimated that $7.4 billion worth of software was lost to piracy in 1993 with $2 billion of that being stolen from the Internet (Meyer and Underwood, 1994). Ryan (1998) puts the cost of foreign piracy to American industry at more than $10 billion in 1996, including $1.8 billion in the film industry, $1.2 billion in music, $3.8 billion in business application software and $690 million in book publishing.

Dissemination of offensive materials

Content considered by some to be objectionable exists in abundance in cyberspace. This includes, among much else, sexually explicit materials (including child pornography), racist propaganda and instructions for the fabrication of incendiary and explosive devices. Telecommunications systems can also be used for harassing, threatening or intrusive communications, ranging from the traditional obscene telephone call to its contemporary manifestation in "cyber-stalking", in which persistent messages are sent to an unwilling recipient.

Digital extortion

Computer networks may also be used in carrying out criminal extortion. The UK's *Sunday Times* reported in 1996 that over forty financial institutions in the United Kingdom and the United States had been attacked electronically over the previous three years. In England, financial institutions were reported to have paid significant amounts to sophisticated computer criminals who threatened to wipe out computer systems (*The Sunday Times*, 2 June 1996). The article cited four incidents between 1993 and 1995 in which a total of £42.5 million was paid by senior executives of the organizations concerned, who were convinced of the extortionists' capacity to crash their computer systems (see Denning, 1999: 233–4).

One case, which illustrates the transnational reach of extortionists, involved a number of German hackers who compromised the system of an internet service provider (ISP) in South Florida, disabling eight of the ISP's ten servers. The offenders obtained personal information and credit card details of 10,000 subscribers, and, communicating via electronic mail through one of the compromised accounts, demanded that 30,000 US dollars be delivered to a mail drop in Germany. Cooperation between United States and German authorities resulted in the arrest of the extortionists (Bauer, 1998).

More recently, an extortionist in Eastern Europe obtained the credit card details of customers of a North American-based on-line music retailer, and published some of them on the Internet when the retailer refused to comply with his demands (Markoff, 2000).

Electronic money laundering and tax evasion

For some time now, electronic funds transfers have assisted in concealing and moving the proceeds of crime. Emerging technologies will greatly assist in concealing the origin of ill-gotten gains. Legitimately-derived income may also be more easily concealed from taxation authorities. Large financial institutions will no longer be the only ones with the ability to achieve electronic funds transfers crossing numerous jurisdictions at the speed of light. The development of informal banking institutions and parallel banking systems may permit central bank supervision to be bypassed, but it will also facilitate the evasion of cash transaction reporting requirements in those nations which have them. Traditional "underground" banks, which have flourished in Asian countries for centuries, will enjoy even greater capacity through the use of telecommunications.

With the emergence and proliferation of various technologies in electronic commerce, one can easily envisage how traditional countermeasures against money laundering and tax evasion may soon be of limited value. It may soon be possible to sell a quantity of heroin, in return for an untraceable transfer of stored value to a "smart-card" which is then downloaded anonymously to an account in a financial institution situated in an overseas jurisdiction which protects the privacy of banking clients. These funds can then be discreetly drawn upon as and when required, downloading them back to the stored value card (Wahlert, 1996).

Electronic vandalism and terrorism

As never before, Western industrial society is dependent upon complex data processing and telecommunications systems. Damage to, or interference with, any of these systems can lead to catastrophic consequences. Whether motivated by curiosity or vindictiveness, electronic intruders cause inconvenience at best and have the potential for inflicting massive harm (Hundley and Anderson, 1995; Schwartau, 1994).

While this potential has yet to be realized, a number of individuals and protest groups have hacked the official web pages of various governmental and commercial organizations (Rathmell, 1997).[2] This may also operate in reverse. Early in 1999, an organized hacking incident was apparently directed at a server which hosted the Internet domain for East Timor, which at the time was seeking its independence from Indonesia (Creed, 1999).

Defence planners around the world are investing substantially in information warfare, researching means of disrupting the information technology infrastructure of defence systems (Stix, 1995).[3] Attempts were made to disrupt the computer systems of the Sri Lankan Government (Associated Press, 1998), and of the North Atlantic Treaty Organization during the 1999 bombing of Belgrade (British Broadcasting Corporation, 1999).

Electronic sales and investment fraud

As electronic commerce becomes more prevalent, the application of digital technology to fraudulent business endeavours will be that much greater. The use of the telephone for fraudulent sales pitches, deceptive charitable solicitations or bogus investment overtures is increasingly common. Cyberspace now abounds with a wide variety of investment opportunities, from traditional securities such as stocks and bonds to more exotic opportunities such as coconut farming, the sale and leaseback of automatic teller machines, and worldwide telephone lotteries (Cella and Stark, 1997: 837). Indeed, the digital age has been accompanied by unprecedented opportunities for misinformation. Fraudsters now enjoy direct access to millions of prospective victims around the world, instantaneously and at minimal cost.

Classic pyramid schemes and "Exciting, Low-Risk Investment Opportunities" are not uncommon. The technology of the World Wide Web is ideally suited to investment solicitations. In the words of two Securities and Exchange Commission (SEC) staff: "[A]t very little cost, and from the privacy of a basement office or living room, the fraudster can produce a home page that looks better and more sophisticated than that of a Fortune 500 company" (Cella and Stark, 1997: 822).

Illegal interception of digital information

Developments in technology also provide new opportunities for electronic eavesdropping. From activities as time-honoured as surveillance of an unfaithful spouse, to the newest forms of political and industrial espionage, information interception has increasing applications. Here again, technological developments create new vulnerabilities. In New York, for example, two individuals recently used a sophisticated scanning device to pick up some 80,000 cellular telephone numbers from motorists who drove past their Brooklyn apartment. Had the two not been arrested, they could have used the information to create cloned mobile telephones which could have resulted in up to $100 million in illegal calls being made (*West Australian*, 9 July 1996: 47).

The electromagnetic signals emitted by a computer may themselves be intercepted. Cables may act as broadcast antennas. In many jurisdictions, existing law does not prevent the remote monitoring of computer radiation. It has been reported that the notorious American hacker Kevin Poulsen was able to gain access to law enforcement and national security wiretap data prior to his arrest in 1991 (Littman, 1997). In 1995, hackers employed by a criminal organization attacked the communications system of the Amsterdam Police. The hackers succeeded in gaining police operational intelligence, and in disrupting police communications (Rathmell, 1997).

Electronic funds transfer crime

The proliferation of electronic funds transfer systems will enhance the risk that such transactions may be intercepted and diverted. Existing systems such as automated teller machines (ATMs) and electronic funds transfer at point of sale (EFTPOS) technologies have already been the targets of fraudulent activity, and the development of stored value cards or smart cards, super smart cards and optical memory cards will no doubt invite some individuals to apply their talents to the challenge of electronic counterfeiting and overcoming security access systems. Just as the simple telephone card can be reprogrammed, smart cards are vulnerable to re-engineering. Credit card details can be captured and used by unauthorized persons. The transfer of funds from home between accounts and in payment of transactions will also create vulnerabilities in terms of theft and fraud, and the widescale development of electronic money for use on the Internet will lead to further opportunities for crime. What for the past quarter-century has been loosely described as "computer fraud" will have numerous new manifestations.

Between June and October 1994, a group of Russian computer hackers attempted to steal approximately 10.7 million US dollars from various Citibank customers' accounts in the United States by manipulating the banks' computerized funds transfer system. One offender, Vladimir L. Levin, was working in a Russian firm, and gained access over 40 times to Citibank's funds transfer system using a personal computer and stolen passwords and account identification numbers. Using a computer terminal in his employer's office in St Petersburg, he authorized transfers of funds from Citibank's head office in New Jersey to accounts which he and his co-conspirators held in California, Finland, Germany, the Netherlands, Switzerland and Israel.

Levin was arrested at the UK's Stansted airport on 3 March 1995 and, after protracted legal proceedings which went to the House of Lords, he was extradited to stand trial before the Federal District Court in New York's Southern District. On 24 February 1998 he pleaded guilty to conspiracy to defraud and was sentenced to thirty-six months imprisonment and to pay Citibank $240,015 in restitution. Citibank was able to recover all but $240,000 of the illegally transferred funds. None of the bank's depositors lost money and, since the fraud was discovered, Citibank requires customers to use an electronic password generator for every transfer of funds. The consequences for Citibank's business reputation were, however, considerable (R. v *Governor of Brixton Prison*; *Ex parte Levin* [1996] 3 WLR 657; *In re Levin*, House of Lords, 19 June 1997).

Common themes and issues

Secrecy and anonymity

A number of common themes and issues are present in each of the forms of digital crime described above. The first concerns the way in which technologies can conceal the content of communications and disguise the identity of users.

Technologies of encryption, for example, can limit access by law enforcement personnel to communications carried out in furtherance of a conspiracy, or to the dissemination of objectionable materials between consenting parties (Denning, 1999).

Also important are technologies for concealing a communicator's identity. Electronic impersonation, colloquially termed "spoofing", can be used in furtherance of a variety of criminal activities, including fraud, criminal conspiracy, harassment and vandalism. Technologies of anonymity further complicate the task of identifying a suspect (Froomkin, 1995).

Victims of digital crime are frequently reluctant to report their victimization to the authorities; in addition the technologies of secrecy and anonymity discussed here often make detection of the offender extremely difficult. Those who seek to mask their identity on computer networks are often able to do so by means of "looping", or "weaving" through multiple sites based in a variety of nations. Anonymous remailers and encryption devices can shield one from the scrutiny of all but the most determined and technologically sophisticated regulatory and enforcement agencies.

Some crimes do not result in detection or loss until some time after the event. Considerable time may elapse before the activation of a computer virus, or between the insertion of a "logic bomb" and its detonation. Finally, technology has greatly facilitated so-called identity-related economic crime in which offenders fabricate documents through the use of desktop publishing equipment to misrepresent their own identity or make use of another's identity for illegitimate purposes (Smith, 1999).

Motivations

Given the diversity of digital crime, it is not surprising that the various types of behaviour discussed here flow from a wide range of motives. Some of these are as old as human society, including greed, lust, revenge and curiosity. Revenge in the modern era can also entail an ideological dimension. Of considerable significance, if not unique to computer related crime, is the intellectual challenge of defeating a complex system. Motivations, whether on the part of individuals or in the aggregate, are very difficult to change. For this reason, the most strategically advantageous approaches to digital crime will be concerned with the reduction of opportunities, and with the enhancement of guardianship.

Opportunities

While motives tend not to change, the variety and number of opportunities for the commission of digital crime have proliferated. The exponential growth in connectivity of computing and communications creates parallel opportunities for prospective offenders, and parallel risks for prospective victims.

The most effective way of eliminating opportunities for digital crime is simply to pull the plug. This is of course unrealistic – the affluent nations of the world are now highly dependent on information technology. For the poorer nations, information technology is probably a necessary, if not sufficient, path to economic development. Thus the challenge lies in managing risk so as to achieve the maximum benefits which flow from new technologies, while minimizing the downside. A merchant could scrutinize every credit card transaction so as to drastically reduce the risk of fraud, but in the process drive away legitimate customers. At a higher level, nations around the world are in the process of developing policies about where to draw the line on such fundamental questions as the balance between the citizen's privacy and the imperatives of law enforcement, and freedom of expression versus the protection of certain cultural values.

There are many technologies which reduce the opportunity to commit digital crime. Given that so much digital crime depends upon unauthorized access to information systems, access control and authentication technologies have become essential. Sophisticated advice and products for computer crime prevention are provided by one of the world's growth industries of today, namely computer security.

Denning (1999) offers a comprehensive inventory of technologies for reducing opportunities for computer crime. She describes technologies of encryption and anonymity which permit concealment of the content of communications, such as a consumer's credit card details, or of the identity of the communicator (not all participants in discussion groups on reproductive health wish to disclose their identities). Denning also outlines technologies of authentication, from basic passwords to various biometric devices, such as fingerprint or voice recognition technology, and retinal imaging, which greatly enhance the difficulty of obtaining unauthorized access to information systems.

Virus detectors can identify and block malicious computer code, whilst blocking and filtering programs can screen out unwanted content. A rich variety of commercial software now exists with which to block access to certain sites (Venditto, 1996).

Guardians

Much digital crime takes place simply because of the absence of a capable guardian. Capable guardianship has evolved over human history – from feudalism, to the rise of the state and the proliferation of public institutions of social control, to the postmodern era in which employees of private security services vastly outnumber sworn police officers in many industrial democracies. Here again, it may be instructive to compare digital crime with more conventional types of crime.

Guardianship against conventional crime involves preventive efforts on the part of prospective victims, contributions by members of the general public or commercial third parties, as well as the activities of law enforcement agencies. Indeed, it is often only when private efforts at crime prevention fail that the criminal process is mobilized. So it is that owners of motor vehicles are encouraged to lock their vehicles at all times, that insurance contracts may offer premium discounts for crime prevention measures such as theft alarms, and that some car parks have video surveillance or private security guards in attendance. Often it is only when these systems fail that the assistance of law enforcement is sought.

Technology can also enhance guardianship. Denning (1999) describes various technologies for detecting attempted intrusions to information systems. Alarms can indicate when repeated login attempts fail because of incorrect passwords, or when access is sought outside of normal working hours. Other anomaly detection devices will identify unusual patterns of system use, including atypical destination and duration of telephone calls, or unusual spending patterns using credit cards.

Guardianship can also be enhanced by market forces. As large organizations begin to appreciate their vulnerability to electronic theft or vandalism, they may be expected to insure against potential losses. It is very much in the interests of insurance companies to require appropriate security precautions on the part of their policyholders. Indeed, decisions to insure and to price insurance may well depend upon the security practices of prospective policy holders. Subcontractors may also be required to have strict IT integrity programs in place as a condition of doing business.

Citizen co-production can also complement activities undertaken by agencies of the state. An example of collaborative public–private effort in furtherance of controlling objectionable content is the Netherlands Hotline for Child Pornography on Internet, an initiative of the Foundation for Dutch Internet Providers (NLIP), the Dutch National Criminal Intelligence Service (CRI), Internet users and the National Bureau against Racism (LBR). Users who encounter child pornography originating in the Netherlands, identifiable by a domain name address ending in "nl", are encouraged to report the site to meldpunt@xs4all.nl.

The policing of terrestrial space is now very much a pluralistic endeavour, and so too is the policing of cyberspace. Responsibilities for the control of digital crime will be similarly shared between agents of the state, information security specialists in the private sector and the individual user. In cyberspace today, as on terrestrial space two millennia ago, the first line of defence will be self-defence – in other words, minding one's own store.

Extra-territorial issues

One of the more significant aspects of digital crime is its global reach. While international offending is by no means a uniquely modern phenomenon, the global nature of cyberspace significantly enhances the ability of offenders to commit crimes in one country which will affect individuals in a variety of other countries. This poses great challenges for the detection, investigation and prosecution of offenders.

Two problems arise in relation to the prosecution of telecommunications offences which have an inter-jurisdictional aspect: first, the determination of where the offence occurred in order to decide which law to apply; and, second, obtaining evidence and ensuring that the offender can be located and tried before a court. Both these questions raise complex legal problems of jurisdiction and extradition (see Lanham *et al.*, 1987).

Even if one is able to decide which law is applicable, further difficulties may arise in applying that law. In a unitary jurisdiction, such as New Zealand's, where there is one law and one law enforcement agency, determining and applying the applicable law is difficult enough. Criminal activities committed across the globe, however, pose even greater problems. Sovereign governments are finding it difficult to exercise control over online behaviour at home, not to mention abroad. A resident of Chicago who falls victim to a telemarketing scam originating in Albania, for example, can expect little assistance from law enforcement agencies in either jurisdiction. As a result, regulation by territorially-based rules may prove to be inappropriate for these types of offence (Post, 1995).

Extraterritorial law enforcement costs are also often prohibitive. The time, money and uncertainty required by international investigations, and if investigations are successful, extradition proceedings, can be so high as to preclude attention to all but the most serious offending. Moreover, the cooperation across international boundaries in furtherance of such enforcement usually requires a congruence of values and priorities which, despite prevailing trends towards globalization, exists only infrequently.

Other issues which may complicate investigation entail the logistics of search and seizure during real time, the sheer volume of material within which incriminating evidence may be contained, and the encryption of information, which may render it entirely inaccessible or accessible only after a massive application of decryption technology.

Traditionally the jurisdiction of courts was local: that is, courts could only entertain prosecutions in respect of offences committed against local laws where there existed a sufficient link between the offence and the jurisdiction in question. There is, however, always the possibility that legislatures will confer extraterritorial jurisdiction for some crimes. Some common examples include offences committed on the high seas, counterfeiting offences, crimes committed by members of the defence forces, and, recently in Australia, sexual relations between Australians and children overseas who are under sixteen years of age.

To the extent that international digital crime is amenable to international enforcement, it will require concerted international cooperation. Past performance in the context of other forms of criminality would suggest that this cooperation is unlikely to be forthcoming except in the relatively infrequent types of illegality where there is widespread international consensus about the activity in question (such as child pornography, or fraud on a scale likely to destabilize financial markets), and about the desirability of suppressing it. In many instances, extradition is likely to be more cumbersome the greater the cultural and ideological distance between the two parties.

Even so, this would assume a seamless world system of stable sovereign states: such a system does not exist today, nor is it likely to exist in the foreseeable future. Law enforcement and regulatory vacuums exist in some parts of the world, certainly in those settings where the state has effectively collapsed. Even where state power does exist in full force, the corruption of individual regimes can impede international cooperation.

Countermeasures

It has long been recognized that the criminal justice system is a very imperfect means of social control, and that effective crime prevention requires the contribution of families, schools and many other institutions of civil society. This is no less the case with digital crime than it is with traditional forms of crime.

It will be immediately apparent that the detection, investigation and prosecution of all of the forms of digital crime described in this chapter pose formidable challenges. Crime in the digital age can be committed by an individual in one jurisdiction against a victim or victims on the other side of the globe. The control of cybercrime lies beyond the capacity of any one agency. What principles can we articulate to assist us in controlling computer crime?

The importance of prevention

It is a great deal more difficult to pursue an online offender to the ends of the earth than to prevent the offence in the first place. The trite homily that prevention is better than cure is nowhere more appropriate than in cyberspace. It applies no less to high-technology crime than it does to residential burglary. Just as one would be most unwise to leave one's house unlocked when heading off to work in the morning, so too is it foolish to leave one's information systems accessible to unauthorized persons.

The role of self help

Another key principle in the prevention of digital crime is the need to raise awareness on the part of prospective victims to the risks which they face. Individuals and institutions should be made aware of the potential consequences of an attack on their information assets, and of the basic precautionary measures which they should take. Those agencies which stand to gain the most from electronic commerce have the greatest interest in developing secure payments systems. Technologies of computer security can provide significant protection against various forms of computer crime. But there are other, "low-technology" measures which should not be overlooked. Perhaps foremost among these is staff selection. Surveys of businesses reveal that one's own staff often pose a greater threat to one's information assets than do so called "outsiders". Disgruntled employees and former employees constitute a significant risk.

Suffice it to say that great care should be taken when engaging and disengaging staff, or in outsourcing IT activities to the private sector.

Similarly, systems and the information contained therein should be backed up regularly. This will not prevent an attack, but it will reduce the risk of irretrievable loss of or damage to data in the event of an attack or system failure.

The use of non-governmental resources

More generally, given the resource constraints which most governments face, it is desirable to enlist the assistance of private sector and community interests in the prevention and detection of digital crime.

Market forces will generate powerful influences in furtherance of electronic crime control. Given the immense fortunes which stand to be made by those who develop secure processes for electronic commerce, they hardly need any prompting from government. In some sectors, there are ample commercial incentives which can operate in furtherance of digital crime prevention. Information security promises to become one of the growth industries of this century. Some of the new developments in information security which have begun to emerge include technologies of authentication. The simple password for access to a computer system, vulnerable to theft or determination by other means, is being complemented or succeeded altogether by biometric authentication methods such as retinal imaging and voice or finger printing.

Detection of unauthorized access to or use of computer systems can be facilitated by such technologies as artificial intelligence, which can identify anomalous patterns of use according to time of day or patterns of keystroke.

Issues of objectionable content can be addressed at the individual level by blocking and filtering software, by which systems administrators can prevent employees' access to certain types of sites. Simple software can track websites visited and the amount of time spent at each site. Internet manager software enables a systems administrator to develop a custom blocking list that could deny access to pages containing certain specified keywords.

Other software can develop customized access categories. When an employee clicks for a page, the software matches the user's ID with the content allowable for the assigned category, then either loads the requested page or advises the user that her request has been denied. The software logs denied requests for subsequent inspection by management. Some software packages can also measure and record the bandwith consumed by Internet applications.

In extreme cases, some would take the law into their own hands. The metaphor of cyberspace as a frontier is not entirely inapposite. There are vigilantes in cyberspace. In some instances, self-help by victims of digital crime may itself entail illegality. "Counter-hacking" by private citizens or by government agencies has been suggested as one way of responding to illegal intrusions. A group calling themselves Ethical Hackers Against Pedophilia have threatened to disable the computers of those whom they find dealing in digital child pornography. Public sector managers would be well advised to avoid becoming either the initiators or the targets of counter-hacking.

Enhancing the capacity of law enforcement

The continuing uptake of digital technology around the world means that law enforcement agencies will be required to keep abreast of rapidly developing technologies. This will entail training in new investigative techniques. As new technologies are exploited by criminals, it becomes even more important for law enforcement not to be left behind. This is a significant challenge, given the emerging trend for skilled investigators to be "poached" by the private sector. The collaboration of law enforcement with specialized expertise residing in the private sector will be a common feature in years to come.

And it will be important for public sector managers to develop close ties with law enforcement, to report suspected illegality to them, as well to provide them with assistance when required. The police, and the institutions which they serve in both public and private sectors, should be familiar with each others' needs.

The importance of international cooperation

As already mentioned, the global nature of cyberspace necessitates the development of new strategies to combat criminal activity which can originate from the other side of the world. The basic approach to overcoming the transnational issues of digital crime lies in developing cooperation between nations. This is more easily said than done, given the significant differences in legal systems, values and priorities around the world.

Enlisting the assistance of overseas authorities is not an automatic process, and often requires pre-existing agreements relating to formal mutual assistance in criminal matters. Nevertheless, there are numerous examples of successful measures, and the web of mutual assistance is being woven ever more tightly.

Conclusion

It has become trite to suggest that the world is a shrinking place. On the one hand, this shrinking is highly beneficial. People around the world now enjoy economic, cultural and recreational opportunities which were previously not accessible. On the other hand, the rapid mobility of people, money, information, ideas, and commodities generally, has provided new opportunities for crime. Linkages between events and institutions at home and abroad are inevitable, and will inevitably proliferate. This will require unprecedented cooperation between nations, and will inevitably generate tensions arising from differences in national values. Even within nations, tensions between such values as privacy and the imperatives of law enforcement will be high on the public agenda. New organizational forms will emerge to combat new manifestations of criminality.

There is a significant danger that premature regulatory interventions may not only fail to achieve their desired effect, but may also have a negative impact on the development of technology for the benefit of all. Over-regulation, or premature regulatory intervention, may run the risk of chilling investment and innovation. Given the increasingly competitive nature of the global market-place, governments may be forced to choose between paternalistic imperatives and those of commercial development and economic growth.

The challenge facing those who would minimize digital crime is to seek a balance which would allow a tolerable degree of illegality in return for creative exploitation of the technology. Even at this early stage of the technological revolution, it may be useful for individuals, interest groups and governments to articulate their preferences and let these serve as signals to the market. Markets may then be able to provide appropriate responses which governments are unwilling or unable to achieve. Digital crime is bound to increase as the new century unfolds. By making effective use of traditional crime control measures, coupled with some sophisticated technological solutions, it may, however, be kept within manageable limits.

Notes

1 This chapter is a revised version of "Digital Crime in the 21st Century" from the *Journal of Information Ethics*, 10, 1, 8–26, reprinted by permission of McFarland and Company, Inc., Box 611, Jefferson NC 28640, USA. Opinions expressed in this chapter are those of the authors and not necessarily those of the Australian Institute of Criminology or the Australian Government.
2 See also www.2600.com/hacked_pages (visited 4 January 2000).
3 See also the website of the Institute for the Advanced Study of Information Warfare (IASIW) www.psycom.net/iwar.1.html (visited 4 May 2000).
4 More information about the Netherlands hotline against child pornography on the Internet can be found at www.meldpunt.org/meldpunt-eng.htm (visited 4 May 2000).

References

Associated Press (1998) "First Cyber Terrorist Action Reported", www.techserver.com/newsroom/ntn/info/050698/info9_25501_noframes.html (visited 4 January 2000).
Bauer, J. (1998) "Testimony to the Subcommittee on Technology, Terrorism and Government Information, Committee on the Judiciary", United States Senate, May 20, 1998. Available at www.securitymanagement.com/library/bauer.html (visited 8 June 2001).
British Broadcasting Corporation (1999) "Nato Under 'Cyber Attack'", www.flora.org/flora.mai-not/10498 (visited 4 January 1999).
Cella, J.J. and Stark, J.R. (1997) "SEC Enforcement and the Internet: Meeting the Challenge of the Next Millennium", *The Business Lawyer*, 52: 815–49.
Creed, A. (1999) "Indonesian Govt Suspected In Irish ISP Hack", *Newsbytes*, 21 February, www.ccurrents.com/newstoday/99/02/21/news8.html (visited 10 January 2000).
Denning, D. (1999) *Information Warfare and Security*, Boston: Addison Wesley.
Edwards, O. (1995) "Hackers from Hell", *Forbes*, 9 October, p. 182.

Froomkin, A.M. (1995) "Anonymity and its Enmities", *Journal of ONLINE Law*, art. 4., June; available at www.wm.edu/law/publications/jol/95_96/froomkin.html (visited 20 June 2001).

Gold, S. (1999) "BT Starts Switchboard Anti-Hacking Investigation", *Newsbytes*, 11 January, www.infowar.com (visited 23 December 1999).

Grabosky, P.N. and Smith, R.G. (1998) *Crime in the Digital Age: Controlling Telecommunications and Cyberspace Illegalities*, Leichhardt: Federation Press; New Brunswick: Transaction Publishers.

Grabosky, P.N., Smith, R.G. and Dempsey, G. (2001) *Electronic Theft: Crimes of Acquisition in Cyberspace*, Cambridge: Cambridge University Press.

Grant, A., David, F. and Grabosky, P. (1997) "Child Pornography in the Digital Age", *Transnational Organized Crime*, 3, 4, 171–88.

Hundley, R. and Anderson, R. (1995) "Emerging Challenge: Security and Safety in Cyberspace", *IEEE Technology and Society Magazine*, 14, 4, 19–28.

Lanham, D. *et al.* (1987) *Criminal Fraud*, Sydney: Law Book Co. Ltd.

Littman, J. (1997) *The Watchman: The Twisted Life and Crimes of Serial Hacker Kevin Poulsen*, Boston: Little Brown.

Markoff, J. (2000) "An Online Extortion Plot Results in Release of Credit Card Data", *New York Times on the Web*, 10 January.

Meyer, M. and Underwood, A. (1994) "Crimes of the Net", *Bulletin/Newsweek*, 15 November 15, 68–9.

Newman, K. (1998) "Phone Call Scams Skim off Millions", *New Zealand Herald*, 20 August, www.infowar.com (visited 23 December 1999).

Post, D.G. (1995) "Anarchy, State, and the Internet: An Essay on Law-Making in Cyberspace", *Journal of ONLINE Law*, art. 3.

Rathmell, A. (1997) "Cyber-Terrorism: The Shape of Future Conflict?", *Royal United Service Institute Journal*, October, 40–6, www.kcl.ac.uk/orgs/icsa/rusi.htm#who (visited 21 December 1999).

Ryan, M. (1998) *Knowledge Diplomacy: Global Competition and the Politics of Intellectual Property*, Washington: Brookings.

Schieck, M. (1995) "Combating Fraud in Cable and Telecommunications", *IIC Communications Topics*, 13, London: International Institute of Communications.

Schwartau, W. (1994) *Information Warfare: Chaos on the Electronic Superhighway*, New York: Thunder's Mouth Press.

Smith, R.G. (1999) "Identity-Related Economic Crime: Risks and Countermeasures", in *Trends and Issues in Crime and Criminal Justice*, 129, Canberra: Australian Institute of Criminology.

Stix, G. (1995) "Fighting Future Wars", *Scientific American*, 273, 6: 74–80.

Stoll, C. (1991) *The Cuckoo's Egg*, London: Pan Books.

Tendler, S. and Nuttall, N. (1996) "Hackers Leave Red-Faced Yard with $1.29m Bill", *The Australian*, 6 August, p. 37.

United States Information Infrastructure Task Force (1995) *Intellectual Property and the National Information Infrastructure: Report of the Working Group on Intellectual Property Rights* (Bruce A. Lehman: Chair), Washington: United States Patent and Trademark Office.

Venditto, G. (1996) "Safe Computing", *Internet World*, September, 48–58.

Wahlert, G. (1996) "Implications for Law Enforcement of the Move to a Cashless Society", in A. Graycar and P.N. Grabosky (eds), *Money Laundering*, Canberra: Australian Institute of Criminology.

West Australian (1996) "Two on Phone Scam Counts", 9 July, p. 47.

4 "Between the risk and the reality falls the shadow"

Evidence and urban legends in computer fraud (with apologies to T.S. Eliot)

Michael Levi[1]

Introduction

The definition, harmfulness, incidence and prevalence of computer-related crime continue to be controversial. Just as the very different behaviours classified as *crimes* are transmogrified into the collective noun "*crime*", almost the only thing that cybercrimes have in common is a claim to be about an activity that is late or postmodern. Sceptics traditionally argue that much of what is described as computer crime is crime that would not have been significantly harder had computers never been invented; but although, as I shall argue, that may be true of *conceptual* categories such as trespass, theft, obscenity and violence (Wall, 1998: 203, also see chapter 1), it is undoubtedly true that computers – and especially the Internet – democratize criminal opportunities by opening up the possibility of virtual access to sites such as financial and defence systems that would not be available physically to many offenders. (For excellent introductions to part of this aspect, see Mann and Sutton, 1998; Wall, 2000.) Even if we were to agree on a definition of the phenomenon, given non-reporting and – even when reported – the difficulty of fitting the crime to existing legal categories, our understanding of when and where "it" occurs is very limited. Wall (1998: 203) goes so far as to assert that "it is…too early even to attempt an assessment of the extent of cybervictimisation, indeed, there are many good reasons as to why this might never be possible." Whilst I agree that this is so in the round, this paper sketches out some brief perspectives on the emergence of computer fraud as a social issue and then goes on to examine what surveys to date tell us about its incidence and prevalence. I will *not* examine what the legal implications of this are, because there is no reason why the legal framework of fraud and attempted fraud should not cope adequately (or any more inadequately than it does in other areas of fraud), though proving that computers were reliable or not on a given date may be harder than less technological forms of evidence.

   It is not my aim here to examine in detail the formal and informal policing of cybercrime (see Wall, 1998). Suffice it to state that electronic activities seem to have been grafted onto existing steam-age and pre-steam-age police roles. In the UK, for example, we have several (and indeed, an increasing number of) Fraud Squads dealing with Internet pornography: why? Because in forces into which personal computers have barely been introduced, Fraud Squads are the only specialist police units which deal with electronic transfers and with documents held on computer which often have to be tested, and with "mirror-imaging" computer disks to search for deleted files: therefore their officers have at least a modicum of computer literacy.[2] Moreover, dealing with Internet pornography helps to convince the police hierarchy that fraud squads serve a socially valuable function: a social value that they only intermittently see when dealing with white-collar crime (Levi and Pithouse, forthcoming).

I commence in this way so as to contextualize how antediluvian the typical interests of both police and academics are. Automatic Fingerprint Recognition and the Police National Computer excepted, the mainstream policing activities – policing public order, juvenile crime and petty persistent adult crime, from "broken windows" upwards – lie outside the scope of "digi-crime"; and most police officers (and researchers who – in biological rather than pejorative terms – are parasitic upon their activities) can go through their entire careers without needing to know anything about its subject matter. Nevertheless, anyone interested in drugs dealing, fraud, the transmission of pornography, transnational crime, money-laundering and the policing methodologies such as electronic eavesdropping that often accompany them, has to have some comprehension of the impact of electronics and computing. This is not *just* the top slice of crime, for even street dealers are able to frustrate easy "analogue" eavesdropping by using digital phones that require different, easier methods for interception but are harder to decrypt. This is merely one example of how technology can alter opportunities for crime concealment, though not necessarily crime commission itself, except in so far as it alters the risk–reward ratio for potential offenders. Another example is payment card fraud, where the introduction of smart cards will not, in the initial phase, prevent people from using stolen cards – such cards do not authenticate the *person* – but will prevent them from re-encoding other people's details onto existing cards or onto simple "white cards" with a magnetic stripe; i.e. they authenticate the *cards*. Except where they can be used in Card Not Present situations – currently this includes many Internet and telephone purchases – this will require counterfeiters to be able to break and remake encrypted cards, ratcheting up the minimum skill requirement very substantially.

The media and the social construction of computer crime

What follows is intended to be a suggestive, rather than a systematic, analysis of media coverage of "computer crime". However, it is useful to set "the problem of cybercrime" in a social context, since seriousness is not – or certainly not *always* – a natural categorization process but rather an interaction between active interpreters of messages and "infotainment" groups conveying them, sometimes at the behest of pressure groups seeking to communicate a particular vision of "the problem" (see Hall, 1994). In constructing forms of crime (and even, arguably, crime in general) as a "social problem", the media both create and reflect conceptions of seriousness. Different groups advocate particular conceptions that serve their material and symbolic interests, though to "expose" these interests tells us nothing about the "truth value" of their statements about the "scale of the problem". The normal methodological tools of victimization surveys and self-report studies are only beginning to be tapped, and a current dilemma is whether to take on trust official assertions or simply to discredit them without any further substantiation. How, for example, does one evaluate statements by computer security experts that events happened, when they refuse to give details either about dates or the corporate identity of victims "for reasons of client confidentiality"? In practice, the media give credibility to elite claims about prevalence, incidence and harm, though defence expert witnesses such as Peter Sommer – the author of the original *Hacker's Handbook* – may receive a fair hearing, especially in liberal newspapers such as the *Guardian* and in the specialist press. It is not suggested here that computer criminals are demonized in the same way as are black people, for computer *use* does not permit the sort of simplistic physical "out of place" definitions of colour and demeanour as does the topography of urban travel. (Though when does active dissent become a "threat to social order", or even potential terrorism? See "Net tightens around the hacktivists", *Guardian*, 2 January 2001.) Anti-counterfeiting groups, in particular, have difficulty in raising the seriousness perceptions of copying software, since many ordinary people find nothing wrong in making extra copies of "overpriced" commodities: the groups therefore have to resort to allegations about the links between counterfeiting and "organized crime", hoping that the negative image of the latter will contaminate all the activities they touch.

It is important to appreciate the interaction between "findings" and news values. Reports on fraud by Parliamentary bodies, accountancy firms, commercial security firms and individual experts can command attention if they assert that the problem is a serious and growing one. For example, if the Ernst & Young surveys of fraud against large companies – discussed on p. 52 – had found high levels of "computer fraud", this fact would have been heavily publicized in both specialist and general news media, since the revelation of large amounts of previously undetected *hi-tech* crime would be very newsworthy. The fact that the surveys did *not* find widespread computer fraud was unattractive to the media, in spite of (or because of) our efforts to suggest that the computer issue contained an element of "hype" and that "the human factor" and corporate cultures were more significant in accounting for fraud. (This was echoed by the Audit Commission, 1994.)

More generally, from the BBC television series *The Consultant* and the Disney movie *War Games* to mid-1990s films such as *The Net* and *Goldeneye*, "computer crime" is used as titillating entertainment which generates fear at the power of technology beyond the control of respectable society. In newspapers, also, the ready market for stories involving young "hackers" remains: in September 1991, prominence was given to the son of an Israeli guided missile expert who allegedly had hacked into Pentagon computers and into the Visa International credit card network. The most substantive error in the front page headline in the *Independent* was that he had not hacked into the Visa network but into the credit reference agencies' network: a rather significant difference. Even had he got into the Visa network, the implication conveyed to readers that untold riches would have become his would have been mistaken, since funds transmission has nothing directly to do with either the Visa network or those of the credit reference agencies. The *Independent* also ran stories during 1994 exposing the vulnerability of private information about senior British politicians and military personnel via the British Telecom network, which, despite some implausibilities, seemed to stack up. Likewise, though speculative and exaggerated, there was a kernel of truth in the threats of computer hacker extortion publicized in *The Sunday Times* (2 June 1996).

One way of enhancing crime seriousness is to associate the activity with "organized crime" or "organized criminals" as if, merely by being organized by a syndicate rather than one or a small group of professional criminals or anarchic "pranksters", that made the impact much worse. This is an arguable point, though under some circumstances people outside traditional crime groups may be regarded as a *less* manageable risk and therefore *more* dangerous even than gangsters. Where technology can be added to gangsterdom, this makes ideal media copy. Illustrations include the Russian technician who hacked into Citibank's phone lines and diverted millions of dollars in 1995 – made into at least one excellent television documentary and endlessly re-cited – and the over-hyped tale of an ATM fraud plot described below. The *Independent* (18 December 1996) caught even the broadsheet mood:

> John "Little Legs" Lloyd, an underworld hardman, and his partner Kenneth Noye, wanted for the M25 road rage murder, hand-picked a team of criminals to pull off an £800m fraud...
>
> The gang was thwarted by an unlikely crime-busting team, made up of a softly spoken prison chaplain and a computer wizard who once tried to burn his wife and child to death.
>
> The swindlers' plan had been to use the help of corrupt British Telecom technicians to tap into the telephone lines which link cash dispensers to bank computers. The taps would have given the gang access to confidential information about tens of thousands of accounts which was to be downloaded onto a computer. The data would have been decrypted and transferred to 140,000 plastic bogus cash cards.
>
> Lloyd...and Noye had established a world-wide network of criminals to carry out fraud on a global scale.

By contrast, in *The Times* of the same day, the well-informed Stewart Tendler told readers that "Noye was never questioned about the cashcard plot and detectives now say they believe he was only peripheral to the plot". One can readily query terms like "hand-picked": how else would one pick a criminal team? And note the "Little Legs" cue that we are not dealing with a member of the social elite here! Lloyd was sent to prison for five years.

The BBC1 television "infotainment" programme "Here and Now" (like other subsequent programmes, for example the counterfeiting of ON Digital smart cards by the BBC's *The Crime Squad* team, 4 September 2000) was similarly obsessed with the ease with which plastic card numbers could be re-encoded and used for fraud, despite evidence that it accounted for only a small proportion of plastic fraud (BBC, 21 April 1997): a "good prog" is one that alarms the public and attacks the competence of large institutions. The publicity accorded to many hacking scares – such as the vulnerability of most pager messages in Britain to simple hacking and recording (*What Cellphone*, November 1996 and several national newspapers) – serves to generate fear of crime and, perhaps, mislead readers into believing mistakenly that "the fraud problem" is technological and external rather than social and internal. This applies especially to cyber-warfare stories, such as "Hackers attack military satellite" (*Daily Telegraph*, 4 March 1999), which did at least go on to point out that there was no evidence of intent to blackmail or disable. There are occasional debunking stories, such as "More Naked Gun than Top Gun" (*Guardian*, 27 November 1997), which deflated US cyber-warriors' claims about their methods, and the threat posed by two British hackers,[3] and "The hacker who turned himself in" (*Guardian*, 26 March 1998): but the general tone is hysterical and "deviance-amplifying".

Disputes about harmfulness are part of the ideological terrain over which defendants and prosecutors battle. According to Sterling (1993), the FBI systematically misrepresented the organized nature of the hacking "group" called "Legion of Doom" and their involvement in crime: in reality, he argues, they did not steal or crash anything. Such battles over social definitions of social harm are not restricted to computer crime, but they are particularly salient to whether those hackings that do not involve pecuniary gain for the perpetrator but may involve substantial pecuniary loss for the victims (and those using allied systems, should they hear about the penetration) should be defined as serious crimes or as what – in the delinquency literature – might be termed "play vandalism". This is especially problematic when many companies and governments themselves hire hackers to test the vulnerability of their systems to penetration: arguably, provided that they leave a trace calling card, freelance hackers are doing for free what the institutions would otherwise have to pay for (except that they are people who might otherwise not be authorized to see the material they see). During 1998, one of a pair of British hackers – the other was acquitted – was given only a modest fine by a judge, in spite of a Pentagon official giving evidence that his activities could have undermined the entire US military defence system. So, was this judgement sound, or did it fail to appreciate a "clear and present danger" or a plausible future risk?

A nice illustration is the Israeli teenager Ehud "The Analyser" Tenenbaum – a member of a group dedicated to fighting racist and paedophile websites – who hacked into NASA and Pentagon computers, before hacking into the Home Page of an FBI officer to tell the FBI that he was the one that 47 FBI agents were looking for. Israeli Prime Minister Netanyahu described him as "damn good", but a director of the ISP Net Decks stated that "The Analyser is a vandal, not a hero". Though the Americans certainly took the opposite view, the Chair of the Israeli Parliament Science and Technology Committee observed in re-integrative mode (after all, Tenenbaum was looking forward to joining the Israeli army very shortly: The *Guardian*, 26 March 1998):

> He didn't cause damage but rather exposed flaws in terms of the protection of important computer information...his huge amount of knowledge should be used to help the state, but this time in accordance with accepted rules and standards.

His activities required all passwords to be changed at Western Michigan University, and cost hundreds of (expensive) hours of repair work. Due to other hackers, two overseas US State Department posts had almost to be disconnected from the global network for most of October 1997, since hacker traces made them insecure. A 1998 study by the General Accounting Office revealed that computer hackers could obtain data such as the travel schedules of US embassy officials – useful for assassinations; while the US Computer Security Institute survey found that 72 per cent of *respondents* from government and business stated that they had suffered financial losses from electronic criminals. In 1996, the Pentagon reported that there had been some 250,000 attempted hackings, only one in 250 of which had been detected at the time: but it is difficult to estimate the economic cost of these attempts other than the cost of security, which has been omitted here on the grounds that security costs are not strictly costs of crime but are costs of doing particular sorts of things about crime. Nevertheless, such an omission has its flaws, in so far as security may be necessary in order to enable an entity to function at all: a good illustration of this is the simulation of warfare in hacker changes to the communications of defence satellites (*Daily Telegraph*, 4 March 1999). The key point is that these attempts are integrated into the necessity to spend billions on fighting cyberterrorism, one of the major issues mentioned in then President Clinton's 1999 "State of the Union" message, and reinforced by subsequent virus attacks. They are also related to battles over encryption and the "need" for the law enforcement/intelligence agencies to retain access to telecommunications without the need for slow and expensive decryption, as noted in the fierce battle over the Regulation of Investigatory Powers Act 2000.

More pragmatically, new forms of technology can also be used to point up the "need" for changes in criminal law, such as the absence of preventative legislation to stop false claims being advertised on the Internet. In "Internet sting lures 82,000 isle 'lairds'", the *Observer* (10 March 1996) warned about a firm selling square-yard plots of remote crofting land to Americans with a fictitious scroll guaranteeing that for a hundred dollars, purchasers will become "an authentic Scottish laird". The article began: "In cyberspace no-one can hear the victim scream." This sort of reporting is part of the general advisory role of the media, but it also reflects the technophobia that is prevalent whenever risks of new technology are exposed (see also Mann and Sutton, 1998; Grabosky and Smith, 1998; Grabosky *et al.*, 2001; Levi and Pithouse, forthcoming, ch. 2).

Finally, it should be appreciated that there is a serious social point about the interaction between computers, trust and security. As Grabosky and Smith (1998: 47) put it:

> [T]rust and confidence in the systems that support commerce, communications, air traffic control, electric power generation and other modern institutions are at the very core of our society. Thus, even the potential for disruption and harm is cause for concern.

The extent of computer fraud

In activities such as computer crime, alongside "organized crime" the normal disciplines by which we evaluate the plausibility of threat levels are absent, for – as in other arenas of white-collar crime (Levi and Pithouse, forthcoming) – the victims are either:

- not asked about their victimization;
- do not respond when asked;
- do not tell us about all their experiences (or so we believe); or
- are unaware of their victimization.

Grabosky and Smith (1998: 8) approach this "harm measurement" issue with some delicacy:

> Quantification can also be deceptive....Often these [financial losses] amount to billions of dollars....Some estimates need to be treated with caution, however, since they are based on figures extrapolated from relatively small surveys to represent losses suffered by industries which have an enormous customer base and daily deal in turnovers amounting to vast sums of money ...However...there are abundant examples of substantial and quantifiable sums being stolen throughout the world.

They add that qualitative dimensions are also important, not least because hackers may inflate their achievements. These statements are true as far as they go, but this does not address the deeper problem that official sources may deliberately or paranoically inflate the threat and may conflate *experience of* with theoretical *risk* from computer crime.[4] This is not simply the attempt to gain more resources, acknowledged by the authors: it is part of the intelligence threat-assessment mental set, encouraged also by the "concerns" (in other words, the self-serving PR) of security consultants whose income depends on shocking (or, as they put it, "creating awareness among") senior executives and government agencies who complacently fail to spend "enough" money on security.

Unlawful (and lawful) major transfers of funds almost invariably involve a financial institution as an intermediary, if not as a victim, of fraud. The definition, incidence and prevalence of computer-related crime continue to be matters of much debate, in which diverse phenomena such as hacking for fun or espionage, theft of computer equipment, counterfeiting of software, criminal damage, blackmail and fraud become intertwined in a single *gestalt*. The Audit Commission (1983) states: "computer fraud is any fraudulent behaviour connected with computerisation by which someone intends to gain dishonest advantage". But there are wide variations in definition, which we will not address here.

It is important to think through whether what we are concerned with is corporate (and national security) *loss* or corporate/individual/governmental *fraud*. The latter speaks to traditional criminal law notions of blameworthiness and the precise allocation of blame to individuals; the former speaks to harm reduction and prevention, irrespective of whether anyone is blameworthy in a way that fits the curious categories of the criminal law. Thus, for example, faulty ambulance dispatch systems or car safety measures can be looked at from a preventative perspective without necessarily seeking simply to dismiss or prosecute the personnel involved. In the light of this sort of consideration, the Audit Commission has shifted its focus to "computer abuse", which it describes (1994: 6) as:

> ...an umbrella term embracing various types of deliberate criminal acts, each of which calls for different skills and techniques in detection. The term embraces computer fraud, virus infections, hacking, theft of data and programs, sabotage, unauthorised private work, invasion of privacy, and unauthorised use of illicit software.

All of these may be subject to shifts in awareness, as different methods of tracking people and their activities highlight a greater proportion of the "dark figure" not only of unreported but of unperceived "abuse". (A return to the 1983 definition would artificially reduce "computer crime".) Fraud includes:

- unauthorized input or alteration of input;
- destruction/suppression/misappropriation of output from a computer process;
- alteration of computerized data;
- alteration or misuse of programs (but excluding by virus infection).

The Audit Commission's sample includes all local authorities and National Health Service bodies in England and Wales, the majority of central government departments and agencies, and a "range of middle- and large-sized companies throughout the UK" (1998: 5); though the response rate from each sector or in aggregate is not specified. Taking all forms of IT fraud and abuse together, the proportion of respondents who were victims rose from 36 per cent in 1994 to 45 per cent in 1997. But the proportion of respondents who reported experiencing fraud fell from 10 per cent in 1994 to 8 per cent in 1997, though the average value of frauds rose from £28,000 to £35,000, making total losses identical. In 1997, input frauds constituted 70 per cent of all frauds by volume. A quarter of all frauds detected were committed by management.

Thirty-seven "computer fraud" cases were reported in 1994–95 to the Treasury (1995: 6) in its survey of internal fraud against government departments, though most were of low value or caused no loss, only two being over £10,000 (of which one was over £60,000, with more being attempted). However, in a further case, a staff member approached a departmental debtor and offered to clear his liability by manipulating records, in exchange for £50,000 (less than half the debt). However, the debtor contacted the police who taped a subsequent conversation, and the civil servant was jailed for attempted corruption. Far heavier losses were generated by the theft of computer hardware and memory, as professional criminals in the mid-1990s targeted computer chips, which were in short supply as a combined result of the Kobe earthquake and the demand for memory to run faster applications. By 1998–99 the number of cases of computer fraud reported had risen to 107, some 18 per cent of the total (Treasury, 2000). A computer fraud had been re-defined as one where information technology (IT) equipment has been used to manipulate computer programs or data dishonestly or where the existence of an IT system was a material factor in the perpetration of the fraud, and this is a slight increase over the previous year, when 92 cases were reported. The monetary loss of £481,400 (£1,300 in 1997–98) was attributed mostly to one case with a value of £477,000: the other cases were mostly unauthorized-access ones.

Since there is so much disagreement about the definition of computer crime, it is hardly surprising that there is little consensus about its cost. If we take telephone fraud, for example, what is termed "shoulder-surfing" – in other words, looking over someone's shoulder while they punch in their credit card code, and then selling it on cheaply to others – costs the phone companies more than any of the hi-tech methods of hackers (Sterling, 1993: 49). The ongoing war of computer fraud prevention resembles that which has occurred with safes, making safe-breaking virtually defunct. The chips on cellular phones can be reprogrammed to generate a false "caller identification", to avoid billing, tapping by the police, and any other unwanted activities. The cost of the theft of long-distance service is in some sense theoretical (though the opportunity cost is real where a significant proportion of the calls would have been made anyway through the official system), but when stolen codes have to be deleted and new ones issued, this is a real cost, as is the trouble for real owners: there are analogies here with plastic card fraud generally, even when the bank pays up.

Some UK data also exist on the prevalence of computer fraud against large private sector organizations (Levi and Pithouse, forthcoming). The Ernst & Young 1986 and 1989 reports showed that, whereas in both the questionnaire and the telephone surveys executives expressed considerable concern about computer fraud and hacking, responses revealed that if simple forgery of input or output documents were to be excluded – which can be effected quite adequately without a computer – only one "worst fraud" was a "real" computer fraud that relied totally on the new technology. Even in a later section of the questionnaire that dealt with *unreported* as well as reported fraud, there were no computer frauds by outsiders, and no computer fraud by users and systems people exceeded £1 million in any case in our sample. Although more than two-thirds of companies stated that computer viruses and hacking were fairly serious or very serious, only 11 per cent had experienced *either* of these and 5 per cent *both* of them.

In 1991, as in previous years, computer frauds again featured very modestly. Only one was committed by systems people – and that was under £10,000; only three – one under £10,000, one £10–100,000, and one over £100,000 – were committed by computer users; and none were committed by outsiders. The number of computer frauds was significantly lower than in 1989, which may be an artefact of responses or may reflect the success of computer security people in selling their message. Finally, international surveys in 1996 and 1998 (Levi and Sherwin, 1996, 1998) turned up very few cases of reported or unreported computer frauds. In making these remarks, we are not debunking the cost to firms of protecting their systems against unlawful use by outsiders of insiders: actual and potential damage to data, for example, can be catastrophic for the operation of computer-dependent businesses and can provide the basis for corporate blackmail in exchange for unravelling the damage (*Sunday Times*, 2 June 1996), but this "cyber-warfare" is different from fraud risks. For example, it may be that thirty British banks detected fraud on their systems in 1998–99, but the amount of money defrauded was modest, and – despite headlines such as "Hackers hold City banks to ransom" (*Sunday Times*, 19 September 1999) – even the amount extorted was modest compared with product contamination threats.

The same difficulties apply to American studies of computer crime. The 1998 Computer Security Institute/FBI study found that based on 520 security practitioners' responses (a 13 per cent response rate), 64 per cent had suffered security breaches in the previous year, at a cost (for the less than half who replied) of $136.8 million. (If one includes those experiencing computer viruses or laptop theft, the proportion victimized rises to 88 per cent.) The cost of financial fraud (against those who could quantify this loss) was stated to be $7.87 million, and telecommunications fraud $17.3 million (with a combined two-year cost of $35 million): a far cry from the claims of private sector specialists, and less than one-fifth of the total imputed cost of computer crime (Computer Security Institute, 1998). The Internet connection was equal to the internal systems as a frequent point of "attack", with over a half of respondents citing it. However, only 15 per cent reported financial fraud, the remainder comprising unauthorized access by employees (44 per cent) and denial-of-service attacks (25 per cent).

A later survey (Computer Security Institute, 2000) did not specify response rates, but 90 per cent of respondents (primarily large corporations and government agencies) detected computer security breaches within the last twelve months. Seventy per cent reported a variety of serious computer security breaches other than the most common ones of computer viruses, laptop theft or employee "net abuse", such as theft of proprietary information, financial fraud, system penetration from outsiders, denial-of-service attacks and sabotage of data or networks. Seventy-four per cent acknowledged financial losses due to computer breaches. Forty-two per cent were willing and/or able to quantify their financial losses. The losses from these 273 respondents totalled $265.6 million (over twice the average annual total over the last three years). Sixty-one respondents quantified losses due to sabotage of data or networks for a total of $27.1 million, well over twice the combined total for the previous three years. As in previous years, the most serious financial losses occurred through theft of proprietary information (66 respondents reported $66.7m) and financial fraud (53 respondents reported $56m).

A British corporate survey by Barnes and Sharp (1998) found that technology was identified very seldom by insurance (6.3 per cent) or retail (13.6 per cent) sector respondents as a cause of the rise in fraud, largely because those sectors were exposed more to thefts and false claims outside the cybersphere. By contrast, 42.9 per cent of services and of oil and gas sectors attributed the rise in fraud to technology. Whether correct or incorrect, this at least focuses us to a more finely-tuned analysis of risk by the nature of the activities.

Hitherto I have focused on cybercrime against the corporate and governmental sectors – which is also the core of political concern, especially in the defence industry – but this is far from the exclusive preserve of organizational real or potential victims. Internet-based misinformation, disinformation and total scams have been a growing focus of the US Securities and Exchange Commission and the FBI, though the UK has not noticed any serious difficulties. The Financial Services Authority has not yet taken legal action against online fraudsters, although one case is thought to be pending in 2001. Most online breaches of the rules were believed to be accidental, and were dealt with by warnings. The UK watchdog will continue regular sweeps of the Internet to identify illegal and unregulated advisers, but a "surf day", carried out in November 2000, identified fewer suspicious UK-based websites than the first sweep, undertaken in the spring of that year. This identified 58 suspicious sites, nine of which remain under investigation. The Washington-based Internet Fraud Watch (IFW) noted an alarming rise in the number and proportion of Internet frauds arising from on-line auctions – where goods are generally paid for by cheque or money order – which rose from 26 per cent of frauds reported in 1997 to 68 per cent in 1998 and 87 per cent in 1999, while the total fraud complaints rose tenfold over the same period. Other top frauds for 1999, in order, are non-auction sales of general merchandise, Internet access services, computer equipment and software, and homeworking plans. In 1999, the IFW reported that consumers lost over $3.2 million to Internet fraud. This figure might look insubstantial compared with other crime costs, but, according to the IFW, "a 38 percent increase in Internet fraud complaints in 1999 coupled with an average consumer loss of as much as $580 indicate an urgent need for consumer education about shopping online". This led to a National Consumers League special warning on "Shopping Safely from Home".

These reported data are partly an artefact of not using credit cards but instead using cheques and money orders, for it seems plausible that the absence of compensation is what leads to reporting to the Internet Fraud Watch: other payment card fraud costs are borne by the card companies and the retailers. Telemarketing frauds, stock price manipulation via Internet "chat group" demand stimulation of interest in lawfully quoted securities, and advertising of offshore investments to tempt the needy and greedy, are all methods by which remote persons can commit frauds with even less human contact and risk of arrest than in normal frauds: they also alter the "capable guardianship" component of fraud prevention. Modern technological changes such as call-forwarding also assist telemarketing and investment fraudsters by enabling them to give as their ostensible phone number one in upmarket areas of London, Miami and other major cities, combined perhaps with an accommodation address there: but in reality, all calls are forwarded instantaneously to some other location, for example in some difficult-to-penetrate offshore finance centre, without the knowledge of the communicators. But notwithstanding the vast estimates offered in some countries like the US (and some huge individual cases involving $200 million of which we are aware), there are no reliable estimates of the aggregate cost to individual or corporate victims. In short, we are *not* suggesting that concern about computer crime is irrational: on the contrary, we agree with Grabosky and Smith (1998), Grabosky *et al.* (2001) and with Mann and Sutton (1998) that computer security is going to be a major issue in the twenty-first century. However, the term must be unpacked into sub-types of crime, and we believe that concern about computer fraud should normally be less than concern about, first, many other types of fraud, and, second, other types of computer crime.

Preventing cyber-fraud

Contrary to the beliefs of Grabosky and Smith (1998), general education about the consequences of computer crime is unlikely to have much impact on inhibiting either destruction, economic, or mischief motivations. By definition, the programmers and operatives of the future are part of the general public, but as with fire-setting and some of the more exotic forms of drug-taking, remote consequences are very difficult to re-educate people about (see Mann and Sutton, 1998), even if one is optimistic about the *possibility* of weaning people away from the sociopathy of their relations with the large, impersonal institutions of late modernity.

Where there is no doubt at all is that the criminal justice process is ill-suited (and inconsistently so) to dealing with these forms of crime. Prevention itself is tough, for the following reasons:

1   because of modest disapprobation among the set of potential abusers – and I would like to see some contextualized research on this, looking at sub-group attitudes and social self-regulation;

2   because, for all the scolding (Grabosky and Smith, 1998: 63) about the importance of controlling public information about telecoms systems, *some* systems information will inevitably leak out and may well be posted on the Internet rather than kept to oneself, as, arguably, a rational *economic* criminal would do (see further, Wall, 2000);

3   because of the continual increase in processor power, which enables unlawful decryption as well as other explorations to take place under circumstances that at one time would have required a massive capital outlay;

4   because it is hard to prohibit criminals from the market, as can be done in some areas of white-collar crime or, increasingly via the civil law (Bamfield, 1997), from stores or even private shopping malls. However, the damage caused even by *individual* acts of computer fraud or vandalism may be entirely disproportionate to offenders' assets and income, far more so than in shop theft or fraud.

Another important theme is the relationship between risk, fear and technological change. It is asserted (Grabosky and Smith, 1998: 75) that, because of high crime risks, consumers may be reluctant to take up new technology and producers may be reluctant to develop it. This is a concept that would benefit from further research. "Fear of crime" is fairly well studied (though often under-theorized) in the settings of conventional crime against individuals and business, but not in the context of purchasing products (or, for that matter, of fraud – see Levi, 2001). For example, until recent improvements, the Internet was a very insecure place over which to give credit card and other personal details, yet many people happily gave away such details, just as they do when ordering goods and services by mail order or on the phone. To what extent does convenience (or relative convenience) overcome fear? Despite publicity given to consumer claims that their accounts have been debited by "phantom withdrawals", most people use ATMs (though they have little choice, given bank opening hours): are they not fearful, and what would it take to make them fearful enough not to use these facilities?

Despite their initial caveat, the "net effect" of Grabosky and Smith's (1998) work and that of other authors in this arena is dealing with crimes by individuals against business and against individuals (a "blue-collar" crime study): there is only a modest amount on the ways that computerized bar coding can facilitate fraud *against* consumers, as the price may not correspond to that advertised (one sees the excuse "programming error by junior staff" flashing before one's eyes), let alone the excellent possibilities for scams on investors by grossly oversold hype about hi-tech products and anti-trust activities by dominant suppliers (though these are not themselves inherently produced by digitization). What we need to know is more about how the organization of work under digitization affects the possibilities of fraud. We also need a more sophisticated and critical awareness of the problematic relationship between the theoretical potential for cybercrime – for example, the possibilities of tapping into databases to discover personal data sufficient to create and/or duplicate identities to use for fraudulent purposes – and the much smaller (as far as we know) incidence and prevalence of computer crime for economic gain. As T.S. Eliot might have said:

> Between the routine activities of anoraks and their situational crimes falls the shadow...Teach us to prevent and not to prevent. Teach us to be still.

Notes

1   A draft version of this paper was presented at the British & Irish Legal Education Technology Association Conference, Cyberspace 1999: Crime, Criminal Justice and the Internet, College of Ripon & York, St John, at York 29–30 March 1999.
2   This is perhaps unduly flippant: forces dealing with large-scale homicide enquiries, and/or with serial murders and rapes, have to utilize computing, but they seldom do anything particularly sophisticated with it.
3   In an interview with me, the former computer science teacher of one of the two British hackers described him as a very moderate student, both in competence and in motivation.
4   This is hardly unique. As debates over "dangerous offenders" illustrate, it is present in violent and sex crimes, too, including paedophilia.

References

Audit Commission (1983) *Computer Fraud Survey*, London: HMSO.
—— (1994) *Opportunity Makes a Thief: an Analysis of Computer Abuse*, London: HMSO.
—— (1998) *The Ghost in the Machine*, London: Audit Commission.
Bamfield, J. (1997) *Making Shoplifters Pay*, London: Social Market Foundation.
Barnes, P. and Sharp, D. (1998) *The Fraud Survey – 1998*, Leicester: Association of Certified Fraud Examiners.
Computer Security Institute (1998) "1998 CSI/FBI Computer Crime and Security Survey", *Computer Security Issues and Trends*, 4, 1: 1–12.
—— (2000) *2000 CSI/FBI Computer Crime and Security Survey*, San Francisco: Computer Security Institute.
Grabosky, P. and Smith, R. (1998) *Crime in the Digital Age*, New York: Transaction.
Grabosky, P., Smith, R. and Dempsey, G. (2001) *Electronic Theft: Unlawful Acquisition in Cyberspace*, Cambridge: Cambridge University Press.
Hall, S. (1994) "Reflections on the encoding/decoding model", in J. Cruz and J. Lewis (eds), *Viewing, Reading, Listening: Audiences and Cultural Reception*, Boulder: Westview Press.
Levi, M. (2001) "Business, cities and fears about crimes", *Urban Studies*, 5, 6: 849-69.
Levi, M. and Pithouse, A. (forthcoming) *White-Collar Crime and its Victims: the Media and Social Construction of Business Fraud*, Oxford: Clarendon Press.
Levi, M. and Sherwin, D. (1996) *Fraud – the Unmanaged Risk: an international survey of the effects of fraud on business*, London: Ernst & Young.
—— (1998) *Fraud – the Unmanaged Risk: an international survey of the effects of fraud on business*, London: Ernst & Young.

Mann, D. and Sutton, M. (1998) "NetCrime: more change in the organisation of thieving", *British Journal of Criminology*, 38, 2: 201–29.

Sterling, B. (1993) *The Hacker Crackdown: Law and Disorder on the Electronic Frontier*, London: Viking.

Treasury (1996), *Frauds against Central and Local Government*, London: HM Treasury.

—— (1997) *Frauds against Central and Local Government*, London: HM Treasury.

—— (1998) *1996–97 Fraud Report. An analysis of reported fraud in government departments*, London: HM Treasury.

—— (2000) *1998–99 Fraud Report. An analysis of reported fraud in government departments*, London: HM Treasury.

Wall, D. (1998) "Catching cybercriminals: Policing the Internet", *International Review of Law Computers and Technology*, 12, 2: 201–18.

—— (2000) *The Theft Of Electronic Services: Telecommunications And Teleservices*, London: Office of Science and Technology Foresight Programme.

5 Hacktivism
In search of lost ethics?

Paul Taylor

Introduction

> Given increasing computer prevalence and the fact our political opponents
> are among the most wired in the world, it is foolish to ignore the computer.
> Rather, it is important to turn our attention toward the computer, to under-
> stand it, and to transform it into an instrument of resistance. For the
> luddites of the world who resist computers, consider using computers to
> resist.
>
> (Wray, 1998a: 1)

Hacktivism is the phrase used to describe the combining of traditional
methods of political protest with the technological knowledge of computer
hacking. Elsewhere (Taylor, 1999), I have illustrated how perceptions of
hacking have been heavily distorted by the effects of the media and the
various social actors who have actively sought to promote negative ethical
interpretations of the activity. Most significantly, recognition of the hackers'
original ethical agenda known as the *hacker ethic* was subordinated to the
much more negative moral judgements used by social groups such as the
computer security industry. Such groups sought to simultaneously distance
themselves from hackers and reinforce their own group solidarity through a
process of stigmatization. This process involved the successful media demo-
nization of hackers and a concomitant failure to appreciate the qualities of the
computer underground that allow it to be represented as a recognizable
culture in its own right (see Jordan and Taylor, 1998). Furthermore, such
internally-oriented, hacker-friendly accounts of hacking suggested that the
original hacker ethic could still be identified within the stigmatized hacking
community. This chapter maintains this focus upon internal accounts of the
hacker ethic and examines its most recent manifestation as embodied in on-
line political activism. While hacktivism combines both political activism
and hacking techniques, this chapter largely limits itself to the specific contribution of hacking practices and culture.[1] Hacktivism is portrayed as a
contemporary refashioning of the original hacker ethic.

Generational ethics

> Access to computers – and anything which might teach you something about the way the world works – should be unlimited and total. Always yield to the Hands-On Imperative!
>
> All information should be free
>
> Mistrust Authority – Promote Decentralisation
>
> Hackers should be judged by their hacking, not bogus criteria such as degrees, age, race, or position
>
> You can create art and beauty on a computer
>
> Computers can change your life for the better
>
> (Levy, 1984: 40–5)

The above manifesto represents Levy's summary of the hacker ethic. Despite the fact that their activity is now synonymous with malicious intrusion into other people's computer systems, this statement of the hacker ethic represented the first generation's putative moral code and political philosophy. However, Levy's manifesto fails to recognize that the phrase *hacking* has a wider application than just to the computing community. Within counter-cultural circles it describes an imaginative and ingenious attitude held, not just to computers, but towards various technologies. The presently more limited and overwhelmingly negative association of hacking with malicious computer intrusion is a relatively recent development. From the mid-1980s onwards, the ethical status of hacking suffered a steady decline, both as a result of social stigmatization by opposing groups, and as hackers began to focus exclusively upon the technological means of their computing activity to the exclusion of any broader political or philosophical ends.

The following schema, despite the innate classificatory difficulties associated with trying to describe the ephemeral environment of computer culture,[2] traces the various generations of hackers to provide a context for the emergence of hacktivism and the claim that it represents a re-emergence of the original hacker ethic.

Levy (1984) identified the following three main hacker generations:

- *"True" hackers*: these were the pioneering computer aficionados of the earliest days of computing who experimented with the capabilities of the large mainframe computers at such US universities as MIT during the 1950s and 1960s.
- *Hardware hackers*: these were the computer innovators who, beginning in the 1970s, played a key role in the personal computing revolution which

served to widely disseminate and dramatically decentralize computing hardware.

- *Game hackers*: in the 1980s these were the creators of popular gaming software applications for the hardware developed by the previous generation.

The following new categories can be added to these initial generations:

- *Hacker/crackers*: from the mid-1980s to the present day, both these terms are used to describe a person who illicitly breaks into other people's computer systems. The choice of the particular phrase to be used by a commentator depends upon his or her moral perspective. *Hacker* tends to be used by those within the computer underground or largely sympathetic to its values, whilst *cracker* tends to be used by those, such as the computer security industry, who oppose it.
- *Microserfs*: in Douglas Coupland's novel (1995) of the same name, *microserfs* is the word used to describe those programmers who, whilst exhibiting various aspects of the hacker subculture, nevertheless became co-opted into the structure of Microsoft or any similar corporate entity.
- *Hacktivists*: the mid-1990s marked the merging of hacking activity with an overt political stance. The previously *ad hoc* political targets of the fourth generation have become increasingly targeted in a much more systematic and focused manner.

From this brief outline of the evolution of hacking it is clear that there has been a rise, a fall, and then a rise again in the perceived ethical content of the activity. The following sections explore the social significance of this ethical ebb and flow.

Early hacker politics

The early hackers were the radicals or guerillas, destined to give the computer a dramatically new image and a political orientation it could never have gained from Big Blue (IBM) or any of its vassals in the mainstream of the industry. At their hands, information technology would make its closest approach to becoming an instrument of democratic politics.

(Roszak, 1986: 138)

Because hacktivism uses computer techniques borrowed from the pre-existing hacker community, it is difficult to definitively identify where hacking ends and hacktivism begins. The political motivations of hacking were identifiable to varying degrees in the earlier generations, but tended to be diluted by the more immediate and pressing concerns hackers had with obtaining access to systems with a complexity commensurate with their technical knowledge. In an era of what Roszak calls "electronic populism", hackers were both instrumental and inspirational figures. This section traces the politicized aspects of the early forms of hacking to illustrate how, despite the temporary loss of the hacker ethic, the activity's inherent values have contributed to the rise of hacktivism. It can be seen from the ethical manifesto of the first generation of hackers cited at the beginning of the chapter that a key issue of concern for the early hackers was the question of unlimited access to computing power and information. For the first and second generations, both the desire to hack and the attempt to make technology more democratic – and therefore accessible – were complementary facets of the hacker agenda.

In May 1971, Abbie Hoffman played a leading role in the establishment of an underground newsletter entitled the *Youth International Party Line* (YIPL), which illustrated this conflation of the technical and the political. Its first issue strenuously opposed the US Government's decision to raise extra revenue for the Vietnam conflict through the taxing of telephone bills, and it contained a form to be filled in and sent to the company which stated: "Because of the brutal and aggressive war the United States is conducting against Vietnam, the amount of federal excise tax has been deducted from this bill. Paying the tax means helping to pay for outright atrocities, for the murder of innocent women and children" (cited in Bowcott and Hamilton, 1990: 49–50). In September 1973, YIPL changed its name to the Technological American Party (TAP) and its newsletters provided a raft of detailed technical information predominantly about how to "phone-phreak" (obtain free telephone calls through the technical manipulation of the telephone system) but also included a range of artefacts including burglar alarms, lock-picking, pirate radio and how to illegally alter gas and electric meters.

TAP ceased publication in 1984, but its mantle was taken up in the same year with the launch of the phone-phreak/hacker magazine *2600*, whose anti-Big Brother government bent was immediately indicated by the editor's choice of the pseudonym Emmanuel Goldstein (the name of the protagonist of George Orwell's *1984*). A few years earlier (1981) a German hacker group called the Chaos Computer Club (CCC) was established which directly addressed the political implications of the original hacker ethic "All information wants to be free", with the following statement of its aims:

> A development into an "information society" requires a new Human Right of worldwide free communication. The Chaos Club…claims a border-ignoring freedom of information which deals with the effects of technologies on human society and individuals. It supports the creation of knowledge and information in this respect.
>
> (cited in Bowcott and Hamilton, 1990: 53)

In the aftermath of the nuclear accident at Chernobyl, the CCC was active in the dissemination of alternative information about the severity of the incident, and worked with the German Green Party in a joint evaluation of the German Federal parliament's introduction of new computer systems.

Anti-corporatist values continued from the earliest hackers and were also an integral element of the second generation, as indicated by the names of some of the early start-up companies such as the Itty-Bitty Machine Company (a parody of the name IBM) and Kentucky Fried Computers (Bowcott and Hamilton, 1990: 142). This spirit was not to last, however, and the initial socially liberating potential of such computers as the Apple II eventually succumbed to their status as mere commodities: "all the bright possibilities seem so disturbingly compatible with corporate control and commercial exploitation" (Bowcott and Hamilton, 1990: 155). The commodification of information proceeded apace, with the third generation's contribution to the huge growth in the computer gaming industry. The counter-cultural hopes pinned upon the computer as vehicle for anti-establishment values remained unfulfilled as the spirit of Thomas Paine gave way to the electronic appetite of PacMan. The fourth generation exhibited ambivalent political credentials, the early hacker desire to promote free access to computers and information as a means of improving a perceived democratic deficit within society at large giving way in time to more selfish concerns about access to computing for its own sake.

Anti-authoritarian attitudes within hacking have been seen less as a form of youthful rebellion and more as a sign of a frustrated desire to consume computing resources (see Taylor, 1999: 53–6), so that "teenage hackers resemble an alienated shopping culture deprived of purchasing opportunities more than a terrorist network" (Ross, 1991: 90). Such a pessimistic assessment is vividly developed in Douglas Coupland's "factional" account of the hacker-type lifestyles of the young programmers working at Microsoft's headquarters in Seattle. *Microserfs* identifies "the first full-scale integration of the corporate realm into the private" (Coupland, 1995: 211), with the supplying of shower facilities for workers who wanted to jog during their lunch break being followed by much more significant developments:

> In the 1980s [when] corporate integration punctured the *next* realm of corporate life invasion at "campuses" like Microsoft and Apple – with the next level of intrusion being that borderline between work and life blurred to the point of unrecognisability. *Give us your entire life or we won't allow you to work on cool projects.* In the 1990s, corporations don't even hire people anymore. People become their own corporations. It was inevitable.
>
> (Coupland, 1995: 211 [emphasis in the original])

The identification of microserfs as the fifth generation of hackers thus marks the nadir of the original hacker ethic. Coupland depicts the extent to which Microsoft's co-option of hacker culture has been so successful that through such corporate-friendly characteristics as "high productivity, maverick forms of creative work energy, and an obsessive identification with on-line endurance (and endorphin highs)", it now merely serves to valorize "the entrepreneurial codes of silicon futurism" (Ross, 1991: 90). The key significance of hacktivism is the way in which it marks a retreat from such a pervasive intrusion of commodified values into social life and a concomitant reassertion of more counter-cultural values.

A short history of hacktivism

As hackers become politicized and activists become computerized, we are going to see an increase in the number of cyber-activists who engage in what will become more widely known as Electronic Civil Disobedience. The same principles of traditional civil disobedience, like trespass and blockage, will still be applied, but more and more these acts will take place in electronic or digital form. The primary location for Electronic Civil Disobedience will be in cyberspace.

(Wray, 1998b: 3)

Denning's comprehensive analysis of hacktivism distinguishes the activity from its close relations in the form of the plainer on-line activism, and the more sinister cyberterrorism: "Activism refers to normal, non-disruptive use of the Internet in support of an agenda or cause–hacktivism...refers to the marriage of hacking and activism...cyberterrorism...refers to the convergence of cyberspace and terrorism" (Denning 1999: 2). She identifies four main types of hacktivist operation (Denning, 1999: 16):[3]

- Virtual sit-ins and blockades
- E-mail bombs
- Web hacks and computer break-ins
- Computer viruses and worms

Virtual sit-ins, blockades and e-mail bombs

A virtual sit-in is little more than a collective, simultaneous requesting of a Web site. If one requests a Web site faster than it can be transferred to and built up on the end user's screen, the server receives, on the one hand, a message telling it that the first request is no longer valid, and on the other hand, the new request. Scripts running on one's own computer or on go-between servers automate this process, and after a certain number of requests the server under attack begins to suffer beneath the strain. One has to differentiate very specifically between knocking out a server for private motives and a political action openly disrupting a Web site for clearly-formulated reasons and for a limited time. That's when it becomes comparable to a warning strike during wage negotiations, a means of civil disobedience signaling that one side has the willingness and courage to fight.

(Grether, 2000: 5)

In 1998, the Electronic Disturbance Theater (EDT) coordinated a series of web sit-ins in support of the Mexican anti-government group the Zapatistas. This incident was perhaps most noticeable for its use of an automated piece of software revealingly called *Flood Net*. The Flood Net software, once downloaded onto an individual's computer, automatically connects the surfer to a pre-selected website, and every seven seconds the selected site's reload button is automatically activated by the software. If thousands of people use Flood Net on the same day, the combined effect of such a large number of activists will disrupt the operations of a particular site. These techniques were also used in the 1999 Etoy campaign by hacktivists responding to a commercial company's attempt through the courts to remove an art collective's website domain name because they felt it was too similar to their own.[4] In what was described as the "Brent Spar of e-commerce",[5] a combination of hacktivist and public relations stunts was used to force an eventual volte-face by the company, aided by a 70 per cent decline in its NASDAQ stock value.

E-mail bombs are used to overload the recipient's e-mail system so that it cannot receive legitimate mail. They are very similar to the techniques used in virtual sit-ins and blockades, and Denning concedes that "an e-mail bomb is also a form of virtual blockade" (Denning, 1999: 19). They have tended to be used by disgruntled groups who have a specific political grievance. For example, e-mail bomb attacks have been targeted against: the Sri Lankan government by Tamil hackers; both NATO and the Yugoslav government by opposing groups during the Kosovo conflict; a San-Francisco-based ISP because it held webpages devoted to the cause of the Basque separatist group, ETA.

Web hacks and computer break-ins

The defacement of websites is as old as the World Wide Web itself. Humour has frequently played a part in these hacks, such as the changing in 1996 of a link title in the pre-election on-line manifesto of the British Labour Party from "The Road to the Manifesto" to "The Road to Nowhere", and the changing of the CIA's website so that it read "Central Stupidity Agency".[6] The hacker group *Cult of the Dead Cow* (CDC) has sought to combine a humorous attitude with a hardened attitude to corporate power on the Internet. Successive versions of its software package "Back Orifice" target computers attached to Microsoft Windows network systems and allow the software's user to access the private files and e-mails of the network user. According to Jordan (forthcoming), at the time of writing Back Orifice had been downloaded 128,776 times since late February 2000, and the CDC argues that it draws attention to the surveillance capabilities written into Microsoft software which allow system administrators access to the private information of users.

In recent years Web hacks have become more explicitly politically moti-vated. In June 1998, for example, a hacker group from various countries called Milw0rm hacked the website of the Indian Atomic Research Centre and inserted their own messages, complete with a mushroom cloud to reinforce their point. In September 1998, Portuguese hackers changed a number of Indonesian websites so that they displayed the words "Free East Timor". Similar attacks have also been directed on a two-way retaliatory basis between Chinese sites and the West, and, in the conflict over Kosovo, between Serbia and the West.

Meanwhile, in 1999, hackers from Taiwan and China conducted an on-line series of Web hacks against each other: "the Chinese government has been accused of attacking a U.S. Web site devoted to the Falun Gong meditation sect, which Chinese authorities outlawed in July 1999" (Denning, 1999: 23); while "Doctor Nuker" of the Pakistan Hacker Club defaced Indian websites in support of Kashmiri separatism. And in the autumn of 2000, Israeli and Palestinian groups targeted each other's websites in support of their conflict.[7]

Computer viruses and worms[8]

In 1988, the first widely disruptive computer worm, known as the Internet Worm, was propagated by Robert Morris Jnr, who ironically was the son of the chief scientist for the US National Computer Security Center. A year later a worm was used for the first time as a form of specific protest when anti-nuclear hackers attempted to stop the launch of a NASA probe which contained nuclear materials. The "WANK" worm (Worms Against Nuclear Killers) was claimed to have cost NASA up to half a million dollars, but failed to prevent the probe's launch. Occurring alongside such indiscriminately targeted viruses as the "Love Bug", more recent examples of virus-based hacktivism include the destruction of an Iraqi government website by an Israeli hacker, and attacks by Serbian hackers upon various public and private sector sites during the Kosovo conflict. Having established some of the main forms of hacktivism, we can now turn to its wider social and theoretical significance.

Hacking *The System*

> Wandering around the labyrinth of laboratories and storerooms, searching for the secrets of telephone switching in machine rooms, tracing paths of wires or relays in subterranean steam tunnels…for some this was common behaviour, and, when confronted with a closed door with an unbearably intriguing noise behind it, there was no need to justify the impulse to open the door uninvited. And then, if there was no one to physically bar access to whatever was making that intriguing noise, how tempting and easy it was to touch the machine, start flicking switches and noting responses, and eventually to loosen a screw, unhook a template, jiggle some diodes and tweak a few connections: things had meaning only if you found out how they worked. And how would you go about that if not by getting your hands on them?
>
> (Levy, 1984: 17)

In Levy's seminal description of early hacking culture, curiosity is shown to be its key determining feature. The hackers' innate intellectual brand of explorative curiosity ultimately constituted a craving to understand *systems*. For the "true hacker", the abstract quality of complexity is of more importance than the specific physical qualities of a particular technological artefact. At the same time, however, such curiosity cannot remain isolated on an abstract intellectual plane: it is inextricably linked to more mundane, physical matters such as the need for access to some form of embodied technology with the subsequent opportunity to exercise the *hands-on imperative*. This combination of interest in both abstract complexity and the physical manifestations of such complexity illustrates a key element of the hacking ethos that in recent times has tended to be overlooked – lost in the minutiae of the most important hacker artifact to date, the computer.

Levy (1984) describes the curiosity of one hacker, Peter Samson, as being effectively interchangeable between such vastly different scales as the labyrinth of MIT's rooms and corridors and the bird's nest of electrical wires underneath the layout table of its *Tech Model Railroad Club* where:

> Underneath this layout was a more massive matrix of wires and relays and crossbar switches than Peter Samson had ever dreamed existed. There were neat regimental lines of switches, and achingly regular rows of dull bronze relays, and a long, rambling tangle of red, blue, and yellow wires – twisting and twirling like a rainbow-colored explosion of Einstein's hair. It was an incredibly complicated system...
>
> (Levy, 1984: 21)

"R", a Dutch hacker, expands upon the heterogeneous nature of hacking by arguing that the phrase should not...

> ...only pertain to computers but to any field of technology. Like if you haven't got a kettle to boil water with and you use your coffee machine to boil water, then that in my mind is a hack. Because you're using the technology in a way that it's not supposed to be used. Now that also pertains to telephones, if you're going to use your telephone to do various things that aren't supposed to be done with a telephone, then that's a hack. If you are going to use your skills as a car mechanic to make your motor do things it's not supposed to be doing, then that's a hack. So for me it's not only computers it's anything varying from locks, computers, telephones, magnetic cards, you name it.
>
> (cited in Taylor, 1999: 16)

Historically, the desire to understand technology's systemic qualities has meant that the curiosity of hackers has been targeted not only at an eclectic range of physical artefacts but also at social structures such as the legal *system*:

> The criminal justice system is a game to be played, both by prosecution and defense. And if you have to be a player, you would be wise to learn the rules of engagement. The writer and contributors to this file have learned the hard way. As a result we turned our hacking skills during the times of our incarceration towards the study of criminal law and, ultimately, survival. Having filed our own motions, written our own briefs and endured life in

prison, we now pass this knowledge back to the hacker community. Learn from our experiences…and our mistakes.

(Petersen, 1997)

The apparently complete dependence of contemporary national governments and global capitalism upon complex communication networks has created room for a more deliberately focused political agenda to be added to the pro-systems but anti-authoritarian tendencies that have always existed within hacking. The huge recent growth in the number of such systems of communication networks has simultaneously increased the global commodification process and its vulnerability to dissenting forces.[9]

Viral, vulnerable times

The damage a successful supervirus could do is almost incalculable. "It would be as if the Millennium Bug has actually done everything it was feared it could do," said one London-based computer security expert last week.…One source close to British intelligence services says MI5 believes both the Basque separatist group ETA and the Kurdish terror organisations have drawn up plans aimed at crashing air traffic control systems through the use of hacking or viruses. Irish Republican terrorists are also thought to have considered similar methods. "The super-virus is going to happen soon," the source said. "There are people out there with that intention. They may coincide their actions with protests against the International Monetary Fund and the World Trade Organisation, just to muddy the water". Many of the organisations connected with anarchist violence in London number hackers in their ranks.

("Coming to a screen near you", *Observer*, 7 May 2000: 19)

The emergence of widespread hacking in the 1980s produced dramatic expressions in the media of the feeling that society was vulnerable to breaches in the smooth running of its new technologies (see Taylor, 1999). A gap seemed to have arisen between society's increasing dependence upon complexly networked communication technologies and its ability to maintain and control them as effectively as it previously had with more physically-based structures. The above excerpt provides an indication of the way in which even broadsheet newspapers dramatize society's vulnerability to computer security weaknesses by loosely grouping together such disparate phenomena as hacktivists, terrorists and computer viruses. Hackers provided a new scapegoat for this nascent feeling of vulnerability and a new target for those fears of the unknown and the "other" that had prospered during the Cold War and which are now recycled in the concept of information warfare.

Hackers have frequently provided a useful embodiment of media-sponsored fears of technology, which have now found a fresh focus in the figure of the cyberterrorist.[10] Just as previous generations of the hacking community have been stigmatized, so too are hacktivists likely to be targeted as scapegoats due to society's increasing dependence upon, but ignorance of, the highly interdependent and complex networks that supply modern society with its extensive needs ranging from the phone calls we make to the food we eat. Perceptions of technologial vulnerability exist within a wider, general social climate of insecurity that is fuelled by the contemporary prominence of a number of infections ranging from AIDS and Ebola to the scarcely detectable prions in BSE-infected meat. Thus there is a culturally-receptive environment for the concerns that have accompanied the advent of IT-based superviruses and which are reflected in the following sample of recent newspaper headlines:

- "Love bug virus creates worldwide chaos": *Guardian*, 5 May 2000 (p. 1).
- "New 'Love Bug' viruses threaten more havoc": *Independent*, 6 May 2000 (p. 12).
- "Supervirus threatens IT meltdown": *Observer*, 7 May 2000 (p. 2).
- "Beware stealthy 'Sons of Love Bug'": *Independent*, 21 May 2000 (p. 11).

George Smith, the editor of the on-line *Crypt Newsletter*, is mordant in his criticism of the formularly weak investigative qualities which consistently feature in press reports of cybersecurity issues and which prosper in the cultural climate of fear. He identifies the phrase "Electronic Pearl Harbor" (Smith, 1998) as a particularly good indicator of the likely inaccuracy of any article that ingenuously uses it, and he defines the phrase as "A bromide popularised by Alvin Toffler-types, ex-Cold War generals, assorted corporate windbags and hack journalists...EPH is meant to signify a nebulous electronic doom always looming over U.S. computer networks...It has been seen thousands of times since its first sighting in 1993" (Smith, 2000). EPH is a slogan for US "info-warriors" whose most potent weapon "appears to be the burying of the enemy with floods of vague military philosophy, impenetrable jargon, clichés, scenarios, and aphorisms gathered from popular books attributed to Alvin Toffler, Tom Clancey, and Sun Tzu" (Smith, 1999: 1).

Smith (2000) claims that EPH articles tend to have consistently identifiable flaws which serve as accurate indicators of media hype in the field of computer security reporting, including:

- Obsession with hypotheses upon what might happen – not what has happened.
- Abuse of anonymous sourcing and slavish devotion to secrecy. All EPH stories usually contain a number of "anonymoids" – from the Pentagon, the White House [etc.]...
- Paranoid gossip...almost any country not USA can be portrayed as taking electronic aim at the American way of life...in a kind of modern techno-McCarthyism.

Such reporting faults and mild paranoia illustrate the way in which hack-tivism highlights an increasingly apparent tension of the modern information age: the uneasy nature of the symbiotic relationship that exists between on-line and off-line activity, and the complex ethical issues that arise due to the growing adoption of virtual technologies. In the following extract, for example, despite the death of an estimated 1,500 civilians during the Kosovo conflict's NATO bombing, US officials seem to place a disproportionate emphasis upon the legal implications of on-line activity compared to the real-world effects of their off-line policies.

> The Pentagon refrained from unleashing an all-out computer attack on Serbia during the Kosovo conflict because the US was worried about the legal implications of launching the world's first "cyberwar"...The Pentagon's computer hackers had the theoretical capacity to plunder Mr Milosevic's bank accounts or bring Serbia's financial systems to a halt. But US defence officials said the plans were shelved for fear of committing war crimes.
>
> (*Guardian*, 9 November 2000)

Similarly, the column inches devoted to the new threat of cyberterrorism seem to be related more to the distorted perspective provided by the prism of media sensationalization than to a considered evaluation of its importance in the wider scale of things. Thus, for example, the e-mail bombing by the Internet Black Tigers in 1998 which was directed against Sri Lankan embassies was, in Denning's view, "perhaps the closest thing to cyberterrorism that has occurred so far, but the damage caused by the flood of e-mail...pales in comparison to the deaths of 240 people from the physical bombings of the U.S. embassies in Nairobi and Dar es Salaam in August of that year" (Denning, 1999: 26). William Church, editor for the Centre for Infrastructural Warfare Studies (CIWARS), underlines this sentiment with his wry observation that, "consid-ering the routinely deadly attacks committed by the Tigers, if this type of activity distracts them from bombing and killing then CIWARS would like to encourage them, in the name of peace, to do more of this type of terrorist activity" (Denning, 1999: 19).

Conclusion

> Computer programmers write software applications that are doomed to become as obsolete as wire recordings or programs for an IBM XT. The infrastructures built by our engineers are equally doomed. Whether a virtual world of digital bits or a physical world of concrete and steel, our civilization is a Big Toy that we both build and use up at the same time. The fun of the game is to know that it is a game, and winning is identical with our willingness to play
>
> (Thieme, undated).

An essential element of hacking that has re-emerged within hacktivism is the ubiquitous targeting of technological ingenuity and curiosity. There are two key aspects of this approach. First, a major element of the hacker aesthetic is *technological re-appropriation*: hackers seek to use a technological artefact for purposes not foreseen by its original designers. Second, the ubiquitous nature of the hacker ethos encourages a tendency to look beyond the specific qualities of individual technologies and instead to treat all technology as part of a broader system that can be played with. The case of the Etoy campaign illustrates the willingness of hacktivists to view the whole of the capitalist system as ripe for hacking. Furthermore, the willingness of hacktivists to combine traditional forms of off-line political protest with new on-line forms exhibits a familiarity and ease with shifting between the virtual and the physical that seems to be lacking in more conventional establishment structures.

Hacking is now almost exclusively associated with computers due to the fact that, more than any other artefact, they embody the abstract, systemic qualities that hackers seek to immerse themselves in. The rise of hacktivism represents a successful additional re-appropriation of this recent close association with computer technology and its recombination with the broader perspective of the more original, atavistic curiosity hackers hold towards not just computers but (technological) systems in general. This chapter has shown that the phenomenon of hacktivism should be viewed in the context of earlier forms of hacking. Hacktivists, however, have sought to excise the way in which hackers tended to privilege access to technological means, or the hands-on imperative, over the actual social ends that such an imperative could help to achieve. They do still remain loyal to the hacker ethic, in so far as they use the communication and media channels of the establishment against itself: rather than just railing against "the system", hacktivists treat it as something to be manipulated and re-engineered for alternative purposes.

We have seen how a key aspect of the original definition of a hack was the way an artefact or system was used either in a way unforeseen by its original designers, or, more than this, in a way diametrically opposed to its original purpose. In so far as the computer code upon which the Internet is based is but a technological instantiation of a broader, less literal capitalist code, hacktivists seek to use that instantiation against this broader political agenda. Debates about hacktivism tend to focus upon whether direct political action is a *non sequitur* if it takes place in virtual environments. In contrast, I would argue that it is hacktivists' imaginative re-engineering of the technological code contained within the Internet that actually enables them to engage more successfully with the more abstract capitalist code that paradoxically has most effect upon the so-called "real world".

Karl Marx argued that the purpose of philosophy is not to understand the world, but to change it. Implicit in the philosophy of hacking is a marked tension between the ultimate goal of the complete understanding of abstract systems which happen to be technologically instantiated, and the contrasting practical potential there is to create real-world effects from the manipulation of the hardware of such systems. With hacktivism, the original ethos of hacking has been resurrected in order to resist presently the biggest system of them all: global capitalism.

Notes

1 See Jordan (forthcoming) for a more detailed analysis of the contributions made by political activism.
2 It is difficult to schematize the evolution of hacking into neat chronological periods. This schema is therefore designed to provide merely a rough, but hopefully useful, overview of some of changes that have emerged within the computer underground. It does not, however, adequately reflect the overlaps in time and ethical quality that exist between the generations, so that, for example, there are hackers from all six generations who claim to share the central ethos of the hackers' first generation. The provisional nature of the schema is further underlined by the fact that definitions of hacking activity are hotly contested both within and outside the computer underground, and there is considerable blurring of the boundaries between "good" and "bad" hacking, and confusion about what constitute the precise differences between hacking and hacktivism.
3 See her web paper (Denning, 1999) for a full account of all four types of hacktivist action, in addition to a detailed contextualization of hacktivism in relation to the related concepts of Internet-based political activism and cyber-terrorism.
4 For a full account see Grether (2000).
5 See the press release available at www.rtmark.com/etoyprtriumph.html (checked on 18 June 2001).
6 These instances are cited in Jordan (forthcoming), and a more detailed list of hacked Web sites can be found at www.hackernews.com/defaced (accessed on 20 January 2001).
7 See the *Guardian Online*, "Wargames on the net: but this time it's for real", by Brian Whitaker, 30 November 2000.
8 Denning (1999: 24) explains the difference between computer worms and viruses in the following manner: "Both are forms of malicious code that infect computers and propagate over computer networks. The difference is that a worm is an autonomous piece of software that spreads on its own, whereas a virus attaches itself to other files and code segments and spreads through those elements, usually in response to actions taken by users (e.g. opening an e-mail attachment)."
9 See Barbrook (2000) for examples of how anti-capitalist values may in fact paradoxically exist in the technologies being used for their dissemination.
10 There is an additional ironic twist that the greater a country's level of technological development, the more vulnerable it is to informational attack by nominally weaker opponents. Thus, in the recent Palestine–Israel conflict: "So far, about 90 Israeli sites have been attacked, and around 20 on the other side, according to iDefense, an electronic security firm. The balance of casualties in cyberspace is the reverse of what has actually happened on the ground, and this may be explained by the scarcity of Palestinian websites" (*Guardian Online*, 30 November 2000).

References

Barbrook, R. (2000) "Cybercommunism: How the Americans are Superseding Capitalism in Cyberspace", *Science as Culture*, 9, 1: 5–40.
Bowcott, O. and Hamilton, S. (1990) *Beating the System – Hackers, Phreakers and Electronic Spies*, London: Bloomsbury.
Coupland, D. (1995) *Microserfs*, London: Flamingo.

Denning, D. (1999) "Activism, Hacktivism, and Cyberterrorism: The Internet as a Tool for influencing Foreign Policy". Available at: www.nautilus.org/info-policy/work-shop/papers/denning.html (checked on 18 June 2001).

Grether, R. (2000) "How the Etoy Campaign Was Won", *Telepolis*, January. Available at: www.heise.de/tp/english/inhalt/te/5843/1.html (checked on 18 June 2001).

Jordan, T. (forthcoming) "Hacktivism: direct action on the electronic flows of information societies", in K. Dowding, J. Hughes and H. Margetts (eds), *Challenges to Democracy: the PSA Yearbook 2000*, London: Macmillan.

Jordan, T. and Taylor, P. (1998) "A Sociology of Hackers", *Sociological Review*, 46, 4: 757–80.

Kaplan, C. (1998) "For Their Civil Disobedience, the 'Sit-In' Is Virtual", *The Cyberlaw Journal*, New York Times on the Web. Available at: www.nytimes.com/library/tech/98/05/cyber/cyberlaw/01law.html (checked on 18 June 2001).

Levy, S. (1984) *Hackers: Heroes of the Computer Revolution*, New York: Bantam Doubleday Dell.

Petersen, J. [aka Agent Steal] (1997) "Everything a hacker needs to know about getting busted by the feds". Available at: www.grayarea.com/agsteal.html (checked on 18 June 2001).

Ross, A. (1991) *Strange Weather*, London: Verso.

Roszak, T. (1986) *The Cult of Information: The Folklore of Computers and the True Art of Thinking*, Cambridge: Lutterworth Press.

Smith, G. (1998) "Electronic Pearl Harbor". Available at: www.nap.edu/issues/15.1/smith.htm (checked on 18 June 2001).

—— (1999) "Future Schlock", excerpted from *Foreign Policy* Magazine. Available at:

—— (2000) "The Big Kahuna of 'Electronic Pearl Harbor' hype 1996–2000". Available at: www.soci.niu.edu/~crypt/other/harbor.htm (checked on 18 June 2001).

Taylor, P. (1999) *Hackers: Crime in the Digital Sublime*, London: Routledge.

Thieme, R. (Undated) "Hacking Chinatown". Available at: www.ctheory.com/a46.html (checked on 18 June 2001).

Wray, S. (1998a) "Transforming Luddite Resistance into Virtual Luddite Resistance: Weaving A World Wide Web of Electronic Civil Disobedience". Available at: www.nyu.edu/projects/wray/luddite.html (checked on 18 June 2001).

—— (1998b) "On Electronic Civil Disobedience". Paper presented to the Socialist Scholars Conference and available at: www.nyu.edu/projects/wray/oecd.html (checked on 18 June 2001).

6 Last of the rainmacs

Thinking about pornography in cyberspace[1]

Bela Bonita Chatterjee

...with *Crash*, Cronenberg has created a future from which he already speaks...
(Grant, 1998: 180)

...the merest mention of "pornography" is followed like a Pavlovian reflex by the word "censorship" as if there was no context other than that of censorship and the law in which the problem of pornography could be raised...
(Kappeler, 1992: 88)

Introduction

As I write this chapter, perhaps the most prominent thought in my mind is how much popular perceptions about pornography have changed over the last few years. I can remember a time – and I'm really not that old – when the word "pornography" would conjure up images of seedy old men in beige rainmacs, furtively edging their way past the racks of sordid magazines in backstreet Soho sex shops. Pornography was something hidden in a stash under the bed; in piles of suspiciously unlabelled videos and crumpled magazines. The glossy lifestyle magazines (in between articles on how to maintain that high-octane lifestyle and still have time for a facial, full wax and manicure) would write utterly sincere articles about what to do if your partner had a porn addiction or if you chanced upon their secret sleaze cache. Worrying stuff.

Yet now, in a high-tech, media-saturated, postmodern culture, the image of pornography in the popular consciousness has changed almost completely. The set of values associated with it have altered quite considerably. As Suzanne Kappeler points out in the epigraph to this chapter, at one time the word "pornography" automatically engendered predictable reflex responses: think of pornography and you thought of censorship. Nowadays, the Pavlovian reaction is still as powerful, but instead of thinking only about censorship and sleaze, think about pornography and you think about the Internet.[2] A current concern in particular is the proliferation of child pornography that has come to the fore in the public consciousness at the same time as the rise of its new digital forum. Leaving child pornography aside for the purposes of this chapter, my interest here lies in the adult pornography debates. To me, it seems that law, cyberspace and pornography have formed a novel and rather unholy trinity against a background of a (sub)culture where it is now socially acceptable and practically expected to use the technology of the Internet to seek out sexually explicit sites.[3]

In addition, the fact that I am researching this as a woman generally raises no eyebrows, as the popular debate on pornography is no longer predominantly framed in terms of whether it degrades women and the automatic assumption that all women are horrified by it.[4] I am not arguing that feminist objections to pornography are now somehow all miraculously negated by the advent of cyberspace, but rather that reconsiderations are needed. Feminism has been undeniably fundamental in shaping attitudes towards pornography in the past, but I would argue that the position of contemporary feminist arguments in relation to this "new wave" of pornography is something that is far from clear. That there is even something as coherent and identifiable as a singular feminist perspective is itself a considerable point of debate and critique within feminist discourses themselves.[5] In seeking to evaluate cyberpornography, problematic from the perspective of feminist analysis is the fact that the greater majority of feminist work that considers pornography was written before cyberspace was a major influence.[6] Feminists have only recently begun to critically engage with cyberspace, and the feminisms that have resulted – known collectively as cyberfeminism – are still developing philosophies (Hawthorne and Klein, 1999: 2).[7] Not only has feminism undergone its own thorough and self-reflexive critique, but the old enemy pornography has changed its shape too, and the context of the debate – the cultural backdrop for the discourse – has altered almost beyond recognition from the world of videos and magazines to that of the postmodern cyber age.

I do not deny that much pornography on the Internet may well reinforce negative and degrading stereotypes, and that the relationship of women with pornography has not always been positive, but new perspectives – and pornographies – are starting to appear. Historians of pornography have long shown that technological developments and pornography are deeply interconnected, with each new medium changing pornography and with pornography in turn driving technological advancements (Williams, 1990; Hunt, 1993; Heim, 1991).[8] Indeed, it cannot be noted without irony that cyberspace owes a considerable part of its development to the pornography industry (Kenny, 1999; O'Toole, 1999; Bradwell, 1998). However, what I intend to argue in this chapter is that the intersection of cybertechnology with pornography has helped to produce new forms of pornography, a development that goes further than a simplistic trade-off in technological advances in production and distribution. These new pornographies, I argue, may be implicated in the construction of new cyber identities – users of pornography in cyberspace can no longer be seen only as passive and inert consumers, but also potentially constructed and deconstructed through their interaction with cyberpornography. What I also argue is that these implications have not been considered by the law. This chapter, then, intends to explore the changing profile of pornography in cyberspace, the implications of this for the construction of the self, and how these changes might be understood in relation to mainstream legal discourse.

Context and theoretical perspectives – some alternative approaches

In order to set this chapter in context, I shall briefly outline some of the approaches that have been already been taken, and explain why I shall not be taking them. There are several ways of writing about pornography, cyberspace and law, but often these three subjects are not discussed as a whole, at the same time. For example, there are several works on pornography which present it as a subject for study in its own right, without a prominent legal theme.[9] For my purposes these types of study are valuable precisely because of their alternative (i.e. non-legal) perspectives. However, my concern is that most of these studies were written before anyone realized the impact that cyberspace would have in this field. As Kendrick says in the new afterword to the 1996 edition of his book, it was not something that could have been foreseen. He goes on to say that he won't attempt to predict the outcome of the current debate, "if it ever yields anything so clear-cut" (Kendrick, 1996: 251). Likewise O'Toole errs on the side of caution at this early stage, observing that "[T]he social impact of new technology often manifests itself through unexpected, less obvious evolutions" (O'Toole, 1998: 282). I have to admit that I share O'Toole's caution, as this area is still emergent, and it is not my intention to dictate the outcomes either, but rather to introduce some new considerations to the debate.

With regard to legal works, often the approach taken is that of "black-letter law", and valuable work already exists that uses this perspective. For example, a body of work is starting to emerge on the interaction of law and cyberspace, the critical focus being predominantly jurisprudential. The debate centres on how law is (or is not) affected by cyberspace. Will an entirely novel jurisprudence be required, or is the reality rather that cyberspace presents no substantively new issues, the implication thus being that extension by analogy from existing law will be sufficient for the purposes of regulation?[10] If, as Barbera Spillman Schweiger writes, "the law must evolve to encompass", then the question becomes what *form* of law will emerge – will this still be recognizable as "law"? (Schweiger, 1998: 225). In contrast, if it is assumed that existing legal rules can apply, then the question becomes one of process and practice – how will those rules be interpreted in order to appreciate the nuances of cyberspace? In addition to this, there are those academics that consider the process of law enforcement in cyberspace, the debate here centring on the practical and theoretical problems of policing the Internet (Wall, 1998: 201).

As I take the view that cyberspace poses *qualitatively* new problems (Kohl, 1999), i.e. problems engendering a novel jurisprudence that may or may not turn out to be "law" in the traditional doctrinal sense (as well as a medium that has implications for pornography), I will not be pursuing a traditional black-letter law analysis. While such approaches are valuable, they tend not to focus on theoretical issues, or to see cyberspace as anything more than a neutral tool or imposition to be subsumed uncritically by the legal hermeneutic, which itself remains uncriticized (Welchman, 1997: 155). What is missing in this approach is a *critique* of cyberspace and the influence of immanent theories (Hawthorne and Klein, 1999: 8). Traditional approaches leave unexplored the wider aspects and potentials of both law and cyberspace, such as the roles of law and cyberspace as sites of the construction of identity. For my purposes, it is these debates that are more interesting. By retaining a narrow, black-letter law focus, the wider and more theoretically informed debates that shadow these questions of identity and its construction, such as how law and cyberspace can be understood using postmodern theoretical frameworks, are omitted.

Considering the body of work that *does* examine those laws which are concerned with regulating pornography on the Internet, the key issues centre on such questions as how they work, how they compare with other legal systems, and how they might be improved. In the absence of any unified or international legal system that relates purely to the Internet, these questions are currently of much interest (Akdeniz, 1996: 235; 1997a; 1997b: 223; Cavazos and Morin, 1995). While such analyses may be useful for lawyers, they tend not to focus on a critical interrogation of what pornography or cyberspace might be, the cultural context that they exist in, the stance of law in relation to pornography as one of either censorship or free speech,[11] and how pornography might be understood, particularly in terms of its interpretation as something other than harmful, in the new medium of cyberspace.[12]

Perhaps of more concern for me is the fact that the current cyberlaw texts do not as yet have much emphasis on gender, which I think is critical to the debate.[13] In choosing to include gender as a focus, my argument is that how we choose to frame the terms of the discourse invariably influences how we understand and analyse those issues involved. As cyberstudies are still in their infancy, still a dialogue as much as a discourse, there is the (relatively) open opportunity to set the agenda. Holly Cullen reminds us that "the introduction of information technology into legal practice and legal education must be informed by gender debates" (Cullen, 1998: 559). Alison Adam, in her work on gender, computer technology and artificial intelligence, highlights how easily questions of gender can be obscured and excluded by the stance of objectivity with which scientific and technological studies tend to be associated. The reality, she argues, is that both science and technology are actually gendered at their most basic levels, being tacitly inscribed with insights and perspectives from mainstream ("malestream"?) epistemology (Adam, 1998: 157).[14] If this is accepted, then attention to gender issues must be central to any critical analysis of cyberspace, including a legal one.[15]

There have been studies on the availability, nature and distribution of pornography on the Internet. For example, there is the UK Home Affairs Committee Report on Computer Pornography (House of Commons, 1994), and the US Carnegie Mellon University study (Rimm, 1995: 1849). These studies have been problematic, for differing reasons[16]. Regarding the UK report, its opening sentence states that "Computer Pornography is a new horror" (House of Commons, 1994: 5). Although it considers "evidence" on pornography from a broad range of sources, the statement betrays what would appear to be a foregone conclusion to the inquiry. While I do not challenge the fact that child pornography poses real questions of abuse and harm, the conclusions seem to be elided with those for adult pornography. The report makes reference to the existing laws, noting that there is legislation in place to cover cases of obscenity, namely the Obscene Publications Acts 1959 and 1964.[17] However, these laws were primarily enacted in response to developments in the production and dissemination of pornography from the mid-nineteenth to the mid-twentieth century and are thus socially, culturally and historically specific. As such, they do not reflect current concerns, debates or understandings of pornography or cyberspace. Relatively recent legislation relating to pornography has attempted to adapt to the conditions of cyberspace as a novel medium, in that digitally created and manipulated images, phenomena that are characteristic of cyberspace, are included.[18] While these changes have been positive for the prevention of child pornography, the manipulation and interpretation of the existing laws to suit has not been entirely progressive for the overall debate. It has not encouraged any detailed consideration of what cyberspace is. Whether the very term "cyberspace" is one that the law is overly familiar with is debatable, the language of legislation still tending to be framed in more narrow and technical terms.[19] Furthermore, it has not forced a legal restatement of obscenity, which remains essentially the same as before. "Pornography" as a term describing sexually explicit material is a relatively recent arrival to the English language, and one that is actually, and rather unhelpfully, unknown to the law. The term known to the UK law is "obscenity", not pornography. "Obscenity" derives from the Latin term *ob scena* which translates as "that which should be hidden" or "off scene", which can be interpreted remarkably broadly. Its common meaning is usually given as "lewd, filthy or disgusting", but to define a word using a series of synonyms does not bring the law closer to a definition (Smith and Hogan, 1999: 270). The UK legislation contains no substantial definition of the term. Rather, the legislation is substantially derived from Common Law, which explains obscenity in terms of its effects. Material is obscene if it has a "tendency…to deprave and corrupt", a test first formulated in *R v Hicklin* in 1868, which still remains in force as the legal test embodied in The Obscene Publications Act 1959 s 1 (1) (1868: 371). A description of effects is not the same as a definition of a term. Legal definitions, then, have been problematic because they have consistently been non-definitions, little more than allusions to equally vague concepts such as obscenity.[20] A thorough evaluation of whether an article is obscene or not is never at stake in UK obscenity law; rather, the inquiry is directed at whether the obscenity is of such a degree that it tends to deprave and corrupt, reducing obscenity to a binaristic evaluation of corrupt/not corrupt, legal/illegal.[21] Thus the law has traditionally eschewed definitions, focusing instead on the effects of material in question and taking it "as read", literally, declaring the fact of its obscenity to be obvious. Legal discussion of pornography is therefore always compromised in a number of ways, in that the law does not recognize the term "pornography", and so the two terms "pornography" and "obscenity" must constantly be used concurrently, and also in that the law's own term, obscenity, has never been effectively defined in legal terms. I choose to understand pornography to reflect a more contemporary understanding, and it is this term that I favour and expand on later in the chapter.[22]

Stewart J.'s (in)famous declaration "I know it when I see it", in the American case of *Jacobellis v Ohio* (1964), points not only to the law's continuing inability and/or reluctance to define what is indeed a mutable phenomenon, but more, I think, to the *constructedness* of pornography: "I know it when I see it" becomes "I define it when I see it". In the absence of any modern definition, obscenity becomes porous for the law, permeable to any prevailing values or morality. At the same time, any contemporary definition runs the risk of being both inflexible and underinformed, still frozen in the framework of the censorship debate. My point is that what we are seeing, and how we see it, has changed considerably with the advent of cyberspace. For law, this lack of critical awareness and issues of definition may well prove problematic, as its nineteenth-century attitudes become increasingly unrealistic. My concern is that, with constant reference to the law and to censorship, our understandings of pornography become self-referential and foreclosed. Legal discourse has provided a highly influential and pervasive way of understanding pornography, but perhaps it has been too pervasive. As Beverley Brown notes in her critique of the law's perspective of obscenity, there is the danger of overdeterminism if the ubiquity of the legal lens remains unchallenged:

> [L]aw's categories of "trouble"…imply a certain perceptual apparatus, specific forms of viewing/reading/looking. These regimes of visibility determine when and how sexual or bodily representations appear on the legal horizon. *They also determine the kind of visual milieu that we inhabit…*
>
> (Brown, 1993: 29 *my emphasis*)

Valuable insights can be gained from considering alternative theories that could in turn inform and enrich the legal discourse (Jackson, 1995). My concern is that without wider (and contemporary) reference, our understanding of pornography may become ossified, precluding diverse, subversive and dynamic interpretations, some of which I hope to explain further and explore in this chapter.

Different problems present themselves with the Carnegie Mellon Report. The Report, apparently most comprehensive, chose to take its definition of pornography from that used in everyday practice by computer pornographers themselves, noting that both the courts and several statutes concur with these categorizations (hard-core, soft-core) (Rimm, 1995: 1849–50). After systematically categorizing the data ("paraphilic, pedophilic, hebephilic", Rimm, 1995: 1852–3) the authors conclude the study with the observation that "[F]inally, the web is browsed predominantly by males" (Rimm, 1995: 1925). However, the study was subsequently revealed to be less than academically rigorous, and has since been widely and substantially discredited. Problems included unsubstantiated statements, misrepresentations as to the nature, status and scale of the study, a lack of objectivity, and methodological flaws that were irresolvable and fatal to the credibility and validity of the study. The members of the research team appeared not to exist, and sources who were implicated in the study later publicly denied their involvement and cooperation.[23]

While the academic credibility of the study is thus fundamentally compromised, I would argue that some useful points can be drawn from it that are in part raised by critics of the study.[24] The Rimm Report's definition of categories of pornography by reference (*inter alia*) to sexual preference raised objections that these categories involved contradictory and subjective classifications (Li, 2000). I would argue that this also draws attention to concerns about interpretation as an issue in its own right. Is objectivity possible here? Is not the meaning of pornography in part dependent on and constructed by the viewer, meaning coming only through interpretation?[25] How congruent can categorizations of sexuality be with subjective experience and understanding? Furthermore, as suggested above, associating definitions of pornography with legal interpretations does little to develop the debate, understandings instead becoming circular and increasingly entrenched.

The emphasis on gender in the report is also interesting. The conclusion of the report would appear to suggest that the gender "stakes" in pornography remain unchanged in a cyber-context. The implicit suggestion is that pornography in cyberspace remains a male interest, as does cyberspace itself. Yet with how much confidence can such statements be made? In this chapter I hope to show that sexualities and identities in cyberspace are increasingly contested, that they are surprisingly elusive, and may no longer be as simple as "male" or "female". What I also hope to show is that cyberspace can no longer be assumed to be a neutral medium, particularly in the context of pornography.

A brief introduction to the cyberlexicon: issues and terms

Every writer makes assumptions of their audience, about their familiarity with various theories and concepts. Usually a "glossary" section is not included, but in this context, for my purposes, some explanation of some of the terms I use is appropriate. Some terms in the field of cyberstudies are still relatively fluid, and which sources are drawn on inevitably shapes understanding. Michael Benedikt, for example, offers no fewer than eleven descriptions of cyberspace, and finds resonance in all of them (Benedikt, 1991: 1–3). It has been argued that the value of cyberspace lies in its ability to resist singular interpretation, and that it would be a mistake to try to impose one (Crang *et al.*, 1999: 1–18). Yet cyberterms are often loaded with multiple, sometimes ambiguous meanings. Following poststructuralist debates on how texts can be deconstructed, terminology and plural interpretations become critical in a political as well as an explanatory sense. As Donna Haraway explains, the terms used to describe new technologies are themselves postmodern interventions, this "cyborg heteroglossia" marks "one form of radical culture politics" in that the spliced, fused terms of cyber-technologies and biopolitics do not follow the prescribed grammatical and syntactical forms (Haraway, 1985: 69–70). For others, this is simply "technophoric cyberdrool" (Squires, in Dovey *et al.*, 1996: 195) that obscures mundane events through the rhetoric of "cyperbole" (Imken, in Crang *et al.*, 1999: 1). These concerns notwithstanding, my understandings are as follows.

Words like "cyberspace", "Internet", "world wide web" and "virtual reality" have now entered the common lexicon and are used interchangeably, but this elision can be confusing as several different sources of understanding inform various meanings of these terms.[26] The term "cyberspace" was first used by the cyberpunk author William Gibson in his 1984 novel *Neuromancer*. A dystopic vision of a high-tech society, *Neuromancer* portrays a dangerous and bleak post-industrial world where, in conjunction with real-life existence, people can inhabit a virtual dimension known as cyberspace. Cyberspace is the three-dimensional, navigable depiction of the world's computer data. This computer-generated space functions as a "consensual hallucination" where computer experts – "console cowboys" – interface with the graphics and forms of the space. They "jack in" to cyberspace through a bodily link with their computers and live in the digital environment (Gibson, 1984).

The cyberpunk version of cyberspace sounds seductive, the physical integration of humanity with technology offering a material realization of the Cartesian mind/body split.[27] By leaving the corporeal body – the "meat" – at the keyboard, the mind is free to explore cyberspace unencumbered by physical limitations.[28] However, the problem is that the vision remains disappointingly literary – the cyberspace described by Gibson doesn't actually exist (Plant, 1998: 12; McRae, 1999). Having said this, its fictional status does not mean that it has no academic use, as cyberpunk is an effective method of critiquing the present. Cyberpunk novels are not abstract but, rather, are closely grounded in contemporary culture. Cyberpunk can be seen as a metaphor for the present, and it is this metaphorical quality that makes cyberpunk writings useful arenas for testing out ideas.[29] The future of cyberspace itself may well be influenced along the model provided by cyberpunk fiction.

The cyberspace in cyberpunk writings sees its closest incarnation to reality in what is known as virtual reality (VR). In everyday language, cyberspace and virtual reality have become synonymous. VR is the closest we have come to realizing the integrated computer-generated world of *Neuromancer*. Short of a physical/neurological link, VR is created by actual computers aiming at creating simulations of the physical world (real or abstract). The environment is immersive, and users interact with the environment via head screens and other sense-linked technology. From its early military, aerospace, robotic and artistic uses, VR has now grown to encompass a wide variety of applications.[30] Shannon McRae writes:

[I]n the decade since William Gibson coined the term "cyberspace", the "consensual hallucination" he envisioned has taken on a reality which is virtual only in so far as it has become a collective, polyvalent and perpetually expanding construct in an imaginary space....."Virtual reality" is most often envisioned in popular culture as: systems that offer users visual, auditory and tactile information about an environment which exists as data in a computer system rather than as physical objects and locations.

(McRae, 1999)

Cyberspace here is less the dystopian hallucination of *Neuromancer* and more the zone of the Internet and the world wide web, as understood in everyday terms. Cyberspace here is a collective, descriptive term for everything from the Internet and the world wide web, and the imaginary or metaphorical space that it exists in.[31] Cyberspace is "where" the information is, an experiential but also an imaginary space, the imaginary "site" of the e-mail conversation and "space" of the chat-room (Lessig, 1996: 1403). To make the image more accessible to lawyers and legal academics, a useful illustration can be taken from intangible property, in that the nature of cyberspace is similar. Like a bank balance, the space of cyberspace exists but is not concrete as such. "Cyber" itself, in common usage, becomes a general (some might venture to say an arbitrary) prefix to denote anything vaguely connected with computers.[32] Strictly speaking, the Internet is not singular but plural, standing for "*inter*connected *networks*". The Internet can be thought of as the skeleton for cyberspace, a network of telecommunications whose cargo is digital information and whose fixed points are computers (Batty and Barr, 1994: 699–701). It is essentially anarchic, "without central points, organising principles, hierarchies" (Plant, 1998: 10, 49). The world wide web, pages of information written in HTML, is just one of the services this skeleton supports, such as chatlines, BBSs (bulletin board systems), e-mail (Kohl, 1998: 124) and MUDs (multi-user dimensions, described by McRae as "text-based virtual worlds, interactive databases from which it is possible to craft highly complex, extremely vivid environments"). These environments resemble communities within which some of their users have participated for a number of years (McRae, 1999).[33]

I choose to use "cyberspace" to mean the metaphorical and social space of the Internet, and the pages of the world wide web, but hopefully this will be a nuanced understanding, carrying with it a knowledge of the underlying concepts, structures and an anarchic nature. The study of cyberspace in academia is growing increasingly popular and has helped to provide valuable theoretical frameworks for more grounded and contextualized understandings of this new medium. These studies, which I draw on, are strongly influenced by postmodern theories on the subject as socially, culturally and discursively constructed, the self being plural, contingent, fragmented and in flux, and also theories on the aesthetics of the postmodernity such as the dominance of image over form, the prevalence of surface and superficiality over depth, textuality over materiality, simulacra and hyperreality over the real, and the deconstruction of monolithic Enlightenment concepts such as "Truth" and binaristic thinking.[34] Postindustrialism is also highlighted as a context for cyberstudies, in addition to the more aesthetic aspects of postmodernity.[35] The theoretical influences of such studies complement the more technical and scientific studies. For example, cyber-theory concerns itself with the new ontics/ontologies of communication systems, cyber-psychology looks at questions of psychology in cyberspace, and cyber-feminism looks at ways of theorizing gender in cyberspace.[36] On these readings, cyberspace can be a unique, transformative space that enables postmodern, fluid subjectivities to be played out and experimented with; a forum that enables imaginative new genders, sexualities and dis/embodiments to be created from scratch. As Thompson suggests, "The use of communication media involves the creation of new forms and interaction in the social world, new kinds of social relationship and new ways of relating to others and oneself" (Thompson, cited in Crang *et al.*, 1999: 11).

Alternative readings of pornography

I have already mentioned that there are alternative readings of pornography beyond that of the simplistic (and overwhelmingly binaristic) legal rhetoric, readings that may help to enrich our understanding and prove of relevance to a cyberspace context. Rather than seeing pornography as a discrete legal problem, these studies articulate and explore the link between pornography and the construction of subjectivities. Actually defining pornography in any encapsulating and concrete way is not the main objective, as these alternative studies recognize it as a shifting and constructed form. An example of this perspective is given by Ann Brooks in her work on postfeminism. Following poststructuralist debates on the construction of meaning through language, postmodernist debates about the centrality of cultural discourse in the formation of identities, and the importance of cultural studies in tracing the politics of postmodernism, she looks at how cultural forms can be sites where the meanings of identities are contested.[37] These forms, she argues, are useful frameworks for examining debates around issues such as "identity, sexuality, ethnicity and image" by understanding them as sites of possible opposition and resistance to hegemonic norms (Brooks, 1997: 135, 139–41, 189). By cultural forms, she means popular types of representation and expression such as art, literature, film, music, dance and drama, but includes pornography also as an important and influential site of meaning and identity construction. Quoting Tania Modleski, she suggests that pornography is a "quintessential postfeminist issue", if it is understood that "the issue of pornography encapsulates debates around sexuality, identity and representation, which have (at least, in part) defined the postfeminist agenda" (Modleski, in Brooks, 1997: 205).

Understanding pornography as a cultural form, then, means that it can be seen as a discourse through which subjectivities are constituted (after Martin, in Brooks, 1997: 192). Pornography becomes a cultural space in which alternative sexualities can be articulated and explored (Brooks, 1997: 206). Thinking about how this might be done, Brooks cites Martin who identifies three main ways that pornography might have positive implications for the creation of alternative identities. First, she argues, such material increases the range of practices and representations available. Second, it offers the possibility of understanding these practices and representations as challenging binary versions of sex and sexuality. Third, it offers a means of subverting dominant cultural forms and establishing new discourses, representations and identities (Martin, in Brooks, 1997: 199). Underpinning this alternative viewing of pornography is a refusal to interpret it as a text that conveys a univocal meaning or a singular "true" interpretation, a perspective that mainstream legal studies have fundamentally overlooked.[38] If there are plural interpretations of texts, then the binary logic behind censorship is destabilized. Legal interpretations import causal and binaristic meanings into texts because censorship is, in essence, a binary proposition. It polarizes its subjects into good and bad, legal and illegal, corrupting and innocent, cause and effect (Olsen, 1990: 199). To interpret pornography as an unstable text is arguably a subversive act in itself. Here, pornography is no longer the simplistic and banal portrayal of men sexually dominating and humiliating women but something infinitely complex with multiple and shifting meanings. It acknowledges that pornography itself may be plural, there may be *pornographies* rather than pornography. Such an understanding makes room for lesbian and gay pornography, as well as for different styles of sexual expression such as fetishism and sado-masochism.[39]

Also important in this alternative analysis of pornography is the concept of performativity. Perhaps the most well known proponent of this idea is the gender theorist Judith Butler, whose work has sought to expose the categories of gendered identity as artificial and reified concepts, the production of acts of parody or performance rather than as natural facts (Butler, 1999). In arguing gender as a performance, the contingent nature of identity construction is highlighted, and further "natural" binaristic structures come under scrutiny as their "factual" basis is undermined:

> [P]arodic contexts…bring into relief the performative construction of an original and true sex. What other foundational categories of identity – the binary of sex, gender and the body – can be shown as productions that create the effect of the natural, the original, and the inevitable?
>
> (Butler, 1999: viii-ix, xi)

A further example of an alternative and postmodern reading of pornography can be found in the work of Carl Stychin (1995). His work adopts several of the ideas explored above but uses them in a more specific analysis, namely the relationship of (gay male) homosexuality to the law. He looks at the way in which law is complicit in the construction of sexual identity through its regime of regulatory discourse, but notes that the very constructed and thus contingent nature of this process invariably means that there is opportunity for resistance and subversion. He argues that, in the law's attempt to consolidate a norm, in other words heterosexuality, it necessarily requires an "other" – homosexuality –

in order to justify that norm. It is this tacit dependence on the "other" that proves to be its weakness. Its discursive nature means that there can never be total closure of meaning and so alternative ("queer") interpretations are always implicit. It means that the legal discourse cannot be simply prohibitive, but provides space for resistance and subversion of the (hetero)normative order each time it attempts to enforce the norm. Such unintentional but inevitable gaps can then be exploited, thus undermining the regulatory project of the law, "[L]egal 'prohibitions' can inadvertently create discursive spaces for the articulation of the identity of the excluded 'other' in a field of legal and political contest" (Stychin, 1995: 7).

Stychin's thesis is also informed by poststructuralist and postmodernist interpretations of identity, seeing the self as discursively constructed, fluid and decentred.[40] He argues that the construction of a political identity in a postmodern environment (i.e., one of discourses) is dependent on the ability to articulate a subjecthood and forge connections though such articulation. The medium of articulation is culture, and so in this way it is through cultural forms and symbols that subjectivities are forged, recognized and circulated. Access to cultural forms, their production and interpretation, thus becomes critical in the successful creation of subjectivity. Drawing on Butler, he explains how performativity is key in this articulation, in that the subject, necessarily partial due to discursive formation, must be continually constituted though repetition. This constant need for consolidation opens up possibilities for alternative, subversive performance strategies such as drag (Stychin, 1995: 31–3).

Having identified the importance of cultural forms, in addition to looking at camp tactics, he considers the role of gay male pornography in the articulation of alternative sexualities. Although his argument centres around contrasting the radical-feminist/legal analysis of pornography with gay male pornography, his analysis, like that of Brooks, is useful because he sees pornography as a cultural form rather than a discrete legal problem that raises purely quantitative issues of censorship. In understanding pornography as a cultural form that is open to multiple interpretation, he manages to transcend the simplistic binary analysis that besets the traditional legal commentaries and offers a quite radical interpretation. Reading pornography as a plural text opens the possibility that it could be a site of alternative performativity that destabilizes heteronormative codes, "a resignification through the misappropriation and subversive use of the signs and codes of dominant patriarchal culture" (Stychin, 1995: 61). On such an understanding, gay male pornography undermines the notion of a coherent sexual subject, and moreover a definitive and thus sound legal reading, if it is understood that legal interpretations presuppose a fixed referent. Seeing pornography as performance allows for fluidity and fantasy to be included in any interpretation, which further complicates the idea of a concrete understanding (Stychin, 1995: 64). As Butler argues, "Fantasy offers the possibility of the fragmentation or proliferation of the identifications which challenges the very locatability of identity" (Butler, in Brooks, 1997: 209). On this analysis, then, pornography is more liberational than harmful, providing an opportunity to create and perform alternative sexual identities. Also important is the role of the viewer, who actively participates in the interpretation of the pornography, as it is the viewer who decodes the performance as "gay".[41] Here, meaning is dependent on interpretation, which is itself shown to be contingent and uncertain. The creative role of the viewer/user in pornography thus imports another contingency into the possible evaluations of pornography, but it is a variable that the standard legal interpretations consistently undertheorize, along with the possibility of open textuality. In imposing specific legal restrictions on the availability, nature and content of pornography (not necessarily gay pornography), the law is seen to play an active part in preventing alternative subjectivities from having access to, and representation in, cultural forms. Although the sites of suppression may in turn obliquely form possibilities for resistance, such a restriction on what is surely a right to articulate a political subjectivity is, he argues, untenable (Stychin, 1995: 74–5).[42]

Further alternative readings? Cyberinterventions

Before I consider the impact of cyberspace on all this, it may be useful to summarize some of the points made so far. What I have suggested is that traditional political and legal perspectives on pornography have been worryingly narrow, being increasingly out of sync (if there ever had been a stage where they were even in) with postmodern and poststructuralist developments in theory and cultural conditions. What has resulted is a rigid and self-referential framework for understanding pornography that has precluded alternative readings and has overbearing and negative influences on the ways in which we choose to think about and analyse pornography, particularly in a legal context. Considering alternative readings of pornography, it has been seen that analysing pornography as a cultural form rather than a legal "problem" yields a far more complex and, importantly, a more contextualized understanding that takes into account the cultural conditions and practices of postmodernity. Here, pornography can be understood as a place of performativity for alternative, fluid subjectivities, as a creative and positive means of communication with the potential for multiple interpretations. As O'Toole writes, "[A] type of cross-subjectivity may occur watching porn, where viewpoints switch and change. 'Identification in porn can be multiple and shifting, bisexual and transsexual, alternately or simultaneously'" (quoting Anne McClintock, in Segal and McIntosh (1992), O'Toole, 1998: 308).

The advantages of the alternative analyses, then, are that immanent theories are included in the picture. The postmodern subject is taken into account, as are ideas about open textuality, plural interpretation and the constructed, discursive nature of pornography. Yet the attempt at a contextualized understanding still lacks a certain something, namely the impact of cyberspace. Although being far from dated in terms of theoretical developments, both Brooks and Stychin omit discussion of cyberspace from their work. What would be useful would be an understanding of pornography, similar to the ones outlined above that appreciate postmodernist and poststructuralist insights, but an understanding that also considers the impact of cyberspace.

The tacit assumption here, of course, is that cyberspace somehow has a significance over and above that of any other media. The essence of the problem is encapsulated by Allucquère Rosanne Stone, who states that the question "What's new?" can have one of two answers, the first being "Nothing", in that computers are just another form of communications technology and give us nothing that we didn't already have, and the second answer being "Everything". In order for the second answer to be true, she argues, some of our assumptions have to be re-examined (Stone, 1995: 115–16). Having explained how I understand cyberspace, I naturally prefer the second answer, but it is worth giving the first response some thought. There are some that would agree with it, such as those who do not use the Internet. This may be out of choice or necessity, but for either reason it is hard to see how it impacts on their lives. I think that there is some truth in this. On a local, personal level perhaps, the effects will only be, at the most, oblique; however, this will not be true for everyone.

Perhaps cyberspace is nothing new because, like all new technology, it is wrapped up in questions of economics and power. Those who are economically disadvantaged may find it hard to become rapturous over technology which they are never likely to be able to experience, let alone afford. The "cultural conditions of postmodernity" may be cynically re-read as the cultural conditions of the economically advantaged and technologically sophisticated postindustrial countries. A cultural form here may well for some be more of a cultural luxury, as has been succinctly argued in the context of feminism and critical race theory: "Women of colour (indeed all women) require a concept of sexuality which expresses the tangible reality of sexual power in *their* lives. For some it may be orgasms: For others, it may be war" (Cox, 1990: 248, emphasis in the original). For some women there may be nothing positive here at all (Hughes, 1999: 157). Discussion about cyberlaw and pornography in an academic context may seem highly inappropriate when the socio-economic context is considered in this way.[43]

Despite these concerns, the fact remains that the emergence of cyberspace has added a whole new dimension to debates around pornography, identity, gender and law. Whether the "cyperbole" is justified or not, it is undeniable that its presence in the public consciousness is more than prominent. Perhaps not "everything" about cyberspace is new, but it does have some unique aspects and novel challenges to pose, which makes it significant when thinking about pornography. In addition to posing challenges to our concepts of temporality and spatiality, it has implications regarding the representation of gender and sexual expression, and the relationship of the body with technology. As Shannon McRae states, "computer networks have drastically refigured the cultural landscape" (McRae, 1999). Thinking about the cultural conditions and symbols of postmodernity, it is seen that the role of the computer and cyberspace is key. As Jean Baudrillard observes, the scene and the mirror have been succeeded by the screen and the network (Baudrillard, in McRae, 1999). The prevalence of cyberpornography, whether actual or feared, is overwhelmingly pervasive, as is illustrated by the contemporary "Pavlovian" reaction to the mention of the word.

But what real significance does it have? Does it simply mean that the consequence of cyberpornography is merely a quantitative increase, that all the new medium brings is easier access and distribution of what are, in essence, the same portrayals of sex that have always existed? Do existing patterns of power and (in)equality inevitably have to map onto the virtual world? I think that the implications are far more complex than a simple transferral of the existing status quo. What I suggest is that cyberspace, as a new space for expression, has engendered an entirely new architecture of sexual expression that did not exist before – a new discourse of pornographies that are suited to the inhabitants and conditions of a postmodern, mediated world. It may be no coincidence that the emergence of cyberpornography coincides with wider debates on the physical, material status of the body itself as well as the coherence of gender, sexuality and identity (McRae, 1999; Springer, in Wolmark, 1999: 35). J. G. Ballard argues that the dominance of "organic sex" is giving way to "a whole new order of sexual fantasies, involving a different order of experiences...the whole overlay of new technologies [that] reach into our lives and change the interior design of our sexual fantasies" (Ballard, in Wolmark, 1999: 34). The potential for interactivity in cyberspace is not present in other media, the access to and authorship of pornography is far wider here, which opens the possibility of alternative constructions and representations of desire not represented by the mainstream pornography industry. It is, in this way, a site for resistance and subversion. On such an understanding, cyberspace is a new space for the articulation of alternative sexualities, and cyberpornography a cultural form.

While highlighting its potential for plural, non-hegemonic meanings, the creation and interpretation of cyberpornography is more complex than in non-cyber texts. Recalling the role of performativity in pornography for producing fluid representations of genders, the medium of cyberspace enables this strategy to be taken to extremes, which start to problematize gender itself. As interaction is remote in cyberspace, in other words it is not face to face: gender cannot be "read" by the usual visual/normative clues used in social space. The gender a user presents online is thus an option from the outset. Images are digitally malleable, so that even visual representations of the body are subverted – Brown's *visual milieu* (Brown, 1993: 29) is recast. The depiction of the body in cyberpornography is essentially chimaeric, a cyborg, whichever fusion the imagination desires that is capable of being graphically represented. Genders and the bodies they represent can be invented *ab initio*, such as the "Spivak" gender in LamdaMOO (Stone, 1995: 64–9) described by McRae as having unique corporeal features as well as pronouns; "e, em, eir, eirs, eirself" (McRae, 1999).[44] She argues that the consequence of this amplified performativity in cyberspace is that the entire concept of gender as a coherent primary marker of identity becomes fundamentally destabilized:

[I]f boys can be girls and straights can be queers and dykes can be fags...then "straight" or "queer", "male" or "female" become problematised...gender becomes a verb, not a noun...the role can be enacted with such focus and intensity that the "I" becomes meaningless.

(McRae, 1999)

The representation of sex in cyberspace, then, becomes pure performativity.[45]

Does the fact that an actual physical presence is still required behind all this provide a fixed point of anchor, bringing the fluid and novel subjectivities and genders back to reality? As Stychin argues, "the ontological status of the body itself grounds subjectivity in a way that it is difficult to imagine transcending" (Stychin, 1995: 21; see also Springer, in Wolmark, 1999; Sofia, in Wolmark, 1999; Stone, 1998). Yet, as Haraway points out, postmodernity has been characterized by the erosion of borders, particularly those that are drawn between organism and machine, which brings into question whether the physical boundaries of the body are impermeable to digital infiltration and hybridity (Haraway, 1985). As we have seen, the relationship of human and cybertechnology is still short of being fully integrational, despite the ubiquity of the cyborg metaphor and cyberpunk visions.

How is the notion of the body problematized in cyberpornography? Apart from the possibility of visual reinvention, McRae suggests that the actuality of erotic interaction and representation in cyberspace forces us to reconsider the way we understand embodied subjectivity. Such interaction "requires a constant phasing between the virtual and the actual, the simultaneous awareness of the corporeal body at the keyboard, the emoting, speaking self on the screen, and the existence of another individual, real and projected, who is similarly engaged". Rather than resulting in a binary split, she argues that the effect of this is to produce a multiple and fractured awareness of the self to the extent that the "self" is rendered "incoherent, scattered, shattered" (McRae, 1999). The projections of such a self in cyberspace leads to debates on traditional concepts of the body as a coherent entity – as Stone puts it, a "physical envelope" – as the locus of agency and the way that representations of body in cyberspace challenge the way we think about corporeality in general. As Stone goes on to suggest, discussions on cyberspace are held against a background where "the accustomed grounding of social interaction in the physical facticity of human bodies is changing" (Stone, 1995: 16–17). For me, the inference to be drawn is that cyberspace, particularly in pornographic contexts where gender and representations are most likely to be destabilized and processes of "phasing" are central, provides a highly tangible experience of the postmodern, fragmented self where both the body and subjectivity can be problematized. This point is underscored by Claudia Springer, who argues that "ambivalence toward the body has been played out most explicitly in texts labelled pornographic...the dispersion of sexual representation across boundaries that previously separated the organic form from the technical" (Springer, in Wolmark, 1999: 35).

Towards theorizing cyberpornography: Where do we go from here?

In commenting on the erosion of boundaries between the organic and the technical and the context of cyberspace, Springer goes as far as to suggest that the era we are in is actually "post-pornographic". Drawing on Kendrick, she argues that pornography has never actually been a stable concept, but rather "constitutes a shifting ideological framework that has been imposed onto a variety of texts since its inception" (Springer, in Wolmark, 1999: 35). For me, her point underscores the general theme of fragmentation and uncertainty that the anarchic and plural conditions of cyberspace only help to amplify. If it is accepted that cyberpornography is a shifting cultural form which significantly problematizes gender, the body and representations of sexuality, then how can it be coherently analysed, and moreover, how can such an analysis be achieved from a legal perspective, in particular that of criminal law? The epistemology of law is, surely, ineluctably pre-postmodern, being grounded in monistic Enlightenment concepts of a unitary self, of binary logic, rationality and predictable cultural conditions.[46] The structure of the criminal law, the concepts of "crime", of a cogent, coherent political agent that could be socially accountable for criminal choices, of certainty, precedent and deviance, were all formed in cultural conditions that did not reflect or accommodate alternative subjectivities, sexualities, lives in cyberspace. The interests of the criminal law are those of a normative structure, necessarily diametrically opposed to the plurality and uncertainty that cyberspace invites. Forcing fluid and shifting concepts into a framework that demands definitive answers to yes/no questions will do them considerable injustice. Yet, if the disruption of gender, the problematizing of the body and the shifting nature of pornography in cyberspace make it less locatable, a floating concept rather than a fixed signifier, then the idea of censorship in this context, of criminality here, is surely undermined. How can pornography be analysed if its new forms and contexts are not acknowledged? How can gender be analysed here when the concept of gender is looking increasingly unstable? A problem for cyberfeminists is locating the political in cyberspace when the concept of woman, of the body as the locus of agency, are challenged. The very process of theorizing cyberspace itself becomes difficult: as Scott Lash asks, how can critique occur in a context which is so immanent that there is no space for reflexivity or critical distance? How can power and inequality be theorized in a context which opens up novel configurations of these issues (Lash, 1999)? Furthermore, how do the very theories employed alter through usage here? As Butler points out:

> ...the face of theory has changed precisely through its cultural appropriations. There is a new venue for theory, necessarily impure, where it emerges in and as the very event of cultural translation...the emergence of theory at the site where the demand for translation is acute and its promise of success, uncertain.
>
> (Butler, 1999: ix)

Clearly, there is much to be reconsidered, but these concepts must also surely force a reconsideration of legal concepts too, of what it means to be political, legally accountable, a legal subject, what is meant by "criminal" itself as well as what is meant by "law".

The problems which cyberspace and cyberpornography may present to law, such as how an essentially binaristic structure can interpret plural identities and sexualities, seem to be similar to those questions that are posed by postmodernism for law in general. Yet perhaps cyberspace and cyberpornography can be seen as postmodern interfaces with law that might not have to result in the stalemate that I envisage above. Perhaps it is a mistake to see law itself as monolithic and immutable, as only when it is seen as such can any involvement with postmodernist theories, and plural and fluid forms such as cyberpornography and the (cyber)identities created through them, be seen as problematic. Jennifer Wicke, in her analysis of postmodern identity and the legal subject, argues that the apoliticism and fragmentation of postmodern identities undermines the politically useful monistic legal subject, even if that subject does leave much to be desired. Important political rights that adhere to the subject become unclaimable with the subject's dissolution through the fragmenting lens of postmodernity (Wicke, 1991: 462). Yet, in responding to Wicke's paper, Mary Joe Frug argues that a marriage of postmodernism and law does not necessarily have to lead to the loss of political effectiveness. Law does not have to be read as more "powerful" than postmodernism, and a progressive politics does not have to depend on preserving the law from postmodernism's fracturing effects (Frug, 1991: 484–5). Law itself can be read as an ambiguous text, as Stella Swain writes: "law exists *as* language and literature" (Swain, 1997: 11). As David Kennedy argues, legal discourse is already starting to admit postmodern themes in the light of its "continual involvement with other social and political forms" (Kennedy, 1991: 476). Surely, on this analysis, it must be open for law to change, in order to accommodate the pluralities and fluidities of cyberpornography, and of cyberspace itself. The advent of cyberspace can be argued as a critical juncture where law can rethink how it creates categories, in order to acknowledge new subjectivities rather than try to fit them into an exclusory, dualistic framework that cannot hope to reflect their complexity. I would therefore argue for subversive readings in cyberlaw that provoke critical re-examinations and re-evaluations, critiques that draw on broad resources and reach down to fundamental epistemological levels, a process that I hope this chapter works towards. Ultimately, the interaction of cyberspace, cyberpornography and law poses complex questions, and rather than attempt to answer them all I prefer to leave some of them open. It will be interesting to see how future discussions develop, but these are discussions that are both theoretically necessary and politically apposite, particularly for lawyers, because, as hinted at by Grant in the second epigraph to this chapter, our futures are already being created, and these futures are ones from which people are already beginning to speak.

Notes

1   I wish to thank Cliff Brown, Megan Comfort, Fiona Cownie, Alison Diduck, Dr Stuart Elden, Debra Ferreday, Sarah Rose, Mathias Klang, Jon Pennycook, Robert Sayer, Dr Frances Simon, Dr Nina Wakeford and Dr David Wall for their valuable comments, encouragement and assistance during the writing of this work. Earlier explorations of ideas in this chapter have appeared elsewhere (see Chatterjee 1999, 2000).

2   Jamie Kenny writes, "In the public mind the words 'internet' and 'pornography' frequently go together, just like 'moral' and 'panic'" (1999: 22).

3   For example, Michael Uebel (2000), drawing on Zillah Eisenstein, notes that the association of pornography with cyberspace has made pornography "cool"; but cf. Lawrence O'Toole's "Afterword" to the second edition of *Pornocopia* (1999: 348) Catherine MacKinnon observes from a (radical) feminist standpoint that pornography in the cyberage seems to have less of a stigma than it used to and cites the following reasons: "As pornography saturates social life, it also becomes more visible and legitimate, hence less visible as pornography...pornography acquires the social and legal status of its latest technological vehicle" (MacKinnon, 1995: 1959). However, cf. Frederick Jameson on this point (1984).

   Having noted in the text that "adult" pornography seems less reviled than it used to be, the reverse is true of "child" pornography. I have chosen to exclude child pornography from my inquiry as I believe the issues involved in that debate to be quite distinct from those surrounding "adult" pornography. Also, a considerable body of work already exists in this area; see, for example, the chapter by Heins in this volume. An interesting perspective can also be found in Tien (1994: 121).

4   See Linda Williams (1990: xi). At the time of writing, the mainstream press reveals that the debate is timely. In *The Independent on Sunday* (6 August 2000: p. 8), Cherry Norton, in a report from The American Psychological Association Conference, announced that "Women take control of cyberporn". Likewise, on the same day, Tracy McVeigh published an article in *The Observer* entitled "Women lead the Porn Revolution" (6 August 2000: p. 12). However, some weeks later, Germaine Greer argued in "Gluttons for Porn" (*The Observer Review*, 24 September 2000, pp. 1–2) that the cyber-aided spread of pornography into mainstream culture is decidedly toxic.

5   See, e.g., Nicholson (1990); Brooks (1997). Of course, "feminist" should not be followed by the equally Pavlovian association of being anti-pornography (Strossen, 1996; Williams, 1990), but MacKinnon (1995: 1957) sees new technology as the latest "trojan horse" for pornography and is very clear indeed on where feminist sympathies should lie. I can't say that I agree with her position, but I acknowledge the invaluable contribution she has made to the feminist debates. It is perhaps easy to criticize positions that appear with hindsight to be essentialist or reductionist, but it is these very critiques that have built the foundations of current debates.

6   Influential feminist studies on pornography include: Itzin (1992); Strossen (1996); MacKinnon (1987; 1989; 1994; 1995); Dworkin (1981); Griffin (1981); Easton (1994); Segal and McIntosh (1993). Useful evaluations from a feminist/legal perspective are given by Eckersley (1987: 149) and also Jackson (1995: 49). For a (radical) feminist discussion of Internet pornography see Adams (1996: 147). I have chosen not to focus on Adams's study because, while I believe she makes some valid arguments, our perspectives fundamentally differ. I understand her argument to be that cyberpornography is nothing more exotic than the modern counterpart of traditional video and magazine pornography, that it reflects (white, straight) male sexuality and thus fosters the oppression of women. However, I would argue that this entails taking uncritical and essentializing interpretations of pornography, gender and sexuality, a stance that this chapter argues against.

7 For a related discussion of prostitution on the Internet (which also includes consideration of pornography from a cyberfeminist perspective) see Hughes (1999: 157).

8 For Michael Heim (1991), there is a deeper, far more fundamental relationship between technology and eroticism itself. For him, cyberspace necessarily has an "erotic ontology"; but cf. McRae (1999) for related critique. The history of obscenity law is also closely linked to technological developments. As writers in this area note, technological advances have consistently provoked legislation that aims at preventing the development being exploited by pornographers, the paradox being that it has been the pornographers who have been instrumental in the developments in the first place. See in general St John Stevas (1956) and Roberston (1979).

9 Examples include historical approaches such as Lynn Hunt's *The Invention of Pornography* (1993) and Walter Kendrick's *The Secret Museum*(1996), media perspectives such as Simon Watney's *Policing Desire*(1997), Linda Williams's *Hard Core*(1990), Brian McNair's *Mediated Sex* (1996) and more contemporary overviews like that given by Lawrence O'Toole in *Pornocopia* (1999). O'Toole includes discussion of cyberspace in his book.

10 The jury would still appear to be well and truly out on this point; see, for example, Johnston and Post (1996: 1367); Lessig (1996: 1403); Schweiger (1998); Gilligan and Imwinkelried (1998: 305); Kohl (1999: 123).

11 Although a notable exception is Edwards and Waelde (1997) who ask in their Preface *whether* the Internet should be regulated as well as *how* it should be regulated.

12 Uebel (2000) examines cyberpornography in relation to masculinity and masochism, stating: "It is my contention that...fantasy is being activated in novel ways. Cyberspace is installing a new regime of sexual representation and, with it, tactical modes of dreaming, thinking, and acting."

13 I prefer to think of these points more as concerns than criticisms, as it has to be acknowledged that the main body of jurisprudence in the emergent field of Internet law is not explicitly feminist, i.e., it is not written *ab initio* along the lines of, say, feminist perspectives on Internet law ("cyberlaw"). Neither is it, as a general observation, overly attentive to matters of, for example, race and age, concerns which some non-legal cyberfeminist texts are trying to explore, for example Hawthorne and Klein (1999). Notwithstanding the difficulties of analysing gender in cyberspace, it is hoped that such perspectives will appear over time.

14 The pun on mainstream was made by Adam (1998) and is far more amusing in the original.

15 There is a considerable body of work that explores the interrelationship of gender and technology; see, for example, Sadie Plant (1998), but also Hawthorne and Klein (1999), Wolmark (1999), Stone (1995), and Kirkup *et al.* (2000).

16 The Rimm/Carnegie Mellon Report does include a substantial methodology appendix, and acknowledges some of the difficulties involved with researching the Internet: for example, the transient nature of some of the material as well as questions of validity and reliability. For a critique of this, see Wallace and Mangan (1996) and Wall (1999).

17 Other relevant (UK) legislation includes the Telecommunications Act 1984; the Video Recordings Act 1984; the Protection of Children Act 1978; the Criminal Justice Act 1988; the Broadcasting Act 1990 and the Computer Misuse Act 1990. Due to constraints of space and time, I have not considered American obscenity law in any real detail in this chapter.

18 This pertains specifically to child pornography. See particularly ss1, 1(1)(a), 2(3), 7(4), 7(7), 7(9) Protection of Children Act (1978) as amended by s.84 (3)(c) Criminal Justice and Public Order Act (1994), s160 (1), 2(1)(a) (b) (c) Criminal Justice Act (1988) as amended by s 160 (4) Criminal Justice and Public Order Act (1994).

19 For example the Computer Misuse Act 1990. It is perhaps partly this continued insistence on a narrow technical understanding of cybertechnologies that precludes the legal debates from considering wider critiques and understandings that see cyberspace as a social space as much as a technical one.

20 See Kendrick (1996: x–xiii).

21 It will be noted from *R v Hicklin* (1868) that the legal test is not even this decisive, couched in the terms of a mere *tendency* to deprave and corrupt only. For further discussion of obscenity law, see specifically Smith and Hogan (1999: 714 *et seq.*).

22 See Li (2000) for an American perspective and a useful discussion on the distinction between pornography and obscenity.

23 See Wallace and Mangan (1996: 125–52) and Wall (1999), Hoffman and Novak (1995) and also Post (1995) as cited in Li (2000).

24 The invalidation of the Rimm study necessarily touches those articles that responded to it in the same volume. However, I do not think that the fact that the Rimm study was discredited necessarily means that the subsequent studies are automatically entirely invalidated themselves as a consequence, and I would argue that the discussions and arguments in them that do not depend on Rimm for validation can still be useful to consider.

25 Following Derrida, language can never adequately encapsulate a fixed meaning; see Arnold (1999: 261).

26 My own wordprocessor does not recognize words like "cyberspace" and "cyborg".

27 The debate on physical, corporeal integration with technology is broadly known as the cyborg debate; see further Haraway (1985: 65), Tomas (1989: 113), Halberstam and Livingston (eds.) (1995). Writing about the non-cyberpunk version of cyberspace, Stone (1995: 40) is careful to note that here the physical/virtual distinction does not map directly on to the mind/body distinction.

28 The promise of transcendence in the rhetoric of cyberpunk (and cyberspace) has been criticized by cyberfeminists, who argue that it has serious political implications.

29 As Tomas (1989: 127) points out, "that fictional world [i.e. cyberspace] is now a very real part of contemporary existence".

30 The term "virtual reality" was coined in the late 1980s by Jaron Lanier, an early developer of the systems (Schroeder, 1993: 963).

31 The nature of cyberspace *qua* space (place?) looks like an interesting debate, but not one that I could adequately address here.

32 The root of the word comes from "cybernetics", developed from the Greek word meaning "steersman". See Plant (1998: 156), Benedikt (1991: 74), Hawthorne and Klein (1999: 1). Pornography also comes from the Greek word meaning writing/painting about prostitutes; see Kendrick (1996: 1,11), Springer (in Wolmark, 1999: 35).

33 See also Wakeford, in Crang *et al.* (1999: 201), who cites a useful definition of a MUD after an early developer, Pavel Curtis. In her chapter, Wakeford also includes valuable discussion on MUDs and gender (Crang *et al.* 1999: 182–3).

34 See Jameson (1984: 53). Interestingly, Jameson sees pornography as a feature of post-modernism and thus unremarkable, as opposed to taboo, being an intrinsic part of this cultural dominant: "...its own offensive features – [including] sexually explicit material...no longer scandalize anyone and are not only received with the greatest complacency but have themselves become institutionalized and are at one with the official culture of Western society" (Jameson, 1984: 56).

35 Writing on cyborgs and "postindustrialism", Tomas (1989: 127) argues that the use of the term "postindustrial" emphasizes "the confluence of bio-technology, information technology, and multinational activity...as opposed to dominant aesthetic confluences", noting that critical works in postmodernism, Lyotard excepted, have tended to gloss over these developments.

36 See, e.g., Wolmark (1999: 19), Braidotti (1996: 9), Plant (1998), Adam (1998), Turkle (1996), Dery (1994), Benedikt (1991), and Hawthorne and Klein (1999).
37 Brooks (1997: 140) writes: "the intersection of postmodernism with popular culture…is profoundly political…the terrain of popular culture articulated in a range of cultural forms and expressed in a range of cultural styles is fundamentally about such a politics." See also Brooks (1997: 162): "the intersection of postfeminist debates with popular culture and popular cultural forms is potentially a rich one for investigating representational politics and issues of identity."
38 After Butler's work on Mapplethorpe, in Brooks (1997: 209); see also Dyer and Henderson, in Brooks (1997).
39 On masochism and cyberpornography see Uebel (2000), who argues in section 3 along similar lines: "we would do well to follow Foucault in replacing the strict 'law and sovereignty' of sex with an open 'technology of sex,' a multiple, positive technology of desire. Such a positive technology of desire opens the possibility of directing our attention, to the specific ways the postmodern apparatus of cyberporn produces, rather than just regulates or prohibits, desires" (footnotes omitted).
40 The queer subject refuses a stable identity, and can be seen as rejecting the very idea of identity *per se*, but a refusal of identity is not a refusal of subjecthood. See Stychin (1995: 21).
41 Or bisexual, or lesbian, depending. Stychin omits the analysis of lesbian pornography (his reasoning given at 1995: 1) but an interesting perspective can be found in Duncker (1995: 5).
42 This is not to say that performativity in itself guarantees subversion. As Judith Butler (1999: xiv) points out in her preface to *Gender Trouble*, "the performance of gender subversion can indicate nothing about sexuality or sexual practice".
43 I acknowledge that I do not adequately address a host of questions including those of race (or power) here. As pointed out by Butler, race is not analogous to gender (Butler, 1999: xiv) and to give a comprehensive analysis would mean exceeding the scope of this chapter. However, I hope such a study may be undertaken elsewhere. For more on race and power see Dery (1994: 179), and Lash (1999).
44 The potential of cyberspace as a place where gender can be destabilized has been a moot point for cyberfeminists, and, although I choose to follow McRae's line of argument, see O'Brien (1999; 76), Donath (1999: 29) and Kendal (1996: 207) for contrasting arguments.
45 Stone notes the work of Brenda Laurel as being invaluable in this debate; see Stone (1995: 17).
46 See further Douzinas *et al.* (1991) for more on the interaction of law and postmodern theories. See also Wicke (1991: 455), Frug (1991: 483), Kennedy (1991: 475) and Boyle (1991: 489).

References

Cases
Jacobellis v Ohio (1964) 378 U.S. 184, 84 S.CT. 1676, 12 L.Ed.2d. 793.
R v Hicklin (1868) L.R. 3 Q.B. 360.

Texts
Adam, A. (1998) *Artificial Knowing: gender and the thinking machine*, London: Routledge.
Adams, C. (1996) "This Is Not Our Father's Pornography: Sex, Lies and Computers", in Charles Ess (ed.), *Philosophical Perspectives on Computer-Mediated Communication*, Albany: State University of New York Press.

Akdeniz, Y. (1996) "Computer Pornography: a Comparative study of the US and UK Obscenity Laws and Child Pornography Laws in Relation to the Internet", *International Review of Law, Computers and Technology*, 10, 2: 235.

—— (1997a) "The Regulation of Pornography and Child Pornography on the Internet", *Journal of Information, Law and Technology*, 1; available at elj.warwick.ac.uk/jilt/issue/1997_1/contents.htm (accessed on 16 June 2001).

—— (1997b), "Governance of Pornography and Child Pornography on the Global Internet: A Multi-Layered Approach", in L. Edwards and C. Waelde (eds), *Law and The Internet, Regulating Cyberspace*, Oxford: Hart.

Arnold, J. (1999) "Feminist Poetics and Cybercolonisation", in S. Hawthorne and R. Klein (eds), *Cyberfeminism, Connectivity, Critique and Creativity*, Melbourne: Spinifex Press.

Batty, M. and Barr, B. (1994) "The Electronic Frontier: Exploring and mapping cyberspace", *Futures*, 26, 7: 699.

Benedikt, M. (ed.) (1991) *Cyberspace, First Steps*, Cambridge, Mass.: MIT Press.

Boyle, J. (1991) "Is Subjectivity Possible? The Postmodern Subject in Legal Theory", *University of Colorado Law Review*, 62: 489.

Bradwell, D. (1998) "Sex Drive", *Internet Magazine*, October, 38.

Braidotti, R. (1996) "Cyberfeminism with a difference", *new formations*, 29: 27.

Brooks, A. (1997) *Postfeminisms: Feminism, cultural theory and cultural forms*, London: Routledge.

Brown, B. (1993) "Troubled Vision, Legal Understandings of Obscenity", *new formations*, 19: 29.

Butler, J. (1990/1999) *Gender Trouble*, London/New York: Routledge.

Cavazos, E. and Morin, G. (1995) *Cyberspace and the Law*, Cambridge, Mass.: MIT Press.

Chatterjee, B. (1999) "'This is not Kate Moss' – An exploration into the viewing of cyberpornography", paper delivered at the 14th Annual BILETA Conference, York, March 1999, available at www.bileta.ac.uk (checked 16 June 2001).

—— (2000) "Cyberpornography, Cyberidentities and Law", *International Review of Law, Technology and Computers*, 14, 1: 89.

Cox, C. (1990) "Anything else is not feminism", *Law and Critique*, 1: 237.

Crang, M., Crang, P. and May, J. (eds) (1999) *Virtual Geographies*, London/New York: Routledge.

Cullen, H. (1998) "Review of Cynthia Cockburn and Ruza Furst Dilic (eds), 'Bringing Technology Home: Gender and Technology in a Changing Europe'", *International Review of Law, Computers and Technology*, 12, 2: 559.

Dery, M. (ed.) (1994) *Flame Wars: The discourse of cyberculture*, London and Durham: Duke University Press.

Donath, J.S. (1999) "Identity and deception in the virtual community", in M.A. Smith and P. Kollock (eds), *Communities in Cyberspace*, London: Routledge.

Douzinas, C., Warrington, R. and McVeigh, S. (1991) *Postmodern Jurisprudence*, London/New York: Routledge.

Dovey, J. (ed.) (1996) *Fractal Dreams*, London: Lawrence and Wishart.

Duncker, P. (1995) "'Bonne Excitation, Orgasme Assure' – The representation of Lesbianism in contemporary French pornography', *Journal of Gender Studies*, 4, 1: 5.

Dworkin, A. (1981), *Pornography*, London: The Women's Press.

Easton, S. (1994) *The Problem of Pornography*, London: Routledge.

Eckersley, R. (1987) "Whither the Feminist Campaign?: An Evaluation of Feminist Critiques of Pornography", *International Journal of the Sociology of Law*, 15, 2: 149.

Edwards, L. and Waelde, C. (eds) (1997) *Law and The Internet, Regulating Cyberspace*, Oxford: Hart.

Frug, M.J. (1991) "Law and Postmodernism: The Politics of a Marriage", *University of Colorado Law Review*, 62: 483.

Gibson, W. (1984) *Neuromancer*, London: HarperCollins.

Gilligan, F.A. and Imwinkelried, E.J. (1998) "Cyberspace: The Newest Challenge for Traditional Legal Doctrine", *Rutgers Computer and Technology Law Journal*, 24: 305.

Grant, M. (1998) "Crimes of the future", *Screen*, 39, 2: 180.

Griffin, S. (1981) *Pornography and Silence*, London: The Women's Press.

Halberstam, J. and Livingston, I. (eds) (1995) *Posthuman Bodies*, Bloomington and Indianapolis: Indiana University Press.

Haraway, D. (1985) "A Manifesto for Cyborgs", *Socialist Review*, 80, 5: 65.

Hawthorne, S. and Klein, R. (eds) (1999) *Cyberfeminism, Connectivity, Critique and Creativity*, Melbourne: Spinifex Press.

Heim, M. (1991) "The Erotic Ontology of Cyberspace". in M. Benedikt (ed.), *Cyberspace, First Steps*, Cambridge, Mass.: MIT Press.

Hoffman, D. and Novak, T. (1995) "A Detailed Analysis of the Conceptual, Logical, and Methodological Flaws in the Article: 'Marketing Pornography on the Information Superhighway'", available at: ecommerce.vanderbilt.edu/novak/rimm.review.html (checked 16 June 2001).

House of Commons (1994) "First Report on Computer Pornography", Session 1993–4, Home Affairs Committee, London: HMSO.

Hughes, D. (1999) "The Internet and the Global Prostitution Industry", in S. Hawthorne and R. Klein (eds), *Cyberfeminism, Connectivity, Critique and Creativity*, Melbourne: Spinifex Press.

Hunt, L. (ed.) (1993) *The Invention of Pornography*, New York: Zone Books.

Itzin, C. (ed.) (1992) *Pornography: Women, Violence and Civil Liberties*, Oxford: Oxford University Press.

Jackson, E. (1995) "The Problem with Pornography: A Critical Survey of the Current Debate", *Feminist Legal Studies*, 3, 1: 49.

Jameson, F. (1984) "Postmodernism, or The Cultural Logic of Late Capitalism", *New Left Review*, 146: 53.

Johnston, D. and Post, D. (1996) "Law and Borders – The Rise of Law in Cyberspace", *Stanmore Law Review*, 48: 1367.

Kappeler, S. (1992) "Pornography: The Representation of Power", in C. Itzin (ed.), *Pornography: Women, Violence and Civil Liberties*, Oxford: Oxford University Press.

Kendall, L. (1996) "MUDder? I Hardly Knew 'Er! Adventures of a Feminist MUDder", in L. Cherny and E.R. Wise (eds), *Wired_Women: Gender and New Realities in Cyberspace*, Seattle: Seal Press.

Kendrick, W. (1996) *The Secret Museum*, London: Methuen.

Kennedy, D. (1991) "Some Comments on Law and Postmodernism: A Symposium Response to Professor Jennifer Wicke", *University of Colorado Law Review*, 62: 475.

Kenny, J. (1999) "Pornography as progress?", *New Times*, 9: 22.

Kirkup, G., Janes, L., Woodward, K and Hovenden, F. (2000) *The Gendered Cyborg, A Reader*, London: Routledge.

Kohl, U. (1999) "Legal Reasoning and Legal Change in the Age of the Internet – Why the Ground Rules are still Valid", *International Journal of Law and Information Technology*, 7, 2: 123.

Lash, S. (1999) "Informationcritique", available at www.brunel.ac.uk/research/virtsoc/ nordic/cbslash.htm (checked 16 June 2001).

Lessig, L. (1996) "The Zones of Cyberspace", *Stanford Law Review*, 48: 1403.

Li, J. (2000) "Cyberporn: the Controversy", *First Monday* (online journal), 5, 8, available at www.firstmonday.org/issues/issue5_8/li/ (checked 16 June 2001).

MacKinnon, C. (1987) *Feminism Unmodified*, Cambridge, Mass.: Harvard University Press.

—— (1989) *Toward a Feminist Theory of the State*, Cambridge, Mass.: Harvard University Press.

—— (1994) *Only Words*, London: HarperCollins.

—— (1995) "Vindication and Resistance: A response to the Carnegie Mellon University Study of Pornography in Cyberspace", *Georgetown Law Review*, 83, 5: 1959.

McNair, B. (1996) *Mediated Sex*, London: Arnold.

McRae, S. (1999) "Coming Apart at the Seams: Sex, Text and the Virtual Body", available at www.usyd.edu.au/su/social/papers/mcrae.html (checked 16 June 2001).

Nicholson, L.J. (ed.) (1990) *Feminism/Postmodernism*, London: Routledge.

O'Brien, J. (1999) "Writing in the body: Gender (re)production in online interaction", in M.A. Smith and P. Kollock (eds), *Communities in Cyberspace*, London: Routledge.

Olsen, F. (1990) "Feminism and Critical Legal Theory: An American Perspective", *International Journal of the Sociology of Law*, 18: 199.

O'Toole, L. (1998) *Pornocopia*, 1st edn, London: Serpent's Tail.

—— (1999) *Pornocopia*, 2nd edn, London: Serpent's Tail.

Plant, S. (1998) *Zeros and Ones*, London: Fourth Estate.

Post, D. (1995) "A Preliminary Discussion of Methodological Peculiarities in the Rimm Study of Pornography on the 'Information Superhighway'", available at ecommerce.vanderbilt.edu/novak/david.post.html (checked 16 June 2001).

Rimm, M. (1995) "Marketing Pornography on the Information Super Highway: A Survey of 917,410 Images, Descriptions, Short Stories, and Animations Downloaded 8.5 Million Times by Consumers in Over 2000 Cities in Forty Countries, Provinces and Territories", *Georgetown Law Journal*, 87, 5: 1849.

Roberston, G. (1979) *Obscenity*, London: Weidenfeld and Nicholson.

St John Stevas, N. (1956) *Obscenity and the Law*, London: Weidenfeld and Nicolson.

Schroeder, R. (1993) "Virtual Reality in the Real World: History, applications and projections", *Futures*, 25, 9: 963–73.

Schweiger, B.S. (1998) "The Path of E-Law: Liberty, Property and Democracy from the Colonies to the Republic of Cyberia", *Rutgers Computer and Technology Law Journal*, 24: 223.

Segal, L. and McIntosh, M. (eds) (1993) *Sex Exposed*, New Brunswick: Rutgers University Press.

Smith, J. and Hogan, B. (1999) *Criminal Law*, 9th edn, London/Edinburgh/Dublin: Butterworths.

Stone, A.R. (1995) *The War of Desire and Technology at the Close of the Mechanical Age*, Cambridge, Mass.: MIT Press.

Strossen, N. (1996) *Defending Pornography*, London: Abacus.

Stychin, C. (1995) *Law's Desire*, London/New York: Routledge.

Swain, S. (1997) "Editorial", *new formations*, 32: 5.

Tien, L. (1994) "Children's Sexuality and the New Information Technology: A Foucaultian Approach", *Social and Legal Studies*, 3: 121.

Tomas, D. (1989) "The Technophilic Body", *new formations*, 8: 113.

Turkle, S. (1996) *Life on the Screen*, London: Weidenfeld and Nicholson.

Uebel, M. (2000) "Toward a Symptomatology of Cyberporn", *Theory & Event* (online journal), 3, 4: ss. 22–4, available at muse.jhu.edu/journals/theory_&_event/v003/3.4u ebel.html (checked 16 June 2001).

Wall, D.S. (1998) "Catching Cybercriminals: Policing the Internet", *International Review of Law, Computers and Technology*, 12, 2: 201.

—— (1999) "Cybercrimes: New wine, no bottles?", in P. Davies *et al.* (eds), *Invisible Crimes: Their Victims and their Regulation*, London: Macmillan.

Wallace, J. and Mangan, M. (1996) *Sex, Laws and Cyberspace*, New York: Henry Holt.

Watney, S. (1997) *Policing Desire: Pornography, Aids, and the Media*, Minnesota: University of Minnesota Press.

Welchman, A. (1997) "Funking up the Cyborgs", review of M. Dery (ed.), *Flame Wars: The Discourse of Cyberculture*, *Theory Culture and Society*, 14, 4: 155.

Wicke, J. (1991) "Postmodern Identity and the Legal Subject", *University of Colorado Law Review*, 62: 455.

Williams, L. (1990) *Hardcore*, London: Pandora.

Wolmark, J. (ed.) (1999) *Cybersexualities: A Reader on Feminist Theory, Cyborgs and Cyberspace*, Edinburgh: Edinburgh University Press.

7 Criminalizing online speech to "protect" the young

What are the benefits and costs?

Marjorie Heins

Introduction[1]

Criminalizing online speech – particularly about sexual subjects – is frequently justified as necessary to protect minors from physical or psychological harm. Certainly this was the rationale underlying the two criminal laws passed in the late 1990s by the United States Congress to control sexual expression on the Internet. The first law, the 1996 Communications Decency Act, or CDA, banned any "indecent" online communications that were "available" to minors – this covered essentially all Internet speech, certainly in newsgroups and websites, where speakers cannot readily determine the age of their listeners or screen the young ones out. "Indecency" was defined in the CDA basically as any words, ideas or images depicting or describing sexual or excretory activities or organs, if deemed "patently offensive" according to "contemporary community standards". Because it unconstitutionally reduced the adult population of the Internet to writing, publishing and reading "only what is fit for children" (*Butler v Michigan*: 383), the CDA was invalidated as a violation of the First Amendment in *Reno v ACLU*.[2]

This first *Reno* decision, now known in legal circles as *Reno I*, did not discourage Congress, "harm to minors" politics being what it is; and a second law, the Child Online Protection Act, or COPA, was passed in 1998. COPA criminalized a narrower category of speech than the CDA: instead of "indecent" or "patently offensive", the standard was now "harmful to minors", or "obscene as to minors". This was basically a variation – watered down for minors – on the three-part US test for constitutionally unprotected obscenity – that is, (1) whether, according to "contemporary community standards", the communication is designed to "pander to the prurient interest"; (2) whether it depicts or describes sexual acts or nudity "in a manner patently offensive with respect to minors"; and (3) whether it "lacks serious literary, artistic, political or scientific value for minors". COPA was also narrower than the CDA in that it applied only to those communicating "for commercial purposes" on the World Wide Web. Yet it had the same basic legal flaw as the CDA: because of the economics and technology of the Web, it forced most speakers to self-censor their material to the level of a hypothetical minor – whether child or teenager was not clear.

The American Civil Liberties Union again went to court, and, in February 1999, a federal judge in Philadelphia struck down COPA as a violation of the First Amendment.

The judge in this second case – *Reno II* – recognized that "perhaps we do the minors of this country harm if First Amendment protections, which they will with age inherit fully, are chipped away in the name of their protection." But he was also clearly uncomfortable with his decision, expressing "personal regret" that it would "delay once again the careful protection of our children" (*Reno II*: 498).[3] Similarly, in *Reno I*, the US Supreme Court had reiterated its often-repeated belief that the government has a "compelling interest in protecting the physical and psychological well-being of minors", which includes "shielding them from indecent messages that are not obscene by adult standards" (*Reno I*: 2343, 2346). The Court in *Reno I* did not elaborate on what this "physical and psychological" harm might be; it simply repeated the mantra – unexplained and unanalysed – that certainly there is *some* sexual material the mere access to which harms youngsters.

But what *is* the harm to minors that is assumed to flow from sexual speech – whether on computers, television or elsewhere – and why is this assumption so powerful that, in the US, politicians continue, by large margins, to pass censorship laws in the purported interest of protecting youth, while in England, the House of Lords urges "industry self-regulation" of "undesirable" Internet content to enable parents and schools to "close off access to the red light districts" (*Agenda for Action in the UK*, 1996); and on the continent, the European Commission tries to figure out how to implement rating and blocking systems – again, ostensibly to protect youth from "potentially harmful" material? Conversely, what has happened to the idea that minors, like adults, have free-expression rights? Are there psychological harms to youngsters when they are *deprived* of information, ideas, or just entertainment that a majority of adults think "unsuitable"?

I became intrigued by these questions as a result of my experiences as an ACLU lawyer specializing in censorship cases. Not only in the area of criminal laws, but in pressures for rating and blocking schemes, in the removal of school texts and library books, and in "explicit lyrics" labels on popular music, the harm-to-minors presumption, largely unexamined, drives a tremendous amount of censorship activity in the US and Europe. As a civil liberties litigator, I thought it obvious by the time of *Reno I* that an intelligent First Amendment challenge to the CDA should include not only arguments about the unconstitutional effect of the law in reducing the adult population of the Internet to reading and publishing "only what is fit for children", but arguments questioning the long-standing assumption that "indecency" harms minors to begin with. This involved introducing evidence of the valuable, non-harmful nature of much potentially "indecent" speech, in the hope of educating courts and persuading them to take a harder look at the harm-to-minors issue. Thus, our clients in *Reno I* included the Planned Parenthood Federation, Human Rights Watch, Stop Prisoner Rape, Wildcat Press (an online magazine for gay and lesbian teens), and the ACLU itself, which, among other things, hosted a teen chatroom on masturbation in the wake of the firing of Surgeon General Joycelyn Elders for daring to make approving public mention of that still-taboo subject.

Our strategy worked – to a point. During the trial (actually a preliminary injunction hearing) in *Reno I*, the judges added their own examples to ours – erotic Hindu sculptures; the word "fuck" used in an online anti-censorship chatroom (as in "fuck the CDA"), the text of Tony Kushner's Pulitzer Prize-winning play, *Angels in America*. When the case got to the Supreme Court, the justices also noted the many educational, non-harmful sorts of sexual information that might be suppressed by the CDA. These included visual art featuring human nudes, safer-sex instructions, discussions about homosexuality, censorship or prison rape; indeed, even a parent's sending birth-control information via e-mail to his or her teenage child (*Reno I*: 2336, 2344, 2347–8).[4] In *Reno II*, likewise, the plaintiffs included OB/GYN.net, Condomania, Artnet, RiotGrrl and Powell's Bookstore, one of the country's leading independent booksellers. None of these plaintiffs are exactly pornographers, but the judge, although following *Reno I* in striking down the law, took scant notice of the value that their communications might have for minors. He credited Congress with simply wanting to protect kids from "commercial pornography", which he assumed would be harmful.

Ultimately, I decided that the presumption of harm to minors – where it came from, what it means to different people, whether it makes sense – merited full-scale, book-length examination. In July 1998, I left the ACLU and began full-time research and writing on this theme. The result is *Not in Front of the Children: "Indecency", Censorship, and the Innocence of Youth* (published by Hill & Wang, 2001). Hopefully, the book will shed some light on this issue that carries such political and emotional weight and that continues to dominate political debates about sex and censorship.

Origins of the concept of harm from sexual speech

The concept of harm to minors is at the very root of modern obscenity law. It was an 1868 English Queen's Bench decision, *Regina v Hicklin*, that established the legal standard for restrictions on sexual speech in England and the United States for most of the next century. *Hicklin* set forth the famous "deprave and corrupt" test for criminally punishable obscenity: that is, "whether the tendency of the matter charged as obscenity is to deprave and corrupt those whose minds are open to such immoral influences and into whose hands a publication of this sort may fall" (*Regina v Hicklin*: 371). Those "whose minds are open to such immoral influences" primarily meant the young; as Lord Chief Justice Alexander Cockburn explained in his *Hicklin* opinion, the danger of prurient literature was that it "would suggest to the minds of the young of either sex, and even to persons of more advanced years, thoughts of a most impure and libidinous character".

In case Lord Cockburn left any doubt as to the precise nature of the harm thought to result from "impure and libidinous" thoughts, the leading anti-sex crusader on the other side of the Atlantic, Anthony Comstock, made it explicit. As head of the New York Society for the Suppression of Vice and a specially deputized prosecutor under recently enacted US obscenity laws, Comstock was probably the most formidable arbiter of what could or could not be published on sexual subjects in late nineteenth-century America. Comstock explained in his 1883 book, *Traps for the Young*, that the printed page is "Satan's chief weapon in his effort to ruin the human family", by stimulating the "secret entertainment" (Boyer, 1968: 20–21, quoting Comstock, 1883: 240). Obsessive fears about this "secret entertainment", fuelled by physicians, reached such heights by the mid-nineteenth century that youngsters were subjected to horrific restraints – chastity belts, penile rings, straitjackets, "cauterisation of the sexual organs" – in order, as historian Peter Gay has put it, to "keep growing or adolescent sinners from getting at themselves" (1984: 303–4). Censorship of erotic literature was but a small addition to this litany of restraints on youthful masturbation.

The obscenity laws' condemnation of "impure and libidinous" thoughts of course reflected not only nineteenth-century myths about masturbation leading to hairy hands, feebleness, idiocy and death, but, more broadly, a long Christian tradition that condemned "genital commotion". The tradition was compounded and intensified by modern institutions of social–sexual control – government, industry, education, the medical profession (Foucault, 1978; 1985; 1986) – and by the unique moral strictures of the Victorian Age. The laughably hypocritical premise of *Hicklin* was that educated adult males reading sexual literature would not get aroused and thus fall into sin, while "those whose minds are open to such immoral influences" (that is, youngsters, women [by definition weak-minded] and members of the lower classes) would, and therefore needed "protection".

Indeed, English determinations of obscenity to this day turn on the perceived vulnerability of the likely audience. In one case in the 1960s, a distributor was acquitted of an obscenity charge because the only proven purchaser of the material in question was a police officer who testified he was unaffected by it; conversely, an obscenity prosecution against a store owner who sold bubble gum cards depicting battle scenes to schoolchildren was reinstated by appellate judges (after acquittal at trial), specifically so that the prosecution could offer expert evidence regarding the capacity of the cards to "deprave and corrupt" the youthful clientele (*R v Clayton and Halsey*; *Director of Public Prosecutions v A. & B.C. Chewing Gum, Ltd.*). In the United States, similarly, the Supreme Court created the "harmful to minors" or "variable obscenity" standard (the one used in the 1998 Child Online Protection Act) in a 1968 case, *Ginsberg v New York*, precisely to criminalize distribution to presumably vulnerable youths of "girlie magazines" that would not be considered obscene, and were thus lawful reading, for adults.

By 1968, of course, anti-masturbation hysteria had abated: "the secret entertainment" was not mentioned in Justice William Brennan's opinion for a majority of the US Supreme Court in the *Ginsberg* case. Instead, *Ginsberg* relied on generalized standards of morality, explained with a touch of psychiatric lingo. The state legislature's justification for the "harm to minors" law in *Ginsberg* was that exposure to erotic material would impair youngsters' "ethical and moral development", (*Ginsberg v New York*: 637) and the Supreme Court considered this vague rationale sufficient. Justice Brennan elaborated by quoting at length from a child psychiatrist, Willard Gaylin, who had written that it is during adolescence, "when sensuality is being defined and fears elaborated, when pleasure confronts security and impulse encounters control…that legalized pornography may conceivably be damaging." Psychiatrists make a distinction, Gaylin explained:

> between the reading of pornography, as unlikely to be *per se* harmful, and the permitting of the reading of pornography, which was conceived as potentially destructive. The child is protected in his reading of pornography by the knowledge that it is pornographic, i.e., disapproved.
> (*Ginsberg v New York*: 642 n.10, quoting Gaylin, 1968: 592–4)

The justification, in other words, was symbolic – the youngster must know that the messages and attitudes reflected in sexually arousing material are disapproved, even while admiring, enjoying or lusting over the ideas and images presented.

Which brings us into present-day conceptions of "harm". That is, youngsters, certainly, will have sexual thoughts; they will seek out information; they will masturbate – nearly all adolescent boys and many girls do (see, e.g., Gagnon and Simon, 1973: 48–57) – but we cannot publicly approve of it. Whether the messages of guilt, shame and disapproval that society sends to youngsters by forbidding their access to sexual explicitness and erotica are ultimately harmful or helpful to them is an open question.

Concepts of harm today

When asked today exactly what harm to minors they believe flows from sexual ideas, entertainment or information, protectionists' answers range from the vaguely spiritual ("they shouldn't be robbed of their innocence") to the specifically reductionist ("if they see sexual acts described or depicted, they will imitate them"). In between are a variety of arguments: minors will pick up bad attitudes (about women, about sex roles, about sexual fidelity) from pornography, or indeed from any sexually suggestive books, TV shows or movies. They will get the wrong ideas about the frequency of unconventional sexual practices, and may aim as a result for an unrealistic athleticism in their own sexual lives, or unrealistic expectations of their partners. Young children may be traumatized by depictions of what appear to be violent acts in which adults are strangely out of control – much as Sigmund Freud once theorized that they were traumatized by witnessing the "primal scene" of their parents copulating. Or, children may get the idea that sex can be pleasurable among relative strangers, without trust or emotional commitment, that it is acceptable for its own sake, without procreation or marriage. Even safer-sex information, it is often argued (in the face of repeated studies that demonstrate the contrary), implicitly approves and therefore encourages youthful sexual activity. And finally, in the words of the 1986 Report of the US Attorney General's Commission on Pornography (the Meese Commission), harm to minors from exposure to erotica "must be seen in moral terms":

> Issues of human dignity and human decency, no less real for their lack of scientific measurability, are for many of us central to thinking about the question of harm....For children to be taught by these materials that sex is public, that sex is commercial, and that sex can be divorced from any degree of affection, love, commitment, or marriage is for us the wrong message at the wrong time.
>
> (US Department of Justice, 1986: 303, 344)

Of course, some cynics take the view that all of these harm-to-minors rationales are a smokescreen for the no-longer politically acceptable belief that *adults* should be barred from controversial or "immoral" information and ideas. On this theory, those who pose as child protectors are, whether consciously or not, simply expressing the common human impulse to suppress ideas or images that they find offensive or threatening. Nevertheless, harm-to-minors arguments are the currency of contemporary censorship, and they must be addressed.

Of the various arguments, imitation and trauma are the only ones that focus on direct physical or psychological harm (rather than the squishy concepts of bad or immoral attitudes). Both the imitation and trauma arguments, however, are empirically unsupported – that is, they rely on anecdotes or appeals to common sense rather than on studies that use random sampling or other scientific techniques. As a practical matter, most young children are not interested in explicit sexual material, and are more likely to consider it "yukky" or boring than intensely frightening. Older ones may be curious, amused, aroused or disgusted, but not likely traumatized.

As for imitation, the fears are based on a reductionist form of thinking that oversimplifies the effects of media and culture on human personality. Certainly, children's, as well as adults', attitudes (and ultimately behaviour) are affected, cumulatively, by information and ideas found in books, visual art, music, films, television and now the Internet. The difficult question is precisely what books, films, songs or Internet sites affect what people, and how; and the answer varies with every individual, according to his or her genetic predisposition, family background, religious training, peer group and general social and cultural environment. Most people, including minors, do not directly mimic antisocial or promiscuous acts that they read about in magazines or see on TV.[5] If they did, we would have to close their eyes and ears not only to explicit or arousing sexual information but to massive chunks of our culture, from the sexual immorality in the Bible to the bloody denouements of Shakespeare's plays. The few who engage in so-called copycat behaviour do so because of their idiosyncratic personal backgrounds. Indeed, a number of studies have found that sexual offenders generally come from repressive environments in which they are less, not more, likely to have been exposed to erotic literature.[6]

Thoughtful protectionists acknowledge that the media are at best a minor factor affecting human attitudes and behaviour, and in ways that are impossible to specify or quantify; but they still maintain that we have to start somewhere. Since we can't transform all parents into paragons of virtue or provide all youngsters with wholesome social environments, the least we can do is protect them from sexually suggestive soap operas, heavy metal music, lascivious condom ads, and pornography on the Internet. In the last two decades, the ideological temperature of this argument has risen, as rhetorical emphasis has shifted from old-fashioned morality to, purportedly, feminism – that is, to theories propagated by the US activists Andrea Dworkin and Catharine MacKinnon, and their acolytes in England and elsewhere, that pornography degrades women and eroticizes male domination. Beyond the heated rhetoric, however, the justification for "protecting" the young remains fundamentally the same as that articulated by more traditional censors: otherwise they will pick up bad ideas.

Which brings us to the "morality" or "bad attitudes" justification that is at the root of pro-censorship protectionism, whether it is explicitly stated, as in the Meese Commission report and the arguments of Dworkin–MacKinnonites, or not. Because we cannot know what specific works are likely to have bad behavioural effects on any particular individual or group, the conclusion is irresistible that protectionism is less about preventing real-world harm (trauma or imitation) than about symbolism. Thus, despite their different phrasings (some in terms of conservative moral values; others pro-censorship feminist; still others wrapped in the language of psychology), almost all of the child-protection rationales are at bottom variations on the symbolic and ideological justifications for censorship approved by Justice Brennan back in 1968, in the US Supreme Court decision in *Ginsberg*. That is, sexual speech conveying "immoral" or disapproved values – whether misogynist attitudes or acceptance of unconventional sex – should not be available to youngsters until they are mature enough to evaluate and (presumably) reject them. A 1997 resolution by the European Parliament made this point explicitly when it explained that "harmful" (as opposed to illegal) Internet content "concerns minors and appertains essentially to the domain of morals" (European Parliament, 1997). Indeed, in numerous European Union documents relating to protection of minors from "harmful" speech, the term "harmful" (or "possibly harmful") is used interchangeably with the perhaps more candid "offensive" or "unsuitable".

Now, moral symbolism is not insignificant, but one must be careful when using it as a basis for censorship. The potential for abuse, and for overbroad restrictions based upon censors' personal reactions to sexual or "offensive" content, is immense. More fundamentally, the premise of a free society – and of free-expression principles – is that governments cannot impose their versions of

morality through censorship of unconventional or "bad" ideas; citizens are entitled to decide these matters for themselves. As a US appeals court explained in
striking down an anti-pornography law drafted by MacKinnon and Dworkin,
"any other answer leaves the government in control of all the institutions of
culture, the great censor and director of which thoughts are good for us"
(*American Booksellers Association v Hudnut*: 330).

Assumptions about harm to minors are in large part premised on the notion
that this free-expression principle does not apply to youngsters – that they have
lesser free speech rights. In the US, the First Amendment rights of minors have
been steadily eroded in the courts, and in Europe, neither Article 10 of the
European Convention on Human Rights nor the child-specific free-expression
guarantee in the 1989 UN Convention on the Rights of the Child has apparently been considered an impediment to legislation designed to restrict minors'
access to online speech.[7] Indeed, in 1976 and again in 1988, the European
Court of Human Rights upheld obscenity judgements that national governments specifically argued were justified by the need to shield minors – in the
first case from a left-leaning Danish sex education text called *The Little Red
Schoolbook*, after it was published in the UK; and in the second, from a Swiss art
exhibit that included explicit sexual scenes (*Handyside*; *Müller and others*).[8]

In addition to infringements on minors' free expression rights, protectionists
rarely consider other countervailing harms to minors from censorship. These
can include feelings of powerlessness; training in authoritarianism; disrespect for
the value of free inquiry; shame or confusion resulting from taboos on erotica;
and the very tangible dangers of STDs and unplanned pregnancies where
contraceptive and safer-sex information is forbidden. Protectionists also
frequently merge all minors, from toddlers to teenagers, into one vast pool of
purportedly vulnerable and impressionable youth. Regardless of whether one
believes in *childhood* innocence, it is not a state that accurately characterizes the
biological and psychological lives of *adolescents*, who are sexually charged, scep-
tical of authority, and hungry for experience and knowledge. Criminal laws, or
elaborate rating and blocking schemes designed to "protect" them from nudity,
sexual discussions, or other broad categories of material deemed potentially
harmful, are arguably an insult to them and to the democratic societies of which
they are soon to become full citizens.[9]

An argument for education instead of protectionism

The protectionist approach, with its assumption of harm to minors from exposure to explicit sexual information and ideas, is not only intellectually and
politically flawed, it is ultimately counterproductive. Youngsters cannot be
expected to mature into competent adults, capable of embracing good ideas and
rejecting bad ones, unless they get some practice at it. Education is in any event
likely to be more effective than censorship in developing sexually sane and
healthy grown-ups. Particularly given the many different attitudes toward sexual
morality prevailing in the world today, and the vagueness and subjectivity of

concepts like "indecent" or "harmful", attempts to criminalize online speech about sex pose grave risks for the ability of minors and adults alike to exchange ideas and information about a subject that is of great public importance, and vital to our physical and mental health.

At the very least, if harm-to-minors ideology continues to be politically irresistible, there ought to be more thoughtful and finely calibrated judgements about it. That is, as children grow older, "protective" censorship should diminish, and their free expression rights to receive controversial information and ideas should increase. Intellectual freedom obviously has little meaning for four-year-olds, but open access to information and ideas – and even just entertainment – is a very different matter for older minors and adolescents.

Europeans have sometimes paid closer attention to these age differences than pundits and advocates in the United States. The former Norwegian Ombudsman for Children, for example, has pointed out the importance of recognizing free-expression rights, and thereby countering feelings of worthlessness and powerlessness, among adolescents who in modern society live for ever-longer periods in situations of dependence. She proposes a graduated framework of minors' "rights and responsibilities" in areas ranging from sexual consent to film attendance (Grude Flekkøy, 1991; see also Freeman and Veerman, 1992). Justices of England's high court, the Law Lords, observed in 1985 that, as teenagers mature, their parents' (and the state's) right to control their decisions in such areas as sexuality dwindle: "if the law should impose on the process of growing up 'fixed limits' where nature knows only a continuous process, the price would be artificiality and a lack of realism in an area where the law must be sensitive to human development and social change" (*Gillick v West Norfolk and Wisbech Area Health Authority*: 421).[10]

I would propose, then, that as youngsters approach majority – arguably, by age 15 – there ought to be a presumption *against* censorship (or "protection"). This would mean that judicial deference to vague moral pronouncements, as in the *Ginsberg* case, would not be acceptable: as with censorship of adults, the state would have to *prove* the need for restrictions. And social science generalizations would not likely suffice as proof, for, short of actual incitement, the propagation of ideas or attitudes that a majority of legislators consider reprehensible is precisely what free expression principles entrust citizens, even young ones (with help from parents and educators), to judge for themselves. Particularly given the efficacy of education – in media literacy, sexuality and alternatives to violence – as a counterweight to pernicious ideas gleaned from television, video games or real-life models, there ought to be focused demonstrations of harm caused by specific works to overcome the presumption of free-speech protection for teenagers.[11] Indeed, even for pre-teens, consideration should be given to the notion of preparing them for adulthood through education and exposure to controversial ideas, rather than the creation of forbidden thought zones and spoon-feeding of only those books, films, cartoons or Internet sites that are considered "kid-safe" by a censoring authority.

Finally, courts, pundits and policymakers should reconsider the long-accepted but mistaken assumption that sexually explicit speech has little value and therefore merits little protection. Sexuality is now recognized as an important cultural and political subject; masturbation is no longer thought to produce idiocy and death; and teenagers are sexually active the world over. Just as the democratic values that secure adults' intellectual freedom should also secure the maturing intellectual freedom of minors, so these same democratic values should protect sexual expression.

Notes

1 The research for this chapter was supported by a grant from the Open Society Institute. A draft version of this chapter was presented at the British and Irish Legal Education Technology Association Conference, *Cyberspace 1999: Crime, Criminal Justice and the Internet*, College of Ripon and York, St John at York, 29–30 March 1999.

2 The June 1997 US Supreme Court decision in *Reno* rejected government arguments for affording cyberspace less than full First Amendment free-speech protection; it described the Internet as a fascinating "new marketplace of ideas" whose growth "has been and continues to be phenomenal" (*Reno I*, 1997: 2351).

3 None of the so-called "defences" written into COPA (e.g., use of credit cards or adult ID systems) were any more effective than those upon which the government had relied in *Reno I* to argue that Internet speakers could and should segregate their speech into "decent" and "indecent" categories, then take action to bar minors from the "indecent" material.

4 Justices O'Connor and Rehnquist, concurring in *Reno I*, questioned whether discussions about prison rape or nude art would have value for minors; (*Reno I*: 2356). Whether they were thinking of seven- or 17-year-olds when they said this is not clear.

5 Those who believe in consistent, predictable imitative effects from sexual content in TV or other media often make analogies to social science studies in the area of media violence. Whatever the usefulness of the analogy, however, and despite overblown claims to the contrary, there is significant disagreement among psychologists about what the media violence literature actually proves – or, indeed, whether the complex and subtle effects of art, information and ideas on different human beings can ever really be quantified. See, e.g., Reiss and Roth (1993), Durkin (1985), Cook (1983: 179–92), Freedman (1994: 836), Zimring and Hawkins (1997), Kellerman (1999) (positing that aggression, like other behaviours, results from the interaction of inborn traits with environmental influences, with media having little direct impact), Committee on Communications and Media Law (1997: 283–6) (noting that "the subject of violence and aggression in psychology is vast", with little agreement among experts about its causes).

6 See, for example, Gebhard *et al.* (1965: 670–8), Thompson (1994: 133), Donnerstein *et al.* (1987: 32–7, 70–1), Carrera (1981: 41), Becker and Stein (1991), Kelley *et al.* (1989: 67), Kronhausen and Kronhausen (1959: 273–4), Williams Committee (1979: 62) (citing a meta-analysis of sexual offender research indicating less exposure to sexual material than other groups).

7 The 1989 UN Convention on the Rights of the Child protects youngsters' right to "seek, receive and impart information and ideas of all kinds". The Charter of Rights of the Child, passed by the European Parliament in 1992, specifically establishes a right to receive sex education, including "information on birth control methods and the prevention of sexually transmitted diseases". The UN Convention on the Rights of the Child, Article 13; European Charter of Rights of the Child, Resolution A3–0172/92, §§ 8.21, 8.32.

8 The court in *Müller* noted: "as at the time of the *Handyside* judgement", it is not possible to discern any "uniform European conception of morals". At p. 22.

9 Space here does not permit a full discussion of non-criminal "protection" systems like television v-chips and Internet rating-and-blocking. The myriad problems with such schemes are by now common knowledge. For one thing, most of them do not distinguish between sexually explicit art or information, on the one hand, and commercial pornography on the other. V-chips rely on either self- or third-party rating of TV content into broad categories such as sex, suggestive language and violence; Internet blocking adds to these two methods a system of "keyword" identification that generally cannot distinguish between the use of terms like "sex" or "breast" in crass pornography and erudite literature or medical information. All of the methods tend to label and block explicit sex education, art, literature and discussions of sexually charged topics like gay rights, Kenneth Starr's report to the US Congress on the activities of Monica Lewinsky and President Bill Clinton, or the effects of Viagra, along with *Penthouse* and *Playboy*. The Yale Biology Department and the American Association of University Women were among the sites blocked by one system, used by a Virginia library, that claimed to filter out only "illegal" material; see *Mainstream Loudoun v Board of Trustees, Loudoun County Library*. The push for self-rating is particularly problematic because it forces Internet speakers to choose among three unpalatable alternatives: they may label their own speech in conclusory, pejorative fashion; they may self-censor to avoid negative ratings and resulting loss of audience; or they may resist self-labelling and risk being automatically blocked because unrated. Both third-party and self-labelling, no matter how elaborately calibrated the scale of different categories for sex, nudity or violence, reduce the complex and highly contextualized process of human communication to a set of simplistic symbols. For more on the frailties of rating-and-blocking programs, see Heins (1998: 38), Akdeniz (1997: 236–9), American Civil Liberties Union (1997), Electronic Privacy Information Center (1997), Computer Professionals for Social Responsibility (1998).

10 The Court rejected a parent's challenge to a health authority guideline permitting physicians in exceptional circumstances to prescribe contraceptives for girls under 16 without parental knowledge or consent. Later decisions of the Court of Appeal narrowed *Gillick*, but did not contradict the Law Lords' recognition of minors' maturing need for autonomy (*Re R*, 1991; *Re W*, 1992).

11 Even the social scientists most frequently cited to support the notion that "pornography" causes bad attitudes and conduct have protested the misuse of their data, pointed out its methodological limitations and stressed the efficacy of educational approaches to combat rape myths or general misogyny. See Linz, Penrod and Donnerstein (1987).

References

Cases

American Booksellers Association v. Hudnut, 771 F.2d 323 (7th Cir. 1985), affirmed, 475 U.S. 1001 (1986).

Butler v Michigan, 352 U.S. 380 (1957).

Director of Public Prosecutions v A. and B.C. Chewing Gum, Ltd. (1967), 1 Q.B. 159, 2 All E.R. 504.

Gillick v West Norfolk and Wisbech Area Health Authority (1985), 3 All ER 402.

Ginsberg v New York, 390 U.S. 629 (1968).

Handyside, Decision of 29 April 1976, Series A, No. 24 (European Court of Human Rights).

Mainstream Loudoun v Board of Trustees, Loudoun County Library, 24 F. Supp.2d 553 (E.D.Va. 1998).

Müller and others, 24 May 1988, Series A, vol. 133 (European Court of Human Rights).

Re R (1991), 4 All E.R. 177.
Re W (1992), 4 All E.R. 627.
Regina v Clayton and Halsey (1962), 3 All E.R. 500.
Regina v Hicklin (1868), 3 Q.B. 360.
Reno I, Reno v American Civil Liberties Union, 117 S.Ct. 2329 (1997).
Reno II, American Civil Liberties Union v Reno, 31 F. Supp.2d 473 (E.D. Pa. 1999), affirmed, 217 F.3d 162 (3d Cir. 2000), review granted *sub nom Ashcroft v. ACLU* (2001).

Texts

Agenda for Action in the UK (1996) 23 July 1996, available at www.parliament.the-stationery-office.co.uk/pa/ld199596/ldselect/inforsoc/contents.htm (checked 17 June 2001).

Akdeniz, Y. (1997) "Governance of Pornography and Child Pornography on the Global Internet: A Multi-Layered Approach", in L. Edwards and C. Waelde (eds), *Law and the Internet*, Oxford: Hart Publishing.

American Civil Liberties Union (1997) *Fahrenheit 451.2: Is Cyberspace Burning?*, available at www.aclu.org/issues/cyber/burning.html (checked 17 June 2001); also published in D. Sobel (ed.) (1999) *Filters and Freedom: Free Speech Perspectives on Internet Content Controls*, Washington, DC: Electronic Privacy Information Center.

Becker, J. and Stein, R. (1991) "Is Sexual Erotica Associated with Sexual Deviance in Adolescent Males?", *International Journal of Law and Psychiatry*, 14, 1–2: 85–91.

Boyer, P.S. (1968) *Purity in Print – The Vice Society Movement and Book Censorship in America*, New York: Scribner's.

Carrera, M. (1981) *Sex – The Facts, the Acts, and Your Feelings*, New York: Crown.

Committee on Communications and Media Law (1997) "Violence in the Media: A Position Paper", *Record of The Association of the Bar of the City of New York*, 52, 3: 273.

Computer Professionals for Social Responsibility (1998) *Filtering FAQ*, avaliable at www.cpsr.org/filters/faq.html (checked 17 June 2001.

Comstock, A. (1883) *Traps for the Young*, New York: Funk & Wagnalls.

Cook, T. (1983) "The Implicit Assumptions of Television Research: An Analysis of the 1982 NIMH Report on Television and Behavior", *Public Opinion Quarterly*, 47, 2: 161.

Durkin, K. (1985) *Television, Sex Roles and Children: A developmental social psychological account*, Milton Keynes: Open University Press.

Donnerstein, E., Linz, D. and Penrod, S. (1987) *The Question of Pornography*, New York: Free Press.

Electronic Privacy Information Center (1997) *Faulty Filters: How Content Filters Block Access to Kid-Friendly Information on the Internet*, available at www2.epic.org/reports/filter-report.html (checked 17 June 2001); also published in D. Sobel (ed.) (1999) *Filters and Freedom: Free Speech Perspectives on Internet Content Controls*, Washington, DC: Electronic Privacy Information Center.

European Parliament (1997) *Resolution on the Commission communication on illegal and harmful content on the Internet*, COM(96) 0487 – C4–0592/96 (Apr. 24), available at www.europarl.eu.int (checked 17 June 2001).

Foucault, M. (1978) *The History of Sexuality: Vol. 1, An Introduction*, New York: Random House.

—— (1985) *The History of Sexuality: Vol. 2, The Use of Pleasure*, New York: Pantheon.

—— (1986) *The History of Sexuality: Vol. 3, The Care of the Self*, New York: Random House.

Freedman, J. (1994) "Viewing Television Violence Does Not Make People More Aggressive", *Hofstra Law Review*, 22: 833.

Freeman, M. and Veerman, P. (eds) (1992) *The Ideologies of Children's Rights*, Dordrecht/Boston/London: Martinus Nijhoff.

Gagnon, J.H. and Simon, W. (1973) *Sexual Conduct – The Social Sources of Human Sexuality*, Chicago: Aldine.

Gay, P. (1984) *Education of the Senses (Part II of The Bourgeois Experience: Victoria to Freud)*, New York: Oxford University Press.

Gaylin, W.M. (1968), "The Prickly Problems of Pornography", (book review), *Yale Law Journal*, 77: 579.

Gebhard, P., Gagnon, J., Pomeroy, W. and Christenson, C. (1965) *Sex Offenders – An Analysis of Types*, New York: Harper & Row.

Grude Flekkøy, M.I. (1991) *A Voice for Children*, London: Jessica Kingsley.

Heins, M. (1998) "Screening Out Sex", *The American Prospect*, July–August, p. 38.

Kellerman, J. (1999) *Savage Spawn – Reflections on Violent Children*, New York: Ballantine.

Kelley, K., Dawson, L. and Musialowski, D. (1989) "Three Faces of Sexual Explicitness – the Good, the Bad, and the Useful", in D. Zillmann and J. Bryant (eds), *Pornography – Research Advances and Policy Considerations*, Hillsdale, NJ: Lawrence Erlbaum.

Kronhuasen, E. and Kronhausen, P. (1959) *Pornography and the Law*, New York: Ballantine.

Linz, D., Penrod, S. and Donnerstein, E. (1987) "The Attorney General's Commission on Pornography: The Gaps Between 'Findings' and Facts", *American Bar Foundation Research Journal*, 4: 713–36.

Reiss, Jr, A. and Roth, J. (eds) (1993) *Understanding and Preventing Violence*, Washington, DC: National Academy Press.

Thompson, W. (1994) *Soft Core – Moral Crusades Against Pornography in Britain and America*, London: Cassell.

US Department of Justice (1986) *Attorney General's Commission on Pornography Final Report* (the Meese Commission), Washington, DC: US Government Printing Office.

Williams Committee (1979) *Obscenity and Film Censorship*, Cambridge: Cambridge University Press.

Zimring, F. and Hawkins, G. (1997) *Crime is Not the Problem – Lethal Violence in America*, New York: Oxford University Press.

8 Controlling illegal and harmful content on the internet[1]

Yaman Akdeniz

Introduction

As the Internet proliferated during the 1990s, public concern grew about the existence of illegal Internet content such as child pornography and also the access to other sexually explicit content by children. Consequently, regulating illegal and harmful Internet content remains one of the greatest concerns for governments, supranational bodies and international organizations. In response to these concerns there have been many initiatives to deal specifically with the existence of illegal and harmful content over the Internet. Most of these initiatives combine co-regulatory efforts with an emphasis upon self-regulation by the Internet industry. They result in the creation of hotlines for reporting illegal Internet content to assist law enforcement agencies, and development of filtering and rating systems to deal with children's access to content which may be deemed as harmful. These issues are quite different in nature and should be addressed separately, as what may not be appropriate for children to see may not necessarily be illegal or even inappropriate for adults to see.

The Internet industry regulatory initiatives are mainly led by bodies such as the Internet Watch Foundation within the UK (www.iwf.org.uk), Internet Content Rating for Europe (www.incore.org), and the Internet Content Rating Association (www.icra.org) both are favoured and supported by the European Commission's Action Plan for the safer use of the Internet within the European Union (European Commission, 1998a; Walker and Akdeniz, 1998). The UK government's policy in relation to these matters remains consistent with the European Commission's Action Plan through the Department for Trade and Industry (DTI) (see Department of Trade and Industry, 1998a; Cabinet Office Performance and Innovation Unit, 1999) and through the quasi-regulatory body, the Internet Watch Foundation (IWF) which works closely with the DTI (see KPMG/Denton Hall, 1999; Cyber-Rights & Cyber-Liberties (UK), 1997).

This chapter will analyse Internet content regulation in the UK with special references to supranational developments within the European Union. Considering the multi-national nature of the Internet, relevant policy initiatives elsewhere (such as in the USA) will also be addressed. The chapter will show that there are flaws in the solutions offered by the policymakers to address content-related problems. Furthermore, it will be argued that solutions that address the issue of harmful content may lead to censorship of perfectly legal content.

The first section will identify the nature of the problem of illegal and harmful content on the Internet. The second section looks at the UK government's approach to the problem, and section three examines the liabilities of Internet Service Providers, which are integral to the process of governance. The fourth section explores the efficacy of self-regulation as a way forward, such as through self-reporting hotlines and the development of rating and filtering systems, whilst section five critiques these systems.

Identifying the problem of illegal and harmful content

Content-related problems have been largely identified, and categorized as illegal and harmful by the European Commission since October 1996 (European Commission, 1996a; 1996b). The European Commission in its October 1996 communication on *Illegal and Harmful Content on the Internet* stated:

> These different categories of content pose radically different issues of principle, and call for very different legal and technological responses. It would be dangerous to amalgamate separate issues such as children accessing pornographic content for adults, and adults accessing pornography about children.
>
> (European Commission, 1996a: 10)

Although the Commission's Action Plan for the European Union for a Safer Use of the Internet (European Commission, 1998a; Akdeniz, 1998; Walker and Akdeniz, 1998), which follows from the earlier EU papers (European Commission, 1996a; 1996b), suggests that "harmful content needs to be treated differently from illegal content", these categories have never been clearly defined by the Commission in its Action Plan or by regulators elsewhere. The Action Plan states that illegal content is related to a wide variety of issues, such as instructions on bomb-making which can threaten national security, and pornography which may harm minors (Akdeniz, 1999b), incitement to racial hatred which threatens human dignity, and libel which threatens individual reputations. But none of these categories provided by the European Commission are necessarily "illegal content" and are not even considered as "harmful content" by many European countries.

The following headings will try to identify the above concerns by the regulators and the possible problems related to the availability of illegal and harmful content over the Internet from a UK perspective, before looking into the approaches that are offered to deal with such content.

Illegal content

It would be wrong to consider the Internet as a "lawless place" (Reidenberg, 1996) and therefore the law of the land would also apply to the Internet in theory. This is also true for the availability of illegal content over the Internet. Content-related criminal laws would also apply to the Internet if the perpetrators are within UK jurisdiction.

The most common and the most referred to example of illegal content is the availability of child pornography over the Internet. This has been a concern for UK law enforcement agencies and the regulators ever since Operation Starburst took place in the summer of 1995 (Akdeniz, 1997a; 2000a). The whole issue of illegal content and how to deal with this sort of Internet content has since revolved around child pornography, even though child pornography and paedophilia are not Internet-specific problems.

Apart from child pornography, law enforcement bodies within the UK are also concerned about the existence of commercial websites featuring sexually explicit content created and maintained by UK citizens, which may be deemed as obscene under the Obscene Publications Act. Another concern for content-related criminal activity by UK law enforcement agencies is the possibility of using the Internet for harassment and threats and the availability of hate-speech material over the Internet. According to the NCIS *Project Trawler Report*, which was launched to study the extent of criminal misuse of information technology and the methods law enforcement officials use, the Internet users "may find themselves repeatedly receiving unwanted and distressing communications, such as threatening, obscene or hateful e-mail" (NCIS, 1999; Uhlig and Hayder, 1997).

Furthermore, and more seriously, the availability of documents over the Internet which contravene the Official Secrets Act 1989 has been a concern for the UK government and security agencies (rather than the law enforcement bodies).[2] Under section 1(1) of the 1989 Act, a person who is or has been a member of the security and intelligence services would be "guilty of an offence if without lawful authority he discloses any information, document or other article relating to security or intelligence which is or has been in his possession by virtue of his position as a member of any of those services or in the course of his work while the notification is or was in force." The 1989 legislation would apply to the dissemination of such information over the Internet.

It should also be noted that law enforcement bodies within the UK remain concerned about the incidental use of the Internet for existing crimes such as fraud (Davis, 1998a), and the emergence of specific cybercrimes (Wall, 1998; Sieber, 1998) such as unauthorized access or hacking into computer networks (Akdeniz, 1996b), distribution of computer viruses such as the ILOVEYOU or the Melissa viruses,[3] and the denial of service attacks to computer networks (*The Independent*, 2000; BBC News, 2000; Royal Canadian Mounted Police, 2000). However, these issues are not so much content-related and therefore will not be further discussed in this chapter.

Harmful content

The difference between illegal and harmful content is that the former is criminalized by national laws, while the latter is considered as offensive or disgusting
by some people but certainly not criminalized by national laws. So, within this
category of Internet content, we are dealing with legal content which may
offend some Internet users or content that may be thought to harm others, e.g.
children with their accessing of sexually explicit content.

This form of Internet content may include sexually explicit content, political
opinions, religious beliefs, views on racial matters, and sexuality. However, it
should be noted that the European Court of Human Rights has confirmed in
Handyside v UK (1976) that freedom of expression extends not only to ideas and
information generally regarded as inoffensive, but even to those that might
offend, shock, or disturb (*Castells v Spain*, 1992), and this sort of information
legally exists over the Internet as well as in other media. But legal regulation of
this sort of Internet content may differ from one country to another; and this is
certainly the case within the European Union, with different approaches to sexually explicit content or to hate-speech by the member states (see Sieber, 1998).

For example, even though publishing or distribution of obscene publications
may be illegal within the UK under the Obscene Publications Act, possession or,
within the context of the Internet, browsing or surfing through sexually explicit
and/or obscene content is not an illegal activity for consenting adults. Furthermore,
there are no laws making it illegal for a child to view such content in a magazine or
on the Internet. The laws normally deal with the *provision* of such content to children.[4] Therefore, harm remains as a criterion which depends upon cultural
differences and this is accepted within the jurisprudence of the European Court of
Human Rights (see article 10(2) of the ECHR and *Handyside v UK*, 1976).

However, the availability of harmful Internet content remains a politically sensitive area, and the UK government and the European regulators continue to be
concerned about the existence of such content on the Internet. The September
1999 Cabinet Office report *e-commerce@its.best.uk*, stated that "there are worries
about the content of the Internet," and according to the report this remains as one
of the major issues that "lead to lack of confidence for the development of e-
commerce within the UK" (Cabinet Office Performance and Innovation Unit,
1999, para. 10.6). However, the main reason for the failure of establishing trust for
e-commerce has been the failure of the UK government to develop a regulatory
framework for the use of strong encryption technologies and not the presence of
harmful, or offensive Internet content (see House of Commons Select Committee
on Trade and Industry, 1999; Akdeniz *et al.*, 2001; and Bowden and Akdeniz, 1999).

UK government approach to illegal and harmful content

This part of the chapter will analyse the UK government approach to the availability of illegal and harmful content over the Internet and will explain the
UK's policy – and to some extent the European Union's position – and the
industry self-regulatory schemes in relation to Internet content.

Within the UK, lead responsibility for content issues lies with the Department for Trade and Industry (DTI) with support from the Department for Education and Employment (DfEE) and the Home Office. However, there is no simple approach for the problems identified in the previous sections and therefore relying on the legal system or the provision of new laws and regulations is not the best way of dealing potential problems that may be encountered with Internet content. Therefore, a multi-layered approach with the involvement of both public and private regulatory bodies at both national and international levels is inevitable to deal effectively with the current problems (see Akdeniz, 1997c). The UK government favours a co-regulatory approach in which there is a role to be played by industry self-regulation. However, whether the current proposals and the policy can address the problems effectively remains to be seen. Therefore, the following sections will also include a critique of the current proposals and the current policy of the UK government.

Enforcement of national laws

This chapter has identified child pornography as the most common and the most referred-to example of illegal content. So far, law enforcement agencies within the UK have been dealing successfully with child pornography-related offences such as creation, possession, and distribution (see *R v Jonathan Bowden*, 2000; Akdeniz, 2000a) ever since the Protection of Children Act 1978 and the Obscene Publications Act 1959 were amended by the Criminal Justice and Public Order Act 1994 to take into account the new technologies, such as computers, computer data and also computer generated images (see Akdeniz, 1996a).

There have been many police operations in relation to the availability of child pornography on the Internet following the relevant laws being amended by Parliament, and these operations resulted in many successful prosecutions involving possession and distribution of child pornography (see further Akdeniz, 2000a; *R v Fellows and Arnold*, 1997; Davis, 1998a, 1998b). However, the application of the Obscene Publications Act 1959 and the availability and distribution of obscene content (not child pornography) have been more problematic from a UK perspective. There have not been many cases brought under the 1959 legislation in relation to the Internet. One notable example is *R v Graham Waddon* (1999; 2000), a case that was brought under the Obscene Publications Act.[5] Waddon was charged with publishing obscene articles contrary to s.2(1) Obscene Publications Act 1959, as he had maintained a commercial website featuring sexually explicit images in the USA. As publishing an article, under s.1(3)(b) of the 1959 Act, included data stored electronically and transmitted, Waddon was successfully prosecuted. He was given an 18-month prison sentence suspended for two years in September 1999 (Wilson, 1999). Such cases are rare and this one certainly does not set up a precedent, as the defendant pleaded guilty to eleven sample counts of publishing obscene articles on the Internet. However, the case stands as a good (or a bad) example of the application of the obscenity legislation to the Internet.

In relation to cyber-stalking and harassment issues, the NCIS Trawler report claimed that "e-mail harassment will increase as Internet usage grows" (NCIS, 1999). However, such claims remain unfounded, as the UK courts only witnessed a single Internet-related case under the Protection of Harassment Act since that legislation was enacted in 1997. The unique prosecution for Internet harassment or cyber-stalking involves the case of *Nigel Harris*, who received a two-year conditional discharge in March 1999 from London's Horseferry Road Magistrates Court followed by a three-year jail sentence in October 1999 for breaching a court order (not Internet-related) (*The Times*, 2000; Seenan, 1999; Born, 1999; Ellison and Akdeniz, 1998, see chapter 9). At the time of writing, there were no cases involving hate-speech and the Internet within the UK.[6] The above examples clearly show that the UK's legal system and law enforcement agencies are capable of dealing with Internet-related illegalities if the perpetrators are within their jurisdiction.

This chapter also identifies the publication of official secrets over the Internet to be a major concern for law enforcement and security agencies within the UK. Although it is not clear, for example, who actually published the list containing the names of more than a hundred MI6 spies, the UK government accused Richard Tomlison, an ex-MI6 officer, of circulating the names over the Internet (*Wired News*, 1999; *The Mirror*, 1999a; Evans, 1999). In this example, the Official Secrets Act 1989 was not applicable because the perpetrators were either outside the jurisdiction, or were unknown. Therefore, the cross-jurisdictional or global nature of the Internet creates instances in which national laws will not be applicable or enforceable because it is hard, or impossible, to identify the perpetrators, or because the criminal activity may be illegal in one jurisdiction and not in another. These cross-jurisdictional problems, combined with the frustration of responding to the pressures brought by the public to restrict the availability of illegal Internet content, inevitably resulted in the development of new approaches to deal with such problems. One resulting action has been a new partnership approach between the Internet Service Providers and the law enforcement agencies which has improved law enforcement techniques in relation to Internet-related crimes.

The 1999 Cabinet Office *e-commerce@its.best.uk*, mentioned earlier, therefore recommended the improvement of the "technical capability of law-enforcement and regulators," and the establishment of an Internet Crime Unit (Cabinet Office Performance and Innovation Unit, 1999, recommendation 10.5) possibly within the Home Office. This idea was initially recommended by the NCIS report and endorsed by the Cabinet Office in its *e-commerce@its.best.uk* report "as a practical way of co-ordinating expertise and ensuring clear lines of responsibility" (para. 10.46). The proposed national unit would have three broad roles: "to investigate the most serious 'IT crimes'; to act as a centre of excellence for 'cybercrime' issues; and to support local forces which encounter offenders using sophisticated IT skills" (NCIS, 1999). The *e-commerce@its.best.uk* report claims that ….

A strengthened law-enforcement ability will send a clear signal to potential Internet criminals that Internet crime does not pay. It will help to boost the

confidence of both e-commerce buyers and sellers. Similarly, stronger detection and presentation effort will deter hackers, spammers and those, such as paedophiles and racists, who place illegal material on the Internet.
(Cabinet Office Performance and Innovation Unit, 1999: para. 10.47)

These recommendations have been accepted by the crime committee of the Association of Chief Police Officers (ACPO) and discussed by the ACPO Council, the NCIS, the National Crime Squad and HM Customs and Excise, and together they have drafted a National Hi-Tech Crime Strategy and Funding Bid. The key elements of the strategy are the development of a multi-agency National Hi-Tech Crime Unit supporting enhanced and nationally coordinated local activity against hi-tech crime. The matter has also been considered by the Home Office and, in January 2000, a proposal for £377,000 to set up a Hi-Tech Crime Planning Unit at NCIS was agreed by the Home Office as part of the overall NCIS levy settlement (Cabinet Office Performance and Innovation Unit, 1999: para. 10.48). This resulted in the establishment of the National Hi-Tech Crime Unit in April 2001 (NCIS, 2001) which will have primary responsibility for investigating the most serious and organized hi-tech crime offences, ranging from attacks on national infrastructure and networks to the more traditional crimes involving new technologies such as the Internet (Home Office, 2000). According to Home Office Minister Charles Clarke, "tackling paedophiles, terror groups, and commercial warfare on the World Wide Web is at the heart of the government's drive to tackle the menace of Internet crime". The Minister stressed that "new methods of co-operation are needed in order to investigate crime on the Internet", and that "it is vital that Internet Service Providers and telecommunication companies are alive to the need for co-operation with the law of enforcement" (Home Office, 1999).

Such cooperation between the law enforcement bodies and the UK Internet Service Providers has been ongoing since late 1997. In November 1997, the ACPO Computer Crime Unit, together with the Internet Service Providers, established the ACPO/Internet Service Providers (ISPs) government Forum with the objective of developing good practice guidelines between Law Enforcement Agencies and the Internet Service Providers Industry, describing what information can lawfully and reasonably be provided to Law Enforcement Agencies and the procedures to be followed. Given the concern over cyber-crimes and cybercriminals, it is entirely understandable that the police and the ISPs should wish to develop mutual understanding and support, and to establish working relationships (Akdeniz and Bohm, 1999). However, such a collaboration process should be transparent and accountable with clearly defined rules which take into account the rights of individual Internet users. Furthermore, those directly affected by such collaboration, for example the users, should also be represented in such a collaboration, and therefore the partnership approach should include public interest groups and users' representatives (Akdeniz, 2000b, 2000c). Cooperation and reliance on the ISP industry is further empha-sized under the Regulation of Investigatory Powers Act (RIPA) 2000 as far as the duty of maintenance of interception capability by the ISPs is concerned (Sections 12–14; see Akdeniz *et al.*, 2001).

Apart from the cooperation of the Internet industry and the law enforcement agencies at the national level, the UK government is also building international cooperation at policy level through a G8 sub-group on Hi-Tech Crime and also taking an active role in the formation of the Council of Europe Cyber-crime Convention (European Committee on Crime Problems, 2000, 2001)[7] as well as contributing to the European Union policy work on cyber-crimes (European Scrutiny Committee, 1998).

The Draft Council of Europe Convention on Cyber-crime was discussed by a House of Commons Select Committee (Select Committee on European Scrutiny, 1999) and, as "this type of crime poses a growing threat", the committee declared that effective action required international collaboration. The work for the Council of Europe Convention started in September 1997, and the Convention will be finalized by September 2001. The Convention would require "state parties to ensure that their criminal law includes offences against the integrity, confidentiality and availability of computer data; copyright and related offences; and content related offences such as the possession and distribution via the Internet of child pornography", among other things (Select Committee on European Scrutiny, 1999). The Convention is also supported outside the member states of the Council of Europe. Given the importance of the subject, non-member states, such as Canada, Japan, South Africa and the United States, actively participated in the negotiations and the Convention is supported by the G8 countries.

Therefore, illegal content issues are dealt both at national and international level by the UK regulators and law enforcement bodies, and governing this sort of content over the Internet requires a multi-layered and international effort. However, as far as UK laws are concerned, some forms of illegal content do exist over the Internet and, to the extent that the perpetrators are within the UK, law enforcement agencies and the courts are dealing with such crimes. Moreover, the National Criminal Intelligence Service (NCIS) in its Project Trawler report "does not assess the risks or scale of criminal activity on the Internet to be as extensive as sometimes portrayed" (NCIS, 1999). Content-related criminal activity remains very low for the moment in so far as such crimes are initiated from within the UK.[8]

Liability of the ISPs

Furthermore, as a result of concerns over Internet content and related criminal activity, mainly because of the availability of child pornography on Usenet discussion groups, the Internet Service Providers (ISPs) were pressured into regulating themselves as they were seen by the law enforcement agencies to be responsible for the content that they carry[9] on their servers, even though they have no control over third-party Internet content (see Cyber-Rights & Cyber-Liberties (UK), 2001). Similar pressures on the ISPs resulted in the successful prosecution of CompuServe in Germany in May 1998, mainly for the distribution of child pornography (see criminal case of *Somm*, 1998. See also Sieber, 1999a, 1999b; Julia-Barcelo, 1998; Bodard *et al.*, 1998).

Although pressured into self-regulation, ISPs have not been prosecuted within the UK, even though they may well be liable for the content they carry (as in the German case of *Somm*) under section 3 of the 1978 Protection of Children Act (Leong, 1998).[10] However, Landgericht Munchen (Regional Court of Munich I, 20th Criminal Division) quashed the *Somm* decision in November 1999 and acquitted Somm following an appeal by both CompuServe and the prosecution in May 1998 (*The Independent*, 1999; note also *LICRA v Yahoo*, 2000). Whilst all the above-mentioned efforts at both national and international level deal with illegal Internet content, the prosecution of Internet Service Providers (ISPs) within the UK remains completely undesirable and cases such as *Somm* need to be avoided at all costs because of the precedents they would set.

The European Parliament and Council Directive on certain legal aspects of electronic commerce in the Internal Market (2000) offers only limited protection to ISPs with the introduction of an "actual knowledge" test for removal of third-party content from ISP servers (European Directive, 2000; articles 13–14). Therefore the procedure known as "notice and takedown" will be common practice for the removal of Internet content through ISP servers. Such notice can be given either by hotlines like the Internet Watch Foundation for the removal of allegedly illegal content, or by private companies or individuals for the removal of other forms of content including content deemed to be defamatory (see Akdeniz, 1999a; Akdeniz and Rogers, 2000; Cyber-Rights & Cyber-Liberties (UK), 1999c) or content that infringes copyright and trademark laws. The "notice and takedown" provisions of the 1996 Defamation Act (section 1) were criticised by Cyber-Rights & Cyber-Liberties (UK):

> It is totally unacceptable that an offended party should simply notify an Internet Service Provider claiming the information to be legally defamatory. The current state of the UK laws forces the ISPs to be the defendant, judge, and the jury at the same time. Notice should not be enough in such cases.
>
> (Cyber-Rights & Cyber-Liberties (UK), 1999b)

Furthermore, law enforcement agencies should act against the real perpetrators – those who create and circulate, or publish, the content over the Internet.[11] Putting pressure on the ISPs to resolve content-related matters should not be the way forward and will only hamper the development of the Internet and electronic commerce within the UK (Akdeniz and Bohm, 1999; Akdeniz *et al.*, 1999; Akdeniz, 2000b).

A self-regulatory approach?

Although the above sections set the scene and provide some criticism about the current national regulatory approach for Internet content, it is important to analyse some of the new approaches that are advocated for Internet content regulation.

Apart from the enforcement of national laws in relation to illegal Internet content, the UK government, unlike, for example, the US government, favours self-regulatory solutions (Department of Trade and Industry, 1996) for Internet content regulation rather than the introduction of any specific legislation (see *ACLU v Reno*, 1997; Akdeniz, 1997b; *ACLU v Reno II*, 1999, 2000). The UK government policy is also consistent with the European Union policy and with the European Commission's Action Plan on Safer Use of the Internet (European Commission, 1998a; Akdeniz, 1998). The EU Action Plan encourages the creation of a European network of hotlines to report illegal content such as child pornography by online users, the development of self-regulatory and content-monitoring schemes by access and content providers, the development of internationally compatible and interoperable rating and filtering schemes to protect users, and measures to increase awareness of the possibilities available among parents, teachers, children and other consumers to help these groups use the networks whilst choosing the appropriate content and exercising a reasonable amount of parental control.

The development of hotlines to report illegal content

Hotlines for reporting illegal Internet content have been promoted by the European Union's Action Plan, and the UK's Internet Watch Foundation (IWF) represents one of the earliest examples of such a hotline. The IWF acts as a hotline for reporting illegal content, and this involves mainly child pornography. The IWF, as an industry-based self-regulatory body, was announced in September 1996, and is supported by the UK government. The organization is a private body financed by the Internet Service Providers, however, it is not an accountable public body.

Its activities concentrate on Usenet discussion groups, and the organization acts upon Internet users reports sent via e-mail, fax or telephone in relation to illegal Internet content. Once the IWF locates the content that is "undesirable" (according to its own judgement) through reports made by Internet users, it informs all British ISPs for the removal of the content located. Furthermore, the hotline also contacts the law enforcement agencies (e.g., NCIS) in relation to these reports.

According to the first IWF annual report (which covers the period between December 1996 and November 1997 and which was published in March 1998) there have been 781 reports to the Foundation from online users in 248 of which action was taken. These reports resulted in the review of 4,324 items, and the Foundation has taken action in 2,215 of them (2,183 were referred to the police and 2,000 to ISPs). Of the total, 1,394 originated from the US while only 125 of the items originated from within the UK. According to IWF's second report (January–December 1998 statistics), the number of reports reached 2,407, and in 447 of these action was taken (430 of the action reports contained child pornography). These involved 14,580 items, upon which the IWF took action on 10,548. Of these, 9,176 were referred to NCIS, 541 to the

UK police, and 9,498 to the UK ISPs. Of the total, 11.79 per cent originated from within the UK, while 49.05 per cent originated from the USA.[12] Furthermore, according to the third-year statistics of the hotline, which cover the period January–December 1999, there were 4,809 reports involving 19,710 items. However, only 4 per cent of the 11,487 items on which the IWF took action originated from the UK, which is an improvement over the 1998 statistics and shows that the problem of child pornography is not a growing problem in the UK and remains an international problem.

These figures tell us little about the actual amount of child pornography on the Internet.[13] It is, therefore, difficult to judge how successful the UK hotline has been so far, despite its own claims and the UK government's claims to its success. While around 10,200 items were removed from the servers of UK ISPs (up until December 1999), it is not known how many new images are posted to various newsgroups, replacing those removed images, within the timeframe of the above activities, nor it is known how much child pornography is located on the World Wide Web while the activities of the hotline are concentrated on Usenet discussion groups.

Another downside of the hotline activities of the IWF is that the efforts of the organization are concentrated on those newsgroups carried by UK ISPs, although hotlines are being developed in other countries and cooperation between these hotlines is expected in the near future through the "Internet Hotline Providers in Europe" project under the EC Daphne Programme.[14] This means that, while illegal material is removed from UK ISPs' servers, the same material will continue to be available on the Internet carried by foreign ISPs on their own servers.

Therefore, expensive monitoring of the Internet at a national level is of limited value, as the few problems created by the Internet remain global ones and thus require global solutions. While the UK government should be involved in finding solutions to global problems with its international partners, global problems do not justify expensive monitoring of the Internet at a national level by industry-based organizations. This is not an attempt to dismiss the role that can be played by hotlines, but there remain serious concerns for the policing role that can be played by such organizations. Privatized policing organizations are not acceptable to judge the suitability or illegality of Internet content, and there is a serious risk for hotline operators to act as "self-appointed judges" with an "encouragement for vigilantism" (ACLU, 1999). According to Nadine Strossen, "these hotlines violate due process concepts that are also enshrined in international, regional, and national guarantees around the world" (ACLU, 1999).

The IWF mainly deals with child pornography, as we have seen, but there are plans to expand its hotline duties and, while child pornography may be an example of clear-cut illegality (even though there are variations in national laws), the same cannot be true for other forms of Internet content such as hate-speech. The new role for the IWF will include "seeking to apply IWF's self-regulation approach to racism on the Internet" (International Watch Foundation, 2000). The IWF hotline model is supported by the European Union's Action Plan and also by the Internet industry (Bertelsmann

Foundation, 1999; Cyber-Rights & Cyber-Liberties (UK), 1999a) which favours the creation of such organizations for assisting ISPs and law enforcement agencies in various countries. However, illegality remains a matter to be decided by courts of law and not by private organizations or by quasi-regulatory bodies, and the industry proposals which advocate that the "task of evaluating the legality or illegality of specific data is difficult for Internet providers and should, therefore, be integrated into the work of hotlines" (Bertelsmann Foundation, 1999; Cyber-Rights & Cyber-Liberties (UK), 1999a) are wrong in principle and would be unacceptable in democratic societies.

Undoubtedly the availability and distribution of child pornography should be regulated along with other illegal activities, whether on the Internet or elsewhere. The main concern of law enforcement and regulatory bodies should, however, remain the prevention of child abuse – the involvement of children in the making of pornography, or its use to groom them to become involved in abusive acts rather than the cleansing of such images from the Internet (Akdeniz, 1997c). At least the former, more serious, issue of prevention of child abuse should be given a priority in national policies, and organizations that deal with Internet policy should align their policies to take into account the prevention of child abuse.

The development of rating and filtering systems

> Internet users are concerned about protecting children and vulnerable people from illegal or immoral material. A May 1999 survey of US parents showed that 78% have concerns about the content of Internet material to which their children have access. In the UK the IWF handled 2,407 reported cases of illegal content in 1998, compared with 898 in 1997. Control of content for consumers is thus a serious, and growing issue and a problem that must be solved.
> (Cabinet Office Performance and Innovation Unit, 1999: para. 10.13)

What the Cabinet Office report refers to as immoral content is often referred to as harmful content by policymakers. However, it should be noted that this type of content is different from illegal content, and in most cases the harmful content category lies within the limits of legality. The concern of the regulators is that certain types of content may be harmful to children and the main self-regulatory initiatives try to address this sort of Internet content.

The Cabinet Office report referred to a US study having not conducted its own survey in relation to Internet content-related concerns within the UK. The reference to illegal content and the role that has been played so far by the IWF's hotline has less serious implications for the issues of harmful content, and the two policy issues should not be confused by policymakers. The apparently confusing debates and arguments about Internet content that are generated by government and industry policymakers are therefore one of the main reasons for the high-profile media coverage about the availability of sexually explicit content and illegal content over the Internet and the consequent public concerns. As a consequence of these concerns, in February 1998 the IWF announced its consultation paper for the development of rating systems at a national level as a solution to dealing with harmful Internet content (Internet Watch Foundation, 1998b; Cyber-Rights & Cyber-Liberties (UK), 1997, 1998).

The Department of Trade and Industry and the Home Office played key roles in the establishment of the IWF. According to the DTI, "as part of its remit to help ensure that the Internet can be a safe place to work, learn and play, the IWF has convened an advisory board comprising representatives of content providers, children's charities, regulators from other media, ISPs and civil liberties groups, to propose a UK-focused system for rating Internet content".[15] In reality, no civil liberties organizations were involved or consulted, as was pointed out by the Cyber-Rights & Cyber-Liberties (UK) November 1997 report, leaving the IWF a predominantly industry-based private organization with important public duties (Cyber-Rights & Cyber-Liberties (UK), 1997). The two *Who Watches the Watchmen* reports by Cyber-Rights & Cyber-Liberties (UK) – a non-profit-making organization – questioned the accountability of the IWF to the public and the openness and transparency of its procedures and decision-making process as a quasi-regulatory body in November 1997 and in September 1998. However, to date there has been no improvement in relation to the structure of the IWF, and a review of this self-regulatory body by the DTI did not address these issues (KPMG/Denton Hall, 1999).

Rating systems such as the Platform for Internet Content Selections (PICS)[16] work by embedding electronic labels in the web documents to vet their content before the computer displays them (Computer Professionals for Social Responsibility, 1998–2001). The vetting system could include political, religious, advertising or commercial topics. These can be added by the publisher of the material, or by a third party – for example, by an ISP – or by an independent vetting body. In addition to rating systems, it is important to mention the availability and use of filtering software programs which are intended to respond to the preferences of parents making decisions for their own children. There are currently around 15 filtering products, which are mainly from the US[17] and which do not necessarily reflect the cultural differences in a global environment such as the Internet.

According to an IWF press release, rating systems would "meet parents' concerns about Internet content that is unsuitable for children" (Internet Watch Foundation, 1998a). The IWF proposals are also supported by the UK government which also supports "the deployment of the Platform for Internet Content Selection (PICS), and the development of ratings systems" (Department of Trade and Industry, 1998a: 13). Furthermore, in many instances the government and Members of Parliament showed their support for the development and use of filtering and rating systems for the protection of children from "immoral and harmful" Internet content or from potentially objectionable material, as referred to by the DTI's *Net Benefit* document (Department of Trade and Industry, 1998a). The Net Benefit document states that:

...some classes of material are legal, and desired by some users, but expressly not desired by others. There is a risk that some users are put off using the Internet and engaging in electronic commerce because they fear unwanted exposure to offensive content.

(Department of Trade and Industry, 1998a: 13)

The Net Benefit document follows on from the DTI's Secure Electronic Commerce Statement (Department of Trade and Industry, 1998b) which was mainly concerned about the regulation of the use of encryption technology and the development of electronic commerce, and was issued in April 1998 (Akdeniz and Walker, 1998). However, that statement also referred to Internet content matters and, in paragraph iv, entitled "Internet content", stated:

As the Internet becomes a mass medium it is only right to ensure that the most vulnerable users are protected. This has meant supporting, and encouraging, such initiatives as the Internet Watch Foundation to ensure that the law is applied on-line in the same way as it is off-line.

The policy developments in relation to Internet content therefore continued with the Net Benefit document (published in October of 1998) which relies on self-empowerment by concerned users as a priority for the UK. To achieve this, the DTI recommended "the use of rating systems which describe the content of a Web site objectively in accordance with a generally recognized scheme, and filtering software which enables the user to block access to Web sites according to their rating or if they are unrated" (Department of Trade and Industry, 1998a). According to John Battle, Minister for Science, Energy and Industry, "such ratings and filtering tools can be extremely useful in helping parents and other adults who care for children to decide on the types of legal material they wish their children to access."[18]

The *e-commerce@its.best.uk* report which was published a year after the Net Benefit document encouraged software companies to supply free content-filtering software (Cabinet Office Performance and Innovation Unit, 1999, recommendation 10.10) but complained about the limited use of such software and tools by the Internet users (Cabinet Office Performance and Innovation Unit, 1999, para. 10.59). However, there are initiatives under the National Grid for Learning programme to develop "parents' Web sites" with the facility to download filtering software (Cabinet Office Performance and Innovation Unit, 1999: para. 10.60).

Self-rating and filtering systems are also promoted by the 1999 Memorandum on Internet Self-Regulation by the Bertelsmann Foundation as empowering user choice. The Memorandum argued that, "used wisely, this technology can help shift control of and responsibility for harmful content from governments, regulatory agencies, and supervisory bodies to individuals". The Memorandum advocated an "independent organisation to provide a basic vocabulary for rating and to oversee updates to the system at periodic intervals" (Bertelsmann Foundation, 1999). However, the organizations that deal with the rating proposals, including the UK's IWF, pursue an undemocratic and unaccountable process for developing such systems, and it is not independent.

Furthermore, according to the *e-commerce@its.best.uk* report, the development of rating and filtering systems and the wide availability of such systems "will make it clear that the Government takes parents' concerns seriously and is prepared to take active measures to meet those concerns" (Cabinet Office Performance and Innovation Unit, 1999, para. 10.60). But the government continues to assume that parents are concerned about Internet content. However, the so-called consultation document by the IWF did not discuss whether these systems are suitable for Britain or whether they are needed at all. In fact, a decision has been taken by the UK organization to develop these systems, and the consultation paper addressed how to develop these systems and had a set of recommendations which suggested that the decision in principle was already taken: rating systems are good and should be developed for use in Britain.

Despite the establishment consensus, it would have been more appropriate to establish a working group, with representatives from both the public and the private sector to assess the real problem of illegal and harmful content at a UK level, rather than trying to find temporary or ineffective solutions to activities which do not necessarily take place within British jurisdiction (Irish Department of Justice, Equality and Law Reform, 1998).

A substantial study, together with a public consultation in this field, was needed in the UK (and is still needed) before moving forward with the current proposals. It therefore remains the duty of the UK government to set up such an "independent" working group or to conduct a Select Committee inquiry to assess the real extent of the problem and to seek the best solutions in an open, transparent and accountable way without infringing the rights of UK citizens. However, the creation of such an independent body or wide public consultation is not expected in the near future (see KPMG/Denton Hall, 1999). At the same time, the IWF continues with its policymaking process and the development of rating and filtering systems within the UK, the European Union[19] and elsewhere,[20] despite the potential problems associated with such systems, as will be explained in the next section (see Sobel, 1999; Akdeniz and Strossen, 2000; Electronic Privacy Information Center, 2001).

A critique of rating and filtering systems

As far as rating and filtering systems are concerned, it is important to provide the whole picture, including the limitations and criticisms of the use and development of rating and filtering systems for the availability of harmful content over the Internet. These limitations and criticisms are not usually considered by government representatives, the European Commission, or by industry bodies (see Sobel, 1999, Electronic Privacy Information Center, 2001).

Originally promoted as technological alternatives that would prevent the enactment of national laws regulating Internet speech, filtering and rating systems have been shown to pose their own significant threats to free expression. When closely scrutinised, these systems should be viewed more realistically as fundamental architectural changes that may, in fact, facilitate the suppression of speech far more effectively than national laws alone ever could.

(Global Internet Liberty Campaign, 1999)

First of all, although the use and development of rating systems are welcome by various governments, including the UK government, the capacity of these tools is limited to certain parts of the Internet, and therefore these tools do not address issue of the availability of harmful content fully. But at no point do the official UK government statements address or warn about the limitations of these technologies.

Rating systems are designed for World Wide Web sites, leaving out other popular Internet-related communication systems such as chat environments, file transfer protocol (ftp) servers, Usenet discussion groups, real-audio and real-video systems which can include live sound and image transmissions, and finally the ubiquitous e-mail communications. These systems cannot be rated with the currently available rating systems, and therefore the assumption that rating systems would make the Internet a "safer environment" for children is wrong as WWW content represents only a fraction of the whole of the Internet content. Although it may be argued that the World Wide Web represents the more fanciful and the most rapidly growing side of the Internet, the problems that are thought to exist by the regulators over the Internet are not WWW-specific.

Second, even when rating technology is applicable to World Wide Web pages, it is not clear what the regulators have in mind when it comes to what sort of content should be rated. Examples from official statements in which the category is referred to as "harmful", "immoral" or as "objectionable" content have been provided in previous sections. However, there is no consensus as to what is actually being referred to by the regulators, apart perhaps from the availability of sexually explicit content over the Internet. In all cases, the targeted category of Internet content remains within the limits of legality rather than illegality.

According to the UK IWF, there is "a whole category of dangerous subjects" that require ratings, and these include information related to drugs, sex and violence, information about dangerous sports like bungee-jumping, and hate-speech material (*Wired News*, 1997). This kind of content would certainly include such publications as *The Anarchist Cookbook* (Powell, 1989; note also Harber, 1990; Feral, 1983; Hutchkinson, 1988) which can be downloaded from not only WWW sites[21] but also can be obtained through ftp servers or through the use of automatic e-mail services. In addition it is also available through well-known bookshops such as Waterstones, Dillons, and Amazon.co.uk within the UK. Therefore, rating systems would not in any way be a complete solution to content deemed harmful to minors.

Third, if the duty of rating is handed to third parties, this would pose free speech problems, and with few third-party rating products currently available, the potential for arbitrary censorship increases. 'Note that no UK-based third party rating body currently exists.' This would mean that there will be no arena for free speech arguments and dissent because the ratings will be made by private bodies and governments will not be involved "directly". When censorship is implemented by government threat in the background, but run by private parties, legal action is nearly impossible, accountability difficult, and the system is not open or democratic. In fact, none of the criticisms in relation to these issues were taken into account by the IWF (Cyber-Rights & Cyber-Liberties (UK), 1997, 1998).

Fourth, another downside of relying on such technologies is that these systems are defective, and in most cases they are used for the exclusion of socially useful websites and information (see Sobel, 1999; Electronic Privacy Information Center, 2001). The general excuse for having them remains the protection of children from harmful content and also the duty of the industry to give more choice to the consumers. Filtering software and rating systems will be used to exclude minority views and socially useful sites rather than to protect children from anything (Gay and Lesbian Alliance Against Defamation, 1997).

Fifth, while children's access is the most cited excuse for the regulation of the Internet, this global medium is not only accessed and used by children. In fact, it is not possible for children to have their own Internet accounts without the involvement of an adult, as it is not possible to get an Internet account through an Internet Service Provider before the age of 18 in almost all countries including the UK. Therefore, children's access to the Internet is already limited, and so there is always a role to play for parents in relation to their children's access to the Internet. Adults should act responsibly towards children's Internet usage rather than relying on technical solutions that do not fully address Internet content-related problems. Librarians and teachers also have a role to play in so far as access to the Internet is provided from public libraries and schools.

Moreover, it has been reported many times that filtering systems and software are over-inclusive, limiting access and censoring inconvenient websites, or filtering potentially educational materials regarding AIDS and drug abuse prevention. Therefore "censorware" enters homes under the guise of "parental control" and purporting to be an alternative to government censorship, but in fact such systems impose the standards of the software developers rather than leaving the freedom of choice to the consumers who buy and rely on such products. The companies creating this kind of software provide no appeal system to content providers who are "banned or blocked", thereby "subverting the self-regulating exchange of information that has been a hallmark of the Internet community" (Computer Professionals for Social Responsibility, 1996).

Last, and importantly, rating and filtering systems with blocking capabilities would allow repressive regimes to block Internet content, or mandate the use of such tools:

> By requiring compliance with an existing rating system, a state could avoid the burdensome task of creating a new content classification system while defending the rating protocol as voluntarily created and approved by private industry.
>
> (Global Internet Liberty Campaign, 1999)

Such a concern on the part of civil libertarians remains legitimate in the light of the recently introduced Australian Broadcasting Services Amendment (Online Services) Act which mandates blocking of Internet content based upon existing national film and video classification guidelines.[22] So there exists governmental support for mandatory rating systems, and this is an option that may be considered not only by repressive regimes but by other democratic societies such as the UK.

Furthermore, any regulatory action intended to protect a certain group of people, such as children, should not take the form of an unconditional and universal prohibition on using the Internet to distribute content that is freely available to adults in other media. The US Supreme Court stated in *Reno v ACLU* (1997) that "the Internet is not as 'invasive' as radio or television", and confirmed the finding of the US Court of Appeal that "communications over the Internet do not 'invade' an individual's home or appear on one's computer screen unbidden." However, the US government tried to regulate the Internet once again with the Child Online Protection Act (COPA) which was enacted by the US Congress as part of an omnibus appropriations bill. COPA intended to punish "commercial" online distributors of material deemed "harmful to minors" with up to six months in jail and a $50,000 fine. However, COPA was immediately challenged by civil liberties organizations including the ACLU and EPIC. Furthermore, COPA was criticized by members of the Global Internet Liberty Campaign (GILC) which stated that:

> "COPA will not be effective in keeping from minors material that might be inappropriate for them. No criminal provision will be more effective than efforts to educate parents and minors about Internet safety and how to properly use online resources. Moreover, we note again that the Internet is a global medium. Despite all the enforcement efforts that might be made, a national censorship law cannot protect children from online content they will always be able to access from sources outside of the United States"
>
> (Global Internet Liberty Campaign, 1998c).

In November 1998, Judge Lowell A. Reed, Jr. stated that the plaintiffs had shown "a likelihood of success on the merits of at least some of their claims" that COPA violates the First Amendment rights of adults. Significantly, the judge emphasized that the temporary restraining order applied to all Internet users, and not just the plaintiffs in the case (*ACLU v Reno II*, 1999). In June 2000, in a unanimous decision, a three-judge panel of the Third Circuit Court of Appeals in *ACLU v Reno II* struck down COPA by stating that the 1998 law "imposes a burden on speech that is protected for adults".

It should therefore be noted that current solutions offered at various regulatory fora, such as the development of rating and filtering systems, may not be the real answer to the existing problems, and the development of such systems may result in censorship of Internet content which is not illegal at all. Furthermore, as the Economic and Social Committee of the European

Commission (1998), in its report on the EC's Action Plan on Promoting Safe Use of the Internet, pointed out that it is highly unlikely the proposed measures will in the long term result in a safe Internet, with the rating and classification of all information on the Internet being "impracticable" (Economic and Social Committee of the European Commission, 1998: para. 4.1). The Committee, therefore, concluded that there is "little future in the active promotion of filtering systems based on rating" (see also Walker and Akdeniz, 1998; Akdeniz, 1999c). None the less the promotion of such tools by the Internet industry and its regulators continues within the UK and elsewhere.

Conclusion

This chapter has provided an overview of Internet regulation within the UK, with special reference to illegal and harmful content. For both categories of Internet content there is no unique solution for effective regulation; the emergence of "Internet governance" entails a more diverse and fragmented regulatory network, with no presumption that its components are anchored primarily in the nation states.

Governance theorists are beginning to recognize that "objects of governance are only known through attempts to govern them" (Hunt and Wickham, 1994: 78) and "governance is not a choice between centralisation and decentralisation. It is about regulating relationships in complex systems" (Rhodes, 1994: 151), and the Internet does provide a great challenge for governance.

Therefore a multi-layered approach to Internet governance (Akdeniz, 1997c) is inevitable, one in which a mixture of public and private bodies will be involved, and which includes the individual Internet users, for control as far as harmful content is concerned. A multi-layered approach will also include layers at a supranational and international level of Internet governance. Furthermore, "if such mechanisms of international governance and re-regulation are to be initiated, then the role of nation states is pivotal" (Hirst and Thompson, 1995: 430). Hence it would be wrong to dismiss the role that may be played by governments, especially for the creation of laws and for maintaining the policing of the state.

However, at a national level, it is now widely accepted that "government cannot simply regulate to achieve its aims in this new global electronic environment",[23] and therefore a "light regulatory touch" is preferred for the development of e-commerce. Although there has been much pressure for a partnership between the government and the industry "to get the right balance", so as to build confidence and protect consumers in the information age, that balance should reflect and respect the rights of individual Internet users as well as those of the business community – an issue often not considered by the regulators and the industry. To achieve such a balance, there is an urgent need for openness, accountability and transparency in relation to regulatory initiatives aimed at Internet content at the national level (Cabinet Office Regulatory Impact Unit, 2000; Cyber-Rights & Cyber-Liberties (UK), 2000), rather than a knee-jerk reaction to such media-hyped coverage, as resulted after the Gary Glitter case (*The Sun*, 1999; *The Mirror*, 1999b, 1999c).

At a supranational level (for example, within the European Union), or at an international level (for example, within the Council of Europe, the OECD, or the United Nations), we will witness more cooperation between police forces, including Interpol which holds regular meetings for law enforcement agencies dealing with cybercrimes, to stimulate further collaboration upon Internet-related criminal activity. However, the alignment of national criminal laws in relation to content (speech) regulation generally seems not to be a feasible option, due to the moral, cultural, economic and political differences between the member states (United Nations, Economic and Social Council, Commission on Human Rights, 1998). This is one reason why the European Commission preferred a self-regulatory approach for the EU with its Action Plan which promotes industry-based proposals for a "safer use of the Internet" (European Commission, 1998a).

Though some sort of consensus may be established as far as some specific crimes such as child pornography are concerned following the development of the Council of Europe's Cyber-crime Convention (see further European Commission, 2001). Furthermore, according to a recent Select Committee on Culture report, "The Multi-Media Revolution", international initiatives will have an important impact on national Internet regulation, but at the same time "the question is whether such attempts at regulation can be anything more than optimistically indicative rather than genuinely effective" (House of Commons Select Committee on Culture, 1998: para. 108). So there is no unique effective solution at an international level, especially for the governance of harmful Internet content, which is the source of arguments for the development of rating and filtering systems to deal with such content. However, current technology does not seem to respect these legitimate differences between nation states. It is argued here that the preferred solutions for the control of harmful Internet content have not been carefully assessed or examined by the UK government. Therefore, some of the initiatives favoured by the government and by the European Commission, but enforced or developed by quasi-governmental bodies, would almost amount to censorship of legal Internet content (Walker and Akdeniz, 1998; Akdeniz, 1999a).

The European Convention on Human Rights, and other international human rights instruments such as the Universal Declaration of Human Rights and the International Covenant on Civil and Political Rights, enshrines the rights to freedom of expression and access to information. These core documents explicitly protect freedom of expression without regard to borders, a phrase especially pertinent to the global Internet (Global Internet Liberty Campaign, 1998a, 1998b).[24] The proposed rating and filtering systems would violate these freedom of expression guarantees (Global Internet Liberty Campaign, 1999). Alternatives to currently available solutions, such as filtering and rating systems, should be considered before trying to build "fortress UK" with too much emphasis on the protection of children from harmful content.

Instead, there should be more emphasis on promoting the Internet as a positive and beneficial medium, and there is urgent need for awareness of Internet usage. If a "light regulatory touch" with an emphasis on self-regulatory or co-regulatory initiatives represents the government's vision, then "self-regulation" should mean individual regulation, rather than self-regulation by the Internet industry without the involvement of individuals and Internet users.

Notes

1 An earlier version of this chapter was published as Akdeniz (2001). The author would like to thank Dr Stephen Saxby, editor, and Elsevier Science Ltd, for permission to republish.

2 For example the NCIS Project Trawler report (NCIS, 1999) did not refer to issues that may be related to the Official Secrets Act.

3 The Melissa virus first appeared on the Internet in March of 1999. It spread rapidly throughout computer systems in the United States and Europe. It is estimated that the virus caused $80 million in damages to computers worldwide. David Smith pleaded guilty on 9 December 1999 to state and federal charges associated with his creation of the Melissa virus. See *United States of America v David Smith (1999)*.

4 See, for example, the Children and Young Persons (Harmful Publications) Act 1955, which was enacted to prevent the dissemination of certain pictorial publications harmful to children and young persons. Under section 2(1) of the 1955 legislation, a person who prints, publishes, sells or lets on hire a work to which this Act applies, or has any such work in his possession for the purpose of selling it or letting it on hire, shall be guilty of an offence and liable, on summary conviction, to imprisonment for a term not exceeding four months or to a fine or both.

5 Another notable case involves the prosecution in November 2000 of a French citizen living in the UK, Stephane Perrin, who was imprisoned for 30 months under the Obscene Publication Act 1959 for the provision of commercial obscene materials through a US-based Internet site. See further www.cyber-rights.org/documents/stephane_perrin.htm (checked 28 June 2001).

6 Note a debate on this issue within the House of Lords: The Internet: Race Hatred Material, House of Lords, Hansard, 11 December 2000.

7 The draft Convention has been approved by the Parliamentary Assembly of the Council of Europe in its 2001 Ordinary Assembly Session held 23–27 April 2001, and the final draft was published on 29 June 2001.

8 See IWF statistics at www.iwf.org.uk/hotline/stat/stat.htm (checked 28 June 2001).

9 See generally the letter from the Metropolitan Police to UK ISPs, August 1996, at www.cyber-rights.org/documents/themet.htm (checked 28 June 2001).

10 Section 3 of the 1978 Act states that "Where a body corporate is guilty of an offence under this Act and it is proved that the offence occurred with the consent or connivance of, or was attributable to any neglect on the part of, any director, manager...he, as well as the body corporate, shall be deemed to be guilty of that offence and shall be liable to be proceeded against and punished accordingly."

11 Note, for example, that in Thailand the Thai police ordered seventeen ISPs to block pornographic websites that superimpose images of Thai actresses on naked images. See "Thai police attempt shutdown of US web server", *GILC Alert*, 3, 8: 9, available at www.gilc.org/alert/alert38.html (checked 28 June 2001).

12 For the statistics, see the IWF's website at www.iwf.org.uk/hotline/stat/stat.htm (checked 28 June 2001).

13 The COPINE project dealt with the availability of child pornography through the newsgroups. See the Proceedings of the First Copine Conference, 20–21 January

1998, Dublin; and Proceedings of the Second Copine Conference, 1–2 April 1999, Brussels.
14 See www.inhope.org (checked 28 June 2001).
15 Mrs Barbara Roche, DTI, Internet, Commons Written Answers, 26 June 1997.
16 Note also the ICRA (Internet Content Rating Association) system which follows from the RSACi system. See for further information www.icra.org (checked 28 June 2001).
17 See www.getnetwise.org (checked 28 June 2001).
18 Adjournment Debate, HMG Strategy for the Internet: Memorandum by the Hon. John Battle MP, Minister for Science, Energy and Industry, House of Commons, 18 March 1998. See, for further support to the rating and filtering systems, Mr Alun Michael, Home Department, (Children (Pornography)), Commons Written Answers, 2 March 1998; Mr Alun Michael, Home Department, (Internet Pornography), Commons Written Answers, 18 February 1998, Column 678; Mr Alun Michael, Home Department, (Internet), Commons Written Answers, 25 June 1997, Column 510 [4902]; Lord Clinton-Davis, The Minister of State, Department of Trade and Industry, Written Answers on Internet: Addiction, House of Lords, 1087, 27 March 1998.
19 The INCORE (Internet Content Rating for Europe) project was set up by a group of European organizations, including the UK's IWF with a common interest in industry self-regulation and the rating of Internet content. It is now focused on a project which aims to create a generic rating and filtering system suitable for European users. This is being funded by the European Commission under the Commission's Action Plan on promoting safer use of the Internet by combating illegal and harmful content on global networks, decision No 276/1999/EC of the European Parliament and of the Council of 25 January 1999.
20 The IWF is also involved with the Internet Content Rating Alliance (ICRA) project with the mission "to develop an internationally acceptable rating system which provides internet users world wide with the choice to limit access to content they consider harmful, especially to children". See the IWF press release, "Consultations on International Internet Self-Rating System launched", 7 October 1998.
21 See, for example, *The Anarchist's CookBook* at www.brandywine.net/users/russell/Hacking/Anarch.zip (checked 28 June 2001); but note that this is not the same as the Powell book and is written by Jolly Roger.
22 See generally www.efa.org.au/Issues/Censor/cens1.html (checked 28 June 2001).
23 Prime Minister Blair, foreword to the Cabinet Office Report, *e-commerce@its.best.uk*, September 1999.
24 Universal Declaration of Human Rights, Article 19 (1) states that "[E]veryone has the right to freedom of opinion and expression includ[ing] [the] freedom to hold opinions without interference and to seek, receive and impart information and ideas through any media and regardless of frontiers."

References

Cases
American Civil Liberties Union, et al., v Janet Reno II (1999), Civil Action No. 98-5591, United States District Court for the Eastern District of Pennsylvania, (February 1, 1999), 31 F. Supp. 2d 473; 1999 U.S. Dist. Lexis 735; at www.epic.org/free_speech/copa/pi_decision.html (checked 29 June 2001).
ACLU v Reno II (22 June, 2000), No. 99-1324. For the full decision see www.epic.org/free_speech/copa/3d_cir_opinion.html (checked 29 June 2001). The

Supreme Court decided to review this case, which is known as *Ashcroft v ACLU*, No. 00-1293, April 2001.

Castells v Spain (1992),App. no.11798/85, Ser.A vol.236, (1992) 14 E.H.R.R. 445.

Handyside v UK (1976), App. no. 5493/72, Ser A vol.24, (1976) 1 E.H.R.R. 737.

LICRA v Yahoo (2000), League Against Racism and Antisemitism (LICRA), French Union of Jewish Students v Yahoo! Inc. (USA), Yahoo France, Tribunal de Grande Instance de Paris (The County Court of Paris), Interim Court Order, 20 November.

R v Fellows and Arnold (1997), 2 All E.R. 548.

R v Graham Waddon (1999), Southwark Crown Court (Judge Hardy) 30 June 1999, Court of Appeal (Criminal Division), 6 April 2000.

R v Jonathan Bowden (2000), 2 All E.R. 418.

Reno v ACLU (1997), 117 S. Ct. 2329.

Somm (1998), Somm, Felix Bruno, File No: 8340 Ds 465 JS 173158/95, Local Court (Amtsgericht) Munich, at www.cyber-rights.org/isps/somm-dec.htm (checked 29 June 2001).

United States of America v David Smith (1999), Criminal No. 99-18 U.S.C.§ 1030(a)(5)(A) information, United States District Court District of New Jersey.

Texts

ACLU (1999) "ACLU Joins International Protest Against Global Internet Censorship Plans", Press Release, no. 9, September, available at www.aclu.org/news/1999/n090999a.html (checked 29 June 2001).

Akdeniz, Y. (1996a) "Computer Pornography: A Comparative Study of the US and UK Obscenity Laws and Child Pornography Laws in Relation to the Internet", *International Review of Law, Computers and Technology*, 10, 2: 235–61.

—— (1996b) "Section 3 of the Computer Misuse Act 1990: an Antidote for Computer Viruses!", *Web Journal of Current Legal Issues*, 3, webjcli.ncl.ac.uk/1996/issue3/akdeniz3.html (checked 29 June 2001).

—— (1997a) "The Regulation of Pornography and Child Pornography on the Internet", *The Journal of Information, Law and Technology*, 1, elj.warwick.ac.uk/jilt/internet/97_1 akdz/default.htm (checked 29 June 2001).

—— (1997b) "Censorship on the Internet", *New Law Journal*, 147: 1003.

—— (1997c) "Governance of Pornography and Child Pornography on the Global Internet: A Multi-Layered Approach", in L. Edwards and C. Waelde (eds), *Law and the Internet: Regulating Cyberspace*, Oxford: Hart Publishing.

—— (1998) "The European Union and illegal and harmful content on the Internet", *Journal of Civil Liberties*, 3, 1: 31–6.

—— (1999a) "Case Analysis: Laurence Godfrey v. Demon Internet Limited", *Journal of Civil Liberties*, 4, 2 (July): 260–7, available at www.cyber-rights.org/reports/demon.htm (checked 29 June 2001).

—— (1999b) *Sex on the Net? The Dilemma of Policing Cyberspace*, Reading: South Street Press.

—— (1999c) "The Regulation of Internet Content in Europe: Governmental Control versus Self-Responsibility", *Swiss Political Science Review*, 5, 22: 123–31.

—— (2000a) "Child Pornography", in Y. Akdeniz, C. Walker and D. Wall (eds), *The Internet, Law and Society*, Harlow: Addison Wesley Longman.

—— (2000b) "New Privacy Concerns: ISPs, Crime Prevention, and Consumers' Rights?" *International Review of Law, Computers and Technology*, 14, 1: 55–61.

—— (2000c) "Policing the Internet: Regulation and censorship", in R. Gibson and S. Ward (eds), *Reinvigorating Democracy? British Politics and the Internet*, Aldershot: Ashgate.

—— (2000d) "The case for free speech", *The Guardian* (Online Section), 27 April.

—— (2001) "UK Government and the Control of Internet Content", *The Computer Law and Security Report*, 17: 4.

Akdeniz, Y. and Bohm, N. (1999) "Internet Privacy: New Concerns about Cyber-Crime and the Rule of Law", *Information Technology and Communications Law Journal*, 5: 20–24.

Akdeniz, Y., Bohm, N. and Walker, C. (1999) "Internet Privacy: Cyber-Crimes vs Cyber-Rights", *Computers and Law*, 10:1, April/May: 34–9.

Akdeniz, Y. and Rogers, W.R.H. (2000) "Defamation on the Internet", in Y. Akdeniz, C. Walker and D. Wall (eds), *The Internet, Law and Society*, Harlow: Addison Wesley Longman.

Akdeniz, Y. and Strossen, N. (2000) "Sexually Oriented Expression", in Y. Akdeniz, C. Walker and D. Wall (eds), *The Internet, Law and Society*, Harlow: Addison Wesley Longman.

Akdeniz, Y., Taylor, N. and Walker, C. (2001) "Regulation of Investigatory Powers Act 2000 (1): Bigbrother.gov.uk: State surveillance in the age of information and rights", *Criminal Law Review*, February: 73–90, available at www.cyber-rights.org/documents/crimlr.pdf (checked 29 June 2001).

Akdeniz, Y. and Walker, C. (1998) "UK Government Policy on Encryption: Trust is the Key?", *Journal of Civil Liberties*, 3, 2: 110–16.

BBC News (2000) "Canada charges hacker suspect", 20 April.

Bertelsmann Foundation (1999) "Memorandum on Internet Self-Regulation', September, available at www.stiftung.bertelsmann.de/internetcontent/english/download/Memorandum.pdf (checked 29 June 2001).

Bodard, K., De Hert, P. and De Schutter, B. (1998) "Crime on Internet: A Challenge to Criminal Law in Europe", *Maastricht Journal of European and Comparative Law*, 5: 222–61.

Born, M. (1999) "Country's first e-mail stalker is convicted", *The Daily Telegraph*, 24 March.

Bowden, C. and Akdeniz, Y. (1999) "Cryptography and Democracy: Dilemmas of Freedom", in J. Cooper (ed.), *Liberating Cyberspace: Civil Liberties, Human Rights, and the Internet*, London: Pluto Press.

Cabinet Office Performance and Innovation Unit (1999) *e-commerce@its.best.uk: The Government's Strategy*, September, available at www.cabinet.office.gov.uk/innovation/1999/ecommerce/ index.htm (checked 29 June 2001).

Cabinet Office Regulatory Impact Unit (2000) *Better Regulation Guide, and the Principles of Good Regulation* available at www.cabinet-office.gov.uk/regulation/taskforce/2000/PrinciplesLeaflet.pdf (checked 29 June 2001).

Cabinet Office Regulatory Impact Unit Task Force (2000) *Regulating Cyberspace: better regulation for e-commerce*, available at www.cabinet-office.gov.uk/regulation/taskforce/ecommerce/default.htm (checked 29 June 2001).

Computer Professionals for Social Responsibility (1998–2001) *Filtering FAQ (Version 1.2)*, available at quark.cpsr.org/~harryh/faq.html (checked 29 June 2001).

—— (1996) Letter sent to Solid Oak, the makers of CyberSitter, 18 December, available at www.cpsr.org/cpsr/nii/cyber-rights (checked 29 June 2001).

Cyber–Rights & Cyber–Liberties (UK) (1997) "Who Watches the Watchmen: Internet Content Rating Systems, and Privatised Censorship", Report, November, available at www.cyber-rights.org/watchmen.htm (checked 29 June 2001).

—— (1998) "Who Watches the Watchmen: Part II – Accountability and Effective Self-Regulation in the Information Age", Report, September, available at www.cyber-rights .org/watchmen-ii.htm (checked 29 June 2001).

—— (1999a) "Memorandum for the Internet Content Summit 1999", 9 September, available at www.cyber-rights.org/reports/summit99.htm (checked 29 June 2001).

—— (1999b) "UK ISP found liable for defamation", Press Release, 26 March, available at www.cyber-rights.org/press (checked 29 June 2001).

—— (1999c) *Hulbert's Case, the Lord Chancellor and Censorship of the Internet*, 11 November, available at www.cyber-rights.org/documents/hulbert.htm (checked 29 June 2001).

—— (2000) "Response to Better Regulation Task Force: Review of E-Commerce", 12 October, available at www.cyber-rights.org/reports/brtf.htm (checked 29 June 2001).

—— (2001) "Response to the Internet Watch Foundation on its discussion paper on the availability of child pornography through the Usenet discussion groups (newsgroups)," available at www.cyber-rights.org/reports/crcl_iwf_newsgroups.htm (checked 29 June 2001).

Davis, D. (1998a) "Criminal Law and the Internet: The Investigator's Perspective", in C. Walker (ed.) "Crime, Criminal Justice and the Internet", *Criminal Law Review* special edition, London: Sweet and Maxwell.

—— (1998b) *The Internet Detective – An Investigator's Guide*, Appendix D, London: Home Office, Police Research Group.

Department of Trade and Industry (1996) "Rating, Reporting, Responsibility, For Child Pornography & Illegal Material on the Internet", Safety-Net proposal, adopted and recommended by the Executive Committee of ISPA (Internet Services Providers Association), LINX (London Internet Exchange) and the Internet Watch Foundation, available at dtiinfo1.dti.gov.uk/safety-net/r3.htm (checked 29 June 2001).

—— (1998a) *Net Benefit: The Electronic Commerce Agenda for the UK*, DTI/Pub 3619, October, available at www.cyber-rights.org/documents/dti_net_benefit.htm (checked 29 June 2001).

—— (1998b) "Secure Electronic Commerce Statement", April, available at www.cyber-rights.org/crypto/secst.html (checked 29 June 2001).

Economic and Social Committee of the European Commission (1998) *Opinion on the Proposal for a Council Decision adopting a Multiannual Community Action Plan on promoting safe use of the Internet* (OJEC, 98/C 214/08, Brussels–Luxembourg, 10 July), pp. 29–32.

Electronic Privacy Information Center (1997) "Faulty Filters: How Content Filters Block Access to Kid-Friendly Information on the Internet", Washington, December, available at www2.epic.org/reports/filter-report.html (checked 29 June 2001).

—— (2001) *Filters and Freedom 2.0: Free Speech Perspectives on Internet Content Controls*, Washington, DC: Electronic Privacy Information Center.

Ellison, L. and Akdeniz, Y. (1998) "Cyber-stalking: the Regulation of Harassment on the Internet", in C. Walker (ed.) "Crime, Criminal Justice and the Internet", *Criminal Law Review* special edition, London: Sweet and Maxwell.

European Commission (1996a) "Illegal and Harmful Content on the Internet", Com (96) 487, Brussels, 16 October, available at europa.eu.int/ISPO/legal/en/internet/communic.html (checked 29 June 2001).

—— (1996b) Green Paper on the Protection of Minors and Human Dignity in Audiovisual and Information Services, Brussels, 16 October, available at europa.eu.int/en/record/green/gp9610/protec.htm (checked 29 June 2001).

—— (1998a) Decision No/98/EC of the European Parliament and of the Council of adopting a Multiannual Community Action Plan on promoting safer use of the Internet by combating illegal and harmful content on global networks, December.

—— (1998b) "Proposal for a European Parliament and Council Directive on certain legal aspects of electronic commerce in the internal market", COM(1998) 586 final, 98/0325 (COD), Brussels, 18.11.1998.

—— (2001) "Creating a Safer Information Society by Improving the Security of Information Infrastructures and Combating Computer-related Crime", COM(2000)890, Brussels, 26 January, available at europa.eu.int/ISPO/eif/InternetPoliciesSite/Crime/CrimeCommEN.html (checked 29 June 2001).

European Committee on Crime Problems (2000) "Committee of Experts on Crime in Cyberspace (PC-CY)", Draft Convention on Cyber-crime Declassified – Public version, PC-CY.

—— (2001) "Committee of Experts on Crime in Cyberspace (PC-CY)", Final Draft Convention on Cyber-crime," CDPC (2001) 17, Strasbourg, 29 June 2001, available at conventions.coe.int/Treaty/EN/projets/FinalCybercrime.htm (checked 29 June 2001).

European Directive (2000), 2000/31/EC of the European Parliament and of the Council of 8 June 2000 on certain legal aspects of information society services, in particular electronic commerce, in the Internal Market ("Directive on electronic commerce") Official Journal of the European Communities, vol 43, OJ L 178 17 July 2000 p.1.

European Scrutiny Committee (1998) "First Report", 7 December, HC 34-I, Session 1998-99, (High Tech Crime).

Evans, M. (1999) "Government fears that rogue web site might put lives at risk", *The Times*, 13 May.

Feral, R. (1983) *Hit Man: A Technical Manual for Independent Contractors*, Boulder, Col.: Paladin Press; available at free.freespeech.org/parazite/hitmanonline-edit.html (checked 29 June 2001).

Gay and Lesbian Alliance Against Defamation (1997) "Access Denied: The Impact of Internet Filtering Software on the Lesbian and Gay Community", New York, December, available at www.glaad.org/org/publications/access/index.html (checked 29 June 2001).

Global Internet Liberty Campaign (1998a) "Regardless Of Frontiers: Protecting The Human Right to Freedom of Expression on the Global Internet", Washington DC: CDT, September, available at www.gilc.org/speech/report (checked 29 June 2001).

—— (1998b) "Member Statement on 'Human Rights and the Internet'", January, available at www.gilc.org/news/gilc-ep-statement-0198.html (checked 29 June 2001).

—— (1998c) Member Statement on the US Child Online Protection Act ("CDAII"), available at www.cyber-rights.org/gilc/gilc-cda.htm (checked 29 June 2001).

—— (1999) "Statement submitted to the Internet Content Summit, Munich, Germany", September, available at www.gilc.org/speech/ratings/gilc-munich.html (checked 29 June 2001).

Hansard (2000) "The Internet: Race Hatred Material", House of Lords, 11 December.

Harber, D. (1990) *The Anarchist Arsenal: Improvised Incendiary and Explosives Techniques*, Boulder, Col.: Paladin Press.

Hirst, P. and Thompson, G (1995) "Globalization and the Future of the Nation State", *Economy and Society*, 24, 3: 408–42.

Home Office (1999) "Making the Internet Safe", Press Release, 306/99, 4 October.

—— (2000) "New hi-tech crime investigators in £25 million boost to combat cyber-crime", Press Release, 359/2000, 13 November, available at www.cyber-rights.org/documents/hi-tech.htm(checked 29 June 2001).

House of Commons Select Committee on Culture (1998) "The Multi-Media Revolution – Volume I", 21 May, Media and Sport Fourth Report, HC 520-I, London: HMSO; available at www.parliament.the-stationery-office.co.uk/pa/cm199798/cmselect/cmcu meds/520-vol1/52002.htm (checked 29 June 2001).

House of Commons Select Committee on Trade and Industry (1999) "Report on Building Confidence in Electronic Commerce: The Government's Proposals", HC 187, seventh report of session 1998–99, 19 May.

Hunt, A. and Wickham, G. (1994) *Foucault and Law: Towards a Sociology of Law as Governance*, London: Pluto Press.

Hutchkinson, M. (1988) *The Poisoner's Handbook*, Port Townsend, Washington, DC: Loompanics.

Internet Watch Foundation (1998a) "Consultations on International Internet Self-Rating System launched", Press Release, 7 October.

—— (1998b) *Rating and Filtering Internet Content – A United Kingdom Perspective*, March, available at www.internetwatch.org.uk/label/index.htm (checked 29 June 2001).

—— (2000) "New Brief for IWF", Press Release, 25 January, available at www.iwf.org.uk/news/press.htm (checked 29 June 2001).

Irish Department of Justice, Equality and Law Reform (1998) *Illegal and Harmful Use of the Internet*. (Pn.5231), Dublin.

Julia-Barcelo, J. (1998) "Liability for On-line Intermediaries: A European Perspective", *European Intellectual Property Review*, 12: 453–63.

KPMG/Denton Hall (1999) "Review of the Internet Watch Foundation", Report for the DTI and Home Office, February.

Leong. G. (1998) "Computer Child Pornography – The Liability of Distributors?", in C. Walker (ed.) "Crime, Criminal Justice and the Internet", *Criminal Law Review* special edition, London: Sweet and Maxwell.

NCIS (1999) *Project Trawler: Crime On The Information Highways*, 22 June, available at www.cyber-rights.org/documents/trawler.htm (checked 29 June 2001).

—— (2001), "Launch of the United Kingdom's first National Hi-Tech Crime Unit", Press Release, 18 January, available at www.cyber-rights.org/documents/ncis_1801. htm (checked 29 June 2001).

Powell, W. (1989) *The Anarchist Cookbook*, Fort Lee, NJ: Barricade Books.

Reidenberg, J.R. (1996) "Governing Networks and Cyberspace Rule-Making", *Emory Law Journal*, 45, 3: 911; available at www.law.emory.edu/ELJ/volumes/sum96/reiden .html (checked 29 June 2001).

Rhodes, R.A.W. (1994) "The Hollowing Out of the State: The Changing Nature of the Public Services in Britain", *Political Quarterly*, 65, 2: 138–51.

Royal Canadian Mounted Police (2000) "Charges laid in the case of attacks against American electronic commerce sites", Press Release, 18 April.

Seenan, G. (1999) "Computer programmer sentenced over banned visit to ex-lover", *The Guardian*, 16 October.

Select Committee on European Scrutiny (1999) Twenty-First Report, HC 34–xxi, 21 June.

Sieber, U. (1998) "Legal Aspects of Computer-Related Crime in the Information Society", Legal Advisory Board, European Commission, January, available at europa.eu.int/ISPO/legal/en/comcrime/sieber.html (checked 29 June 2001).

—— (1999a) "Control possibilities for the prevention of criminal content in computer networks", *Computer Law Security Report*, 15, 1–3: 34–9; 90–100; 168–81.

—— (1999b) "Responsibility of Internet Providers – A comparative legal study with recommendations for future legal policy", *Computer Law Security Report*, 15, 5: 291–310.

Sobel, D. (ed.) (1999) *Filters and Freedom: Free Speech Perspectives on Internet Content Controls*, Washington, DC: Electronic Privacy Information Center.

The Independent (1999) "Germany clears Net chief of child porn charges", 18 November.

—— (2000) "From hackers with love: the computer bug that brought world business to its knees", 5 May.

The Mirror (1999a) "TRAITOR: Ex-spy puts names of MI6 agents on Internet in revenge for getting the sack", 13 May.

—— (1999b) "No tears if he dies in prison", 13 November.

—— (1999c) "Voice of the Mirror acts to net perverts like Glitter", 13 November.

The Sun (1999) "Fury as Glitter gets only 4 months", 13 November.

The Times (2000) "E-mail 'stalker' jailed for nine months", 25 February.

Uhlig, R. (1999) "Libel setback for Demon", *The Daily Telegraph*, Connected Section, 1 April.

Uhlig, R. and Hayder, K. (1997) "E-mail open to police scrutiny", *The Daily Telegraph*, 9 June.

United Nations, Economic and Social Council, Commission on Human Rights (1998) *Racism, Racial Discrimination, Xenophobia and Related Intolerance: Report of the expert seminar on the role of the Internet in the light of the provisions of the International Convention on the Elimination of All Forms of Racial Discrimination*, (Fifty-fourth session, Geneva, 10–14 November 1997), E/CN.4/1998/77/Add.2, 6 January.

Walker, C. and Akdeniz, Y. (1998) "The governance of the Internet in Europe with special reference to illegal and harmful content", in C. Walker (ed.) "Crime, Criminal Justice and the Internet", *Criminal Law Review* special edition, London: Sweet and Maxwell.

Wall, D. (1998) "Policing and the Regulation of the Internet", in C. Walker (ed.) "Crime, Criminal Justice and the Internet", *Criminal Law Review* special edition, London: Sweet and Maxwell.

Wilson, J. (1999) "Net porn baron escapes jail", *The Guardian*, 7 September.

Wired News (1997) "Europe Readies Net Content Ratings", 7 July.

—— (1999) "Britain Shuts Down Spy Sites", 12 May.

9 Cyberstalking
Tackling harassment on the Internet

Louise Ellison

Introduction

The problem of on-line harassment has received considerable and, in many cases sensationalized, press coverage in recent years; for example, see *BBC On-line* (1999). These reports suggest that a woman who uses the Internet instantly risks becoming the target of a cyberstalker and finds herself the victim of a campaign of electronic abuse. Disturbing pronouncements as to the nature and impact of harassment on-line have become commonplace. Some commentators, such as Brail (1996), have gone as far as to state that on-line harassment is already killing free speech on the Internet, in particular the free speech of women. Women are engaging in self censorship, it is claimed, in order to avoid harassment and are, as a result, being further marginalized in cyberspace (Spender, 1995). In February 1999, the Vice President of the United States, Al Gore, called for a fight against cyberstalking, stating that the Internet had inadvertently become a sinister new avenue for carrying out violence against women (*Washington Post*, 1999). This chapter examines the phenomenon of cyberstalking and the issues surrounding its regulation.

What is on-line harassment?

Harassment on the Internet can take a variety of guises. A direct form of Internet harassment may involve the sending of unwanted e-mails which are abusive, threatening or obscene, from one person to another (McGraw, 1995). It may involve electronic sabotage, in the form of sending the victim hundreds or thousands of junk e-mail messages (the activity known as "spamming") or sending computer viruses. Indirect forms of harassment may involve a cyberstalker impersonating his or her victim on-line and sending abusive e-mails or fraudulent spams in the victim's name. Victims may be subscribed without their permission to a number of mailing lists, with the result that they receive hundreds of unwanted e-mails everyday.

Unsurprisingly, it is the more dramatic cases of on-line harassment which have grabbed the media headlines. The majority of incidents so far reported have occurred in the United States. One such case is that of Cynthia Armistead of Atlanta, who received threatening and obscene e-mail messages from her cyberstalker as well as harassing telephone calls.[1] Her harasser posted phoney advertisements to a USENET discussion group, offering Armistead's services as a prostitute and providing her home address and telephone number, which led to more obscene e-mail messages and telephone calls. Jayne Hitchcock posted a warning on the Internet about a New York literary agency asking for $225 to review her book. She was then "mail bombed" with more than 200 e-mail missives (*Washington Times*, 1998). Her name, telephone number and address appeared on racist and sex newsgroups inviting men to call her or come to her home day or night. In January 1999, Gary Dellapenta, a 50-year-old security guard from Los Angeles, was arrested and charged under California's "cyber-stalking" laws (Goodin, 1999). Dellapenta allegedly posted messages in AOL (America On-line) chatrooms that appeared to come from his victim, a 28-year-old woman. The messages claimed that the woman had an unfulfilled sexual fantasy of being raped, and included her name, address and telephone number. Six men visited the woman's apartment in response to the messages and the woman also received dozens of telephone calls from men. Dellapenta pleaded guilty to one charge of stalking and three counts of soliciting others to commit rape, and faces a maximum sentence of six years' imprisonment (*New York Times*, 1999).

There have also been a number of well publicized cases involving death threats sent via the Internet. In 1998, the first US federal case involving hate e-mail resulted in the conviction of Richard Machado. Machado had sent derogatory e-mail messages to Asian students at the University of California, in which he threatened to kill them. He was convicted on one civil rights charge and sentenced to time served (Macavinta, 1998). In another case, Kingman Quon of California was accused of e-mailing death threats to Hispanic professors, students and officials across the country. In January 1999 he pleaded guilty to seven misdemeanour counts of interfering with federally protected rights, specifically threatening to use force against his victims with the intent to intimidate or interfere with them because of their national origin or ethnic background (Deutch, 1999). In June 1999 Kingman Quon was sentenced to two years' imprisonment (*Wired*, 1999).

While undoubtedly distressing for the victims involved in these cases, there is, as yet, no evidence to suggest that persistent campaigns of on-line harassment which involve death threats or escalate into "real-life" stalking are commonplace. There have, however, been numerous pronouncements that cyberstalking activity is set to increase. In August 1999 a report published by the US Justice Department examined the problem of cyberstalking and sought to estimate the extent of the problem of harassment on-line (Attorney General, 1999). The report accepts that the nature and extent of cyberstalking are difficult to quantify but states that ISPs and local law enforcement agencies are receiving a growing number of complaints about harassing and threatening behaviour on-line. The report suggests that the potential magnitude of the problem may be estimated by reference to the problem of real life stalking:

In the United States, there are currently more than 80 million adults and 10 million children with access to the Internet. Assuming the proportion of cyberstalking victims is even a fraction of the proportion of persons who have been the victims of off-line stalking within the preceding 12 months, there may be potentially tens or even hundreds of thousands of recent cyberstalking incidents in the United States.

(Attorney General, 1999)

In the UK, the National Criminal Intelligence Service warned that e-mail harassment will increase as Internet usage grows.

Innocent users may find some unpleasant material coming their way. Junk mail may be received, containing pornography or other distasteful or obscene material. The user may find themselves repeatedly receiving unwanted and distressing communications, such as threatening, obscene or hateful e-mail. Vicious rumours may be spread on-line, or blackmail demands received.

(NCIS, 1999)

Do the characteristics of computer-mediated communications encourage harassment?

Concern surrounding on-line harassment has been fuelled by the claims of some commentators that characteristics peculiar to the Internet and to computer-mediated communications (CMCs) make the medium particularly attractive to the stalker and harasser. These claims are examined below.

Although the nature of CMC and its societal and behavioural effects have been the subject of much research, it is, as Walther (1996) notes, "still debated, tested, and not very well understood when one examines the literature on the subject". It has, however, been suggested that CMC differs in many ways from traditional communication technologies. One striking and highly valued feature of CMC is its general potential for pseudonymity. Pseudonymity on the Internet can be achieved by simply forging or "spoofing" an e-mail header so as to create an on-line digital persona, while many ISPs and on-line service providers allow their users to adopt pseudonyms as their user ID.[2] In CMC the gender, race, age and physical appearance of others is not immediately evident. It is for the user to decide what information she or he will or will not reveal in Internet communications. This gives users greater control over self-representation (Parks and Floyd, 1996). For example, researchers of human behaviour on CMC systems observe that identity manipulation is commonplace in CMC. Users often create alternative personae for their on-line interactions with others that bear little resemblance to their real-life identities. The comparative anonymity or pseudonomity of CMCs, it is claimed, means that users tend to be less inhibited in their on-line interactions with others (Kiesler *et al.*, 1984). It is commonly asserted that people will write things in electronic communications that they would not ordinarily say or write in "real life"

(Greenberg, 1997). For example, it is claimed that e-mail users are often more blunt and direct in their communications and are less concerned with the possible impact their speech may have; the words they choose, it is suggested, are more harsh or crude than those used in other contexts (McGraw, 1995).

Disinhibition among CMC users has also been attributed to a lack of regulating feedback in electronic communications. There is no body language, no change in tone of voice or facial expression in CMC; there are only letters, numbers and symbols. Reid (1991) claims that this lack of social context cues obscures the boundaries that would generally separate acceptable and unacceptable forms of behaviour. According to Reid, this can lead to extremes of behaviour on-line, including hostility and aggression:

> Protected by the anonymity of the computer medium, and with few social cues to indicate "proper" ways to behave, users are able to express and experiment with aspects of their personality that social inhibition would generally encourage them to suppress.
>
> (Reid, 1991)

It is also suggested that people continue to attach less significance and weight to their electronic correspondence. Electronic messages are often regarded as casual and transitory and are, it is alleged, less reflective as a result. This is in part due to the fact that people assume that their one-to-one messages are private and will be seen only by the recipient, and because users are often unaware that most e-mail systems can create a complete record of a communication. Harassment on-line has also been linked to sex differences in computer-mediated communications. While research in this area has only recently begun, a number of researchers have argued that men tend to be more adversarial in their on-line interactions and use intimidation tactics to dominate and control on-line discourse. Susan Herring (1993) is one such researcher who claims that men are more belligerent on-line and more likely to use angry and abusive language. The practice of flaming is given as an example. Flames are highly aggressive, sarcastic, vulgar or critical responses sent to a user. The general acceptance of flaming on-line is reflected in rules of netiquette (rules regarding appropriate behaviour on-line). Virginia Shea, author of *Netiquette*, explains that although flames often get out of hand they have a purpose in the ecology of cyberspace. Flames are aimed at teaching someone something or stopping them from doing something. While conceding that flame messages often use more brute force than is strictly necessary, Shea maintains that that is half the fun (Shea, 1994). It has been argued that these rules, which have been developed largely by men, assume confrontation and a combative communication style. For example, Dale Spender, author of *Nattering on the Net*, likens net rules to those governing a boxing match: "[n]o hitting below the belt, no fighting dirty; may the best man win." Most netiquette statements acknowledge that the going can get rough but, according to Spender (1995: 196), the answer is invariably that if you cannot take the heat, stay out of the kitchen.

Tackling harassment on-line

This section examines the various means available, both legal and non-legal, for tackling harassment on-line.

Legal regulation

In the United States, concern that existing laws are inadequate to deal with on-line harassment has led to calls for specific cyberstalking legislation. A number of US states now have specific cyberstalking statutes. The first US state to include on-line communications in its statutes against stalking was the state of Michigan in 1993. Other states which have anti-stalking laws that include electronic harassment include Arizona, Alaska, Connecticut, New York, Oklahoma and Wyoming. The recent US Justice Department report, however, identified significant gaps in current federal and state law. The report calls on states to review their existing stalking and other statutes to determine whether they address cyberstalking and, if not, to expeditiously enact laws that prohibit cyberstalking. It further recommends that federal law be amended "to make it easier to track down stalkers in cyberspace" (Attorney General, 1999).

In the UK, in contrast, existing laws are sufficiently flexible to encompass on-line stalking and e-mail harassment. A person sending offensive or threatening messages may, for example, commit an offence under section 43 of the Telecommunications Act 1984, which makes it an offence to send by means of a public telecommunications system a message or other matter that is grossly offensive or of an indecent, obscene or menacing character. The Protection from Harassment Act 1997 may also be invoked in cases of on-line harassment. This Act provides a combination of civil and criminal measures to deal with stalking. It creates two criminal offences, the summary offence of criminal harassment and an indictable offence involving fear of violence. Under section 2 it is an offence to pursue a course of conduct which amounts to the harassment of another where the accused knew or ought to have known that the course of conduct amounts to harassment. A person commits an offence under section 4 if he pursues a course of conduct which causes another to fear, on at least two occasions, that violence will be used against him. It is sufficient that the accused ought to have known that his course of conduct would cause the other to so fear on each of those occasions. Harassment includes alarm and distress, but these terms are not defined in the Act; they are to be given their ordinary meaning. The range of behaviour covered by the Act is thus potentially extremely wide. The sending of abusive, threatening e-mails or the posting of offensive material would constitute an offence under section 2 of the Act as long as it amounts to a course of conduct (for example, more than one e-mail must be sent) and the offender knew or ought to have known that his conduct amounted to harassment. In March 1999, Nigel Harris, a 23-year-old computer programmer, became the first person to be convicted under the Act of harassment by e-mail. Harris had sent a girlfriend abusive and threatening electronic messages after she ended their two-year relationship. Harris was given a two-year conditional discharge (*Daily Telegraph*, 1999).

Legal regulation of cyberstalking will not only hinge upon laws which are sufficiently flexible to deal with electronic harassment. A lack of training and specialized expertise on the part of law enforcement agencies may result in reports of threatening or offensive behaviour on-line not being taken seriously or not being thoroughly investigated. There have been reports, for example, that alleged victims of on-line harassment have been told by police officers, unfamiliar with the technology involved, simply to turn off their computers (Attorney General, 1999). The US Justice Department report recognizes a lack of appropriate training and expertise as a significant potential obstacle to the effective regulation of harassment on-line. The report recommends training to promote technological proficiency among investigators and the establishment of specialized units to investigate and prosecute cyberstalking cases. Similar concerns have been raised in the UK by the National Criminal Intelligence Service (NCIS): "Organisations and law enforcement must overcome their lack of familiarity with the technologies and inexperience in dealing with IT crimes" (NCIS, 1999). Concerns have also been expressed in relation to the retrieval and preservation of electronic evidence by criminal investigators who may not be adequately trained or simply not equipped with the appropriate computer forensic software. If the evidential integrity of electronic evidence is to be safeguarded, criminal investigators must be sufficiently aware of computer forensic methods. According to Sommer (1993), "…many investigators and regulators seem so far broadly unaware of the problems of acquiring evidence sufficiently robust against hostile criticism in court". Lawyers and judges must similarly become acquainted with the technical issues involved if computer evidence is to be treated appropriately by the criminal courts (Davis, 1998).

The challenge of anonymity

Given the nature of the Internet, legal regulation may not always be the most effective solution when dealing with threatening and harassing behaviour on-line. The Internet presents law enforcement bodies with unique problems. These pertain mainly to the international aspects of the Internet; it is a medium that can be accessed by anyone throughout the globe with a computer and a modem. This means that a potential offender may not be within the jurisdiction where an offence is committed. Anonymous use of the Internet also promises to create challenges for law enforcement authorities. True anonymity on-line is achieved by using an anonymous re-mailer such as (www.anonymizer.com) (accessed on 16 June 2001). Re-mailers are computer services which cloak the identity of users who send messages through them by stripping all identifying information from an e-mail and allocating an "anonymous ID". The most sophisticated re-mailer technology is called MixMaster (Cottrel, 1996) which uses public key cryptography, granting unprecedented anonymity to users who wish to communicate in complete privacy. By chaining together several re-mailers, a user could create a trail so complex that it would be impossible to follow. The ease with which users can send anonymous messages would render legal regulation of on-line harassment a difficult, if not impossible, task. Tracing a cyberstalker may prove an insurmountable obstacle to any legal action when the electronic footprints which users leave behind are effectively eliminated by re-mailer technology.

Given these enforcement problems, some commentators have called for the prohibition of anonymous communications while others have called for restrictions to be placed on anonymity (Kabay, 1998). Opponents of anonymity argue that it threatens civility and accountability on-line. Those who call for such restrictions, however, fail to recognize the cost of such action to the on-line community in terms of fundamental freedoms. Placing restrictions upon anonymity on-line would have serious negative repercussions for freedom of expression and privacy on the Internet (Wallace, 1999). Free speech is facilitated by anonymity on-line; it allows human rights activists, political and religious dissidents and whistleblowers throughout the world to engage in confidential communications free from intrusion. In March 1999, for example, Anonymizer launched the Kosovo Privacy Project, providing free and confidential web browsing and e-mail to people in the region (Kahney, 1999). Anonymity is also important for on-line discussions and newsgroups dealing with sensitive issues such as sexual abuse, domestic violence and alcoholism. Users seeking access to information on AIDS, for example, or seeking guidance from the Samaritans, clearly benefit from remaining anonymous. Anonymity can also facilitate the protection of privacy on the Internet. On-line users can currently use web-based services such as Anonymizer to surf the web anonymously, thus enabling them to evade surveillance and monitoring of their activities on the Internet. The positive value of anonymous communication more than offsets the dangers associated with its illegitimate use. The imposition of restrictions upon anonymity on-line would be both premature and harmful to individual users and to the Internet community at large.

Non-legal solutions

It is now increasingly accepted that self-regulatory solutions to problems such as cyberstalking will have to be sought to compensate for the inevitable limitations of legal regulation, given the potential for anonymity on-line and the global nature of the Internet. A new multi-layered governance approach to undesirable and unlawful conduct on line will be necessary if Internet users are to be adequately protected (Akdeniz, 1997). Non-legal solutions to harassment on-line are considered below.

Ignore it!

Some advocates of free speech on the Internet have been quick to urge against legislative or regulatory solutions and to advise users simply to ignore on-line harassment. These commentators present harassment as an inescapable, if regrettable, feature of life on-line. Jensen, for example, argues that women should take a "sticks and stones" approach to abusive and offensive e-mail messages (Jensen, 1996). However, such a view assumes that "minor" incidents of harassment do not have a real and significant impact on users. Advising users simply to put up with the more mundane everyday instances of on-line harassment fails to acknowledge that this type of "dripping tap harassment" (Wise and Stanley, 1987) may well cause some individuals to curb their activity on-line.

Industry efforts

The US Justice Department report recognizes that ISPs and system administrators have an important role to play in empowering users and protecting consumers from harassment on-line:

> Ultimately...the first line of defence will involve industry efforts that educate and empower individuals to protect themselves against cyberstalking and other on-line threats.
>
> (Attorney General, 1999)

Individuals who receive unwanted e-mails or find that offensive information about them has been posted on the Internet are indeed advised to contact the offender's ISP, who may eliminate the offending account. The federal report, however, criticizes ISPs for not adequately addressing electronic harassment. According to the report, complaint procedures are often hard to locate, and acceptable-use policies are frequently vague as to what constitutes prohibited conduct. While many ISPs do have anti-harassment policies in place, it is claimed that they are not being widely and consistently enforced.[3] The report recommends that the Internet industry should establish clear and understandable procedures for individuals to register complaints and should actively seek to educate consumers on how to protect themselves on-line. The Internet industry is further called upon to cooperate fully with law enforcement agencies when investigating complaints and to develop and distribute training material for law enforcement on the investigation of Internet crime.

Self-protection

Self-protection is arguably the least problematic solution to stalking and harassment on the Internet. There are many websites and books which provide information for self-protection from cyberstalkers for on-line users. One such site is Women Halting On-line Abuse (WHOA),[4] launched in 1997, which aims to educate the Internet community about on-line harassment and to formulate voluntary policies that system administrators can adopt in order to create harassment-free environments. In general, women are advised, where possible, to adopt either a male or gender-neutral user name. All users are advised to keep personal information divulged on-line to a minimum. To guard against on-line impersonation, it is also recommended that users use strong encryption programmes such as "Pretty Good Privacy" (PGP) to ensure complete private communications. New and innovative software programmes which enable users to control the information they receive are also being developed (Spertus, 1996). There are, for example, technical means by which users may block unwanted communications. Tools available include "kill" files and "bozo" files which delete incoming e-mail messages from individuals specified by the user, and such tools are included with most of the available e-mail software packages. There is also specially designed software to filter or block unwanted e-mail messages. In the future, advanced filtering systems which recognize insulting e-mail may be available.

Conclusion

As use of the Internet has grown, so too have fears that it will facilitate undesirable and unlawful behaviour. The nature of the Internet, as a faceless medium, makes it an ideal tool, it is claimed, for the would-be cyberstalker as well as the would-be hacker, fraudster and cyberterrorist (Greenberg, 1997). Moreover, it is commonly alleged that the Internet's specific characteristics, its global reach and potential for anonymity, render it immune to effective regulation (Jensen, 1996). This chapter has sought to challenge this increasingly pervasive view. The Internet simply demands new approaches and, where necessary, new solutions. A multi-layered approach to regulation is required that seeks to educate and empower users; an approach which involves individual users, the Internet industry, technical solutions such as the use and development of privacy enhancing technologies,[5] specialized policing practices and, inevitably, global cooperation between law enforcement bodies (Ellison and Akdeniz, 1998: 29–48). Furthermore, the need to safeguard fundamental freedoms such as privacy and free speech on-line must, as this chapter has sought to highlight, inform future regulatory initiatives at each level.

Notes

1   See, for example, the harassment section on the Technomom pages at www.technomom.com/harassed/ (checked 17 June 2001).
2   The providers will usually have a record of the user's identity and can trace the user if necessary.
3   For example, ChaTciRCuiT has a Chat Policy for their IRC Chat site which states that the "use of speech as a means to hurt others, such as threats, harassment, racism, or obscenity will not be permitted." See www.chatcircuit.com/fyi/policies.html (checked 17 June 2001). TalkCity has adopted a similar policy, simply stating that expressions of bigotry, hatred, harassment or abuse will not be tolerated. See www.talkcity.com/csa/ (checked 17 June 2001).
4   whoa.femail.com/ (checked 17 June 2001).
5   See, for example, www.hushmail.com and www.pgpi.org (both checked 17 June 2001).

150   *Louise Ellison*

References

Akdeniz, Y. (1997) "Governance of Pornography and Child Pornography on the Global Internet: A Multi-layered Approach", in L. Edwards and C. Waelde (eds), *Law and the Internet: Regulating Cyberspace*, Oxford: Hart.

Attorney General (1999) "Cyberstalking: A New Challenge for Enforcement and Industry", *A Report from the Attorney General to the Vice President*, available at www.usdoj.gov/ag/cyberstalkingreport.htm (checked 17 June 2001).

BBC On-line (1999) "Cyberstalking: Pursued in Cyberspace", available at www.bbc.co.uk/hi/english/uk/newsid_378000/378373.stm#top (checked 17 June 2001).

Brail, S. (1996) "The Price of Admission: Harassment and Free Speech in the Wild, Wild West", in L. Cherny and E. Reba Wise (eds), *Wired Women: Gender and New Realities in Cyberspace*, Washington: Seal Press.

Cottrel, L. (1996) "Mixmaster FAQ", available at www.obscura.com/~loki/remailer/mixmaster-faq.html (checked 17 June 2001).

Daily Telegraph (1999) "Country's first e-mail stalker is convicted", 24 March.

Davis, D. (1998) "Criminal Law and the Internet: The Investigator's Perspective", *Criminal Law Review*, December Special Edition: Crime, Criminal Justice and the Internet.

Deutch, L. (1999) "Man to plead guilty to e-mailing death threats to Hispanics across the country", *Nando Times*, January 28.

Ellison, L. and Akdeniz, Y. (1998) "Cyber-stalking: the Regulation of Harassment on the Internet", *Criminal Law Review*, December Special Edition: Crime, Criminal Justice and the Internet.

Goodin, D. (1999) "Cyberstalking law snags alleged violator", *CNET.COM*, January 25, available at news.cnet.com/news/0-1005-200-337787.html?tag=st.cn.sr.ne.1 (checked 17 June 2001).

Greenberg, S. (1997) "Threats, Harassment and Hate On-line: Recent Developments", *Boston Public Interest Journal*, 6: 673–96.

Herring, S. (1993) "Gender and Democracy in Computer-Mediated Communication", *Electronic Journal of Communication*, 3, 2: 1–30.

Jensen, B. (1996) "Cyberstalking: Crime, Enforcement and Personal Responsibility in the On-line World", available at www.sgrm.com/art-8.htm (checked 17 June 2001).

Kabay, M. (1998) "Anonymity and Pseudonymity in Cyberspace: Deindivduation, Incivility and Lawlessness Versus Freedom and Privacy", paper presented at the *Annual Conference of the European Institute for Computer Anti-virus Research*, March 1998.

Kahney, L. (1999) "Email Assist for Yugoslavs", *Wired News*, March 26, available at www.wired.com/news/news/politics/story/18765.html (checked 17 June 2001).

Kiesler, S., Siegel, J. and McGuire, W. (1984) "Social Psychological Aspects of Computer-Mediated Communication", *American Psychologist*, 39, 10: 1123–34.

Macavinta, C. (1998) "Prison time for email threats", May 4, available at news.cnet.com/news/0-1005-200-328979.html (checked 17 June 2001).

McGraw, D. (1995) "Sexual Harassment in Cyberspace: The Problem of Unwelcome E-mail", *Rutgers Computer and Technology Law Journal*, 21: 491–518.

NCIS (1999) "Project Trawler: Crime of the Information Highway", available at www.cyber-rights.org/documents/trawler.htm (checked 17 June 2001).

New York Times (1999) "Internet Stalking Case Ends in Plea", 29 April, available at www.nytimes.com/library/tech/99/04/cyber/articles/29stalk.html (checked 17 June 2001).

Parks, M., and Floyd, K. (1996) "Making Friends in Cyberspace", *Journal of Communication*, 46, 1: 80–97.

Reid, E. (1991) "Electropolis: Communication and Community on Internet Relay Chat", unpublished manuscript available at www.aluluei.com/ (checked 17 June 2001).

Shea, V. (1994) *Netiquette*, San Rafael: Albion.

Sommer, P. (1998) "Digital Footprints: Assessing Computer Evidence", *Criminal Law Review*, December Special Edition: Crime, Criminal Justice and the Internet.

Spender, D. (1995) *Nattering on the Net*, Melbourne: Spinifex Press.

Spertus, E. (1996) "Social and Technical Means for Fighting On-line Harassment", paper presented at *Virtue and Virtuality: Gender, Law, and Cyberspace – MIT Artificial Intelligence Laboratory*, May 5; available at www.ai.mit.edu/people/ellens/Gender/glc (checked 17 June 2001).

Wallace, J. (1999) "Nameless in Cyberspace: Anonymity on the Internet", Cato Institute Briefing Papers no. 54, available at www.cato.org/pubs/briefs/bp-054es.html (checked 17 June 2001).

Walther, J. (1996) "Computer-Mediated Communication: Impersonal, Interpersonal, and Hyperpersonal Interaction", *Communication Research*, 23 February: 1–43.

Washington Post (1999), "Gore wants 'cyber-stalking' fought", 26 February.

Washington Times (1998) "Author's real-life story is cyberspace nightmare", 19 February.

Wired (1999) "Nailing Net Hate Mail", June 29, available at www.wired.com/news/print_version/politics/story/20470.html (checked 17 June 2001).

Wise, S. and Stanley, L. (1987) *Georgie Porgie: Sexual Harassment in Everyday Life*, London: Pandora.

10 The language of cybercrime

Matthew Williams

Introduction

The study of computer-mediated communication has primarily been the privilege of media and communications disciplines, yet over the past decade or so the pervasiveness of new communications technology upon everyday life inevitably stirred up interest in other fields of study. It seems only recently that criminology and legal studies have taken an interest in these new forms of communication, identifying them as contemporary vehicles for criminality. To date the majority of interest has been in the ability of these new forms of social interaction to facilitate and expand upon existing criminal activity – the extension of paedophile networks (O'Connell, 2000), the dissemination of subversive hate-related propaganda (Whine, 2000; Mann and Tuffin, 2000), the facilitation of financial crimes (Kaspersen, 1988; Denning, 1995; Holland, 1995; Neumann, 1995), and the forging of hyper-criminal networks, such as the Locksmith newsgroup identified by Mann and Sutton (1998). However, there has been little interest and a paucity of empirical research into the more subtle or hidden forms of deviance on-line.

As within off-line communities, on-line populations are subjected to a myriad of quasi-criminal activities such as verbal abuse, defamation, harassment, stalking and, to an extreme extent, "virtual rape" (Mackinnon, 1997a). These forms of on-line deviance might be dubbed simply as misbehaviour, highlighting the "virtual" element of these acts and as such playing down their significance in relation to "real-world" affairs. However, basing assumptions of the seriousness of on-line deviant acts on the separateness of the "real" and the "virtual" only serves to shift accountability away from the on-line offender. The notion that a deviant act is mitigated due to its "virtuality" is short-sighted. To argue that an act of racial or sexual harassment carried out on-line through text is any less serious than an equivalent verbal act in the off-line world is to grant the would-be offender the right to defame and humiliate individuals on the basis that it is simply not "real". A contrary position is advanced in this chapter, stating that both the "real" and the "virtual" are not separate experiences and as such the nature of on-line communication enables a perpetrator to inflict recognizable levels of harm upon a victim via textual slurs and abuse. It is further argued that, due to the unique conventions and ways of "being" experienced by many on-line users, certain acts of harassment might be afforded with more "force" to harm a victim than is otherwise found in off-line equivalents. While this article does not aim to identify an aetiology of on-line abusive acts, it does convey the way in which forms of abuse on-line have the ability to harm the objects of derision significantly enough to warrant a closer examination of these acts, and subsequently to consider suitable forms of redress. To accomplish this the chapter delineates the mechanics of abusive acts within the on-line environment, which in turn indicates how individuals are susceptible to harm from these acts. Understanding that abuse on-line manifests through text is imperative, and identifying which forms of abusive text pose significant enough threat to an individual's identity becomes necessary if any form of redress is to be made possible both on- and off-line.

Virtually criminal

As a precursor to understanding how on-line offenders harm their victims through text, it is important to understand that events within on-line settings are not wholly separate from those in the off-line world. Such a strict dichotomy between the "real" and the "virtual" must be nullified if the consequences of abusive acts on-line are to be fully acknowledged. It seems a common trait for many researchers and philosophers in understanding cultural formations and phenomena to view them as a set of opposing, interrelated or complementary forces. Cognitive maps that delineate social groups, sets of beliefs and the like clearly help in calming the chaos that social scientists are often faced with in the real world. However, there is always a clear danger of oversimplifying what might be a far more complex and interactive social process for the sake of a presumed theoretical, methodological or philosophical bias. Those theorists and empiricists who make a stark distinction between "real" and "virtual" phenomena are arguably guilty of such bias (see Baudrillard, 1998; Jameson, 1991). The focus on virtuality as the defining feature of the Internet may have had less to do with the nature of the technology itself than with various intellectual projects at the time. As Miller and Slater identify:

> The Internet appeared at precisely the right moment to substantiate postmodern claims about the increasing abstraction and depthlessness of contemporary mediated reality…and poststructuralists could point to this new space in which identity could be detached from embodiment and other essentialist anchors, and indeed in which (some) people were apparently already enacting a practical, everyday deconstruction of older notions of identity.
>
> (Miller and Slater, 2000: 4; parentheses in original)

The barriers between the real and the virtual are subject to erosion, with arguably less nascent forms of postulation advocating the idea of a reciprocity between on- and off-line life. That is to say, "Internet media is continuous with and embedded in other social spaces, that they happen within mundane social structures and relations that they may transform but that they cannot escape into a self-enclosed cyberian apartness" (Miller and Slater, 2000: 4). More importantly, if on-line arenas were to be viewed as places apart from off-line life, one would expect to find behavioural patterns, such as deviant acts, that were abstracted and alien from off-line interactions. Crimes carried out on computer networks seem to be extensions of everyday crimes in the real world. Essentially crimes are re-engineered to function in the on-line environment, utilizing the technologies they are faced with (Williams, 2000). It is, then, important to understand that both acts of deviance and experiences on-line are inexorably linked to the "real" world. As such, the consequences of on-line abuse and harassment can manifest in the "real" world even if the act was performed in a "virtual" setting. To better understand how on-line abuse harms individuals in the off-line world, an examination of how language both constitutes and de-constitutes the victim's identity is required. Recognizing that language is a sustaining force behind "being", utilizing it as an abusive tool may result in the victim experiencing degrees of ontological precariousness.

"Being" through language and text

The need to deconstruct virtual deviance in order to understand its conse-quences requires an examination of the vehicle through which derision is made possible – the speech act. Althusser (1971) gives an account of the constitution of bodies through language that proves useful in the analysis of on-line deviance. The point made is that language is one of the sustaining entities or forces behind the individual. The social existence of the body is made possible partly by being interpellated within the terms of language (Althusser, 1971). In short, a non-defined body is called into existence, or being, by language. In Althusser's example of interpellation a policeman calls out "Hey, you there" in a crowded street, and everyone who hears him turns around, ready to be recog-nized. The answer from any member of the crowd does not pre-exist the policeman's call, so the passer-by turns precisely to acquire an identity. In short, the address animates the addressee into existence. But one must not fall into the trap of thinking that language "discovers" the body; language only funda-mentally constitutes the "self". This calls into question the possibility of the "first address" a body must undergo to become constituted within a system of language. The fundamental question to be asked is how can a body be addressed if it has no ability to be recognized. Butler (1997) contends that Althusser's reversal of Hegel shows how the act of being addressed itself constitutes "being", and that the context of the address, or the meaning, is unimportant in the initial process of "fabrication". The outcome of the address may either include the body in the language system, or marginalize it outside of the system, in abjection. In summary, individuals come to recognize themselves as individuals with an identity through their objectification by others in language; this objectification places them in a hierarchy of the social/language system where relationships with others are recognized through difference.

Speech acts – illocution and perlocution

If the body is constituted through language, then it follows that language can also de-constitute an individual's identity. Butler (1997) examines the ways in which language can be used as a weapon to wound individuals through "verbal assaults" and similar derisory acts. When individuals claim they have been injured by an insult, they are ascribing a certain agency to language, a force that allows it to harm an individual in similar ways to physical acts. Indeed, to claim that language injures is to combine both linguistic and physical vocabularies. The choice of title in Matsuda *et al.*'s (1993) text *Words that Wound* suggests that "language can act in certain ways that parallel the infliction of physical pain and injury" (Butler, 1997: 4). Indeed, the psychological and physiological battering from racial and homophobic slurs can mirror that of physical assault: "it's like receiving a slap in the face, it's instantaneous" (Lawrence, 1993: 68). The ability for language to harm with such force draws on the body's reliance on the language system. A verbal insult draws on that initial process of interpellation, recasting and subordinating the individual within the social/language hierarchy. So the essential point remains that the contemporary address recalls and re-enacts the formative ones that gave *a priori* certification. As Butler (1997: 5) summarizes, "If language can sustain the body, it can also threaten its existence".

Yet before any analysis can be made of offensive or harassing text from within the on-line environment, it would be prudent to ascertain what speech or text could be deemed as offensive. Yet, as Becker *et al.* (2000: 36) note in attempting to define hate-speech: "in constructing a definition...one is really crafting unspoken rules regarding discourse". Any attempt to map the pains of verbal or textual performances, in terms of content, individual susceptibility and the multitude of contexts derisory speech can take would be fruitless. For this reason a broader mechanical approach can be adopted to identify wider frameworks of derisory speech, theorizing the mechanics which allow for such agency in language. Here the "form" injurious speech takes is examined, not the "content". By adopting a broader approach it is possible to identify a bifurcation in forms of language, particularly speech or text of a derisory content. Austin (1975) delineates illocutionary and perlocutionary speech acts. Although a clumsy dyad, with a substantial "grey" area between them, this way of proceeding can be beneficial in understanding forms of on-line derision. The illocutionary speech performance is one where at the same time as what is being said, something is also being done: the policeman stating "I am charging you with assault" is not saying something which has a delayed consequence; the consequence is immediate. The speech is the act of doing, where a certain "force" is acted upon another. Perlocutionary acts, however, have a delayed effect: what is said at one point in time may have a consequence that is temporarily distant. Austin gave the examples of "warning" ("I warn you") as an illocutionary act, and persuading ("I persuaded him") as a perlocutionary act. The speech act of warning has an instantaneous effect, where the act of warning occurs at the same time as the utterance. Persuasion itself implies that the consequences of a persuasive speech act are temporarily removed from the utterance. The reason for the disparity in speech acts derives from social and linguistic conventions. The illocutionary speech act is only so due to its ability to refer and draw from convention and ritual in society at points in time, such as the wedding ritual ("I do") and the naming of a ship. Indeed, instances of failed speech performances can help explain the illocutionary act's reliance on the temporal social milieu.

It is the illocutionary performance that harbours the force to effectively harm an individual in a derisory context. The possibility for the abusive illocutionary act to simultaneously convey action in speech means that it does more than represent violence; it is violence. The forceful utterance "reinvokes and reinscribes" a relation of domination (Butler, 1997: 18).

Illocution and computer-mediated communication

Illocutionary performances also exist within synchronous forms of computer-mediated communication (CMC). Synchronous (such as chat), as opposed to asynchronous on-line communication (such as e-mail and newsgroups), allows for temporal co-presence, an effect that intensifies on-line interactions, creating an atmosphere where discussions can flourish. The immediacy of synchronous communication on-line makes it akin to that of off-line communication. This heightened sense of immediacy in chat leads to the expression of more emotion and heated exchanges. Emotion can be readily expressed within synchronous forms of communication, due to the realization that IRC (Internet Relay Chat) is more oral than literate – the latter being characteristic of asynchronous communication. Although synchronous communication is written and not spoken, many of its linguistic characteristics mirror the spoken word. This is seen in the increased used of phatic communication, such as "gee", "hmm" and "grrr", which is typical of speech, not of writing (Sternberg, 1998). It is within this medium that injurious illocution can flourish.

Injurious illocutions on-line can appear in two quite distinct forms. The first is a textual adaptation of the spoken illocution, so what would have been a vocal insult now appears as text on screen. This type of injurious speech has already met with legal rationalization and proceedings in the "real" world (*Stratton Oakmont, Inc. v Prodigy Services Co., 1995; Cubby v Compuserve 1991; California Software, Inc. v Reliability Research, Inc. 1986)*. Indeed, Internet Service Providers or bulletin board operators who regulate on-line discourse can be held liable as publishers of defamatory material. More so, users of CMC could also be found liable for defamatory on-line statements (Davis, 2000). The second form of injurious illocution on-line differs from the first in that it draws on several textual conventions that have emerged from within the virtual environment itself. This form of illocution allows for traditional forms of violent behaviour (i.e., forms of physical or actual violence within an off-line environment) to be re-engineered as textual violent performances on-line. The very nature of interaction inherent within computer-mediated communication has forged a convention that allocates more "functions" to text than is usually granted to the spoken word. Where speech partly functions as dialogue, description and emotion off-line, text on-line is solely responsible for these functions. On-line text allows for "physical" performances to occur in a virtual environment and is the only vehicle through which individuals can create an on-line context. Consequently, on-line text carries a heavier burden than off-line language in sustaining individual identities.

As Markham found, many individuals in her study conceptualized CMC as a "*way of being*", emphasizing how they and others were able to express self through text, talking of experiences "*in* or *as* the text" (1998: 85). The example of "virtual rape" can be understood from this perspective, where text is the sustaining force behind the "body's" identity on-line, and where "physical" performances are expressed textually (Mackinnon, 1997a). When, in the case of "virtual rape" described by Dibble (1993: 240), the assailant Mr Bungle forced his victim to "eat his/her own pubic hair" by typing in a detailed description of the process in real time, the textual act bore a two-fold performance; the act of "eating pubic hair" occurred at the same time as the assailant's utterance. Virtual perceptions of time and environment (where what is said often has no temporal lag to what is done) mean that such textual performances have immediate consequences. Such a burden and reliance on text arguably leaves it susceptible to misuse, being employed as an effective vehicle for derision.

If this act of "virtual rape" were to occur in the actual environment in a verbal or a printed form the consequences would possibly be less harmful. Arguably, individuals are more ontologically secure in the off-line world in comparison to those on-line whose identities are made vulnerable through an over-reliance on text (Turkle, 1995). In order to understand why acts of textual violence lack illocutionary force outside of the on-line environment, two of the three requirements needed for a successful injurious illocution can be drawn upon. The initial success of any kind of illocution depends on what Austin called "securing uptake" (1975: 118). This process is best explicated by a reciprocal process between two interlocutors. For example, once A utters a potentially injurious illocution to B, the object of potential derision, B, must be open to the idea that A might be telling B what in fact she means to tell him/her. At first thought one might assume that a verbal expression of "virtual rape" in the off-line world would be possible if the criteria of reciprocity were met between two interlocutors, essentially the offender and the victim. Indeed, a harassing telephone call ensures reciprocity by evoking a convention between the caller and the called. The called performs the convention by greeting the caller, who proceeds to deliver a verbal account of "virtual rape", whereupon the called understands that they are subject to a harassing telephone call. If the victim decides not to continue with the exchange, reciprocity can be severed by a refusal to respond or by responding in an unconventional manner. However, the argument made here is that such an exchange differs from the second type of textual illocution on-line, in that the effects are likely to be less harmful. The on-line illocution is able to involve and invade the potential victim to a greater extent due to their over-reliance on text as the sustaining force behind their identity. While vocalized language has the role of sustaining the body in the harassing telephone call, the burden on verbalized language is less. Essentially, while reciprocity between two interlocutors off-line can be secured in order to perform a "virtual rape", the absence of the on-line context reduces the illocutionary force to harm.

To reiterate, the role that convention has in securing uptake has already been detailed (e.g., the statement "I do" in the wedding ceremony), yet neither convention nor reciprocity can account for the success of an illocutionary performance alone. When an injurious illocution is delivered, there must be a conducive context. Taking the above example, it is noted that the second type of illocution found in the virtual arena could not secure a successful uptake in other off-line settings. This is precisely because the illocution would be used in a non-conducive context – the convention of text as description, emotion and action within the on-line environment allows for the mechanical reproduction of physical violence in text, but the same cannot be done off-line, as the conventions and contexts do not apply. In his performance of "virtual rape" on-line Mr Bungle further secured a conducive social context by his unmistakable entrance to the community described in text as "A fat, oleaginous, Bisquick-faced clown dressed in cum-stained harlequin garb and girdled with a mistletoe-and-hemlock belt whose buckle bore the quaint inscription 'KISS ME UNDER THIS YOU BITCH!'" (Dibble, 1993: 239). The assailant's intentions were made clear from the outset, with the creation of a sexually oppressive and insidious social context. To clarify, an example of a non-conducive context in the off-line world might be a judge saying "I sentence you to life imprisonment" outside of the courtroom. The object of the illocution would clearly question the utterance and hence both reciprocity and uptake would be at fault, creating an unsuccessful illocution.

The final ingredient to a successful illocution is subordination. The feminist claim that the female voice has gone unheard, overshadowed by male dominance and its replication in language, highlights the way in which powerful groups in a community determine the scope of reciprocity and hence restrict the illocutionary potential of certain groups. This is not to say these groups cannot literally be heard; it is more the case that they can do less with speech than others, they are lacking certain ingredients to secure successful illocution. The same perspective can be applied to the successful uptake of injurious illocutions; someone who is in a privileged position within a language/social hierarchy is able to subordinate another with more success. The use of racist slurs against Afro-Caribbeans or Asians by a white individual would have a more forceful illocutionary effect than another Afro-Caribbean or Asian person using similar language. This is supported by the adoption of once-insulting words by these subordinate groups, for example the use of "queer" in friendly exchanges between gay males. Further, research into the emotion humiliation, a possible harm of an injurious illocution, indicates subordination as a precursor to harm. According to Klein (1991), humiliation occurs within relationships of unequal status where the humiliator dominates the victim. Humiliation or injurious illocution is essentially the practice of social control, where an individual's sense of identity is undermined (Silver *et al.*, 1986).

The manifestation of subordination and hierarchy within the on-line environment calls for a revaluation of the mechanics behind the illocutionary act. Both on- and off-line personae harbour differing power relations for the individual, akin to Goffman's (1971) multiple selves; individuals have the opportunity to carry out two distinct lives, both with differing social relations. The question here is what self does a potential illocution draw its power from when performed within the virtual environment. At first thought we might assume it to be the on-line persona, but one cannot ignore the reciprocal relationship between the real and the virtual, identifying that each influences the other. So, in the case of textual insults, it becomes less obvious who is delivering and who is the object of the attempted illocution. However, status relations are more apparent in the second type of illocution on-line. During his act of virtual rape, Mr Bungle harboured a unique kind of power that enabled a successful injurious illocution. His knowledge of the technical aspects of the on-line community allowed him to control and deliver injurious illocutions while his victims were immobilized; arguably, without this technological power, the objects of his derision may have silenced his illocutions as power relations would have been equalized. With his grotesque entrance, Mr Bungle secured uptake by ensuring reciprocity, his esoteric technical knowledge allowed for both the physical and the social control of his victims, while the context of the environment ensured that Mr Bungle's textual performances were effective in victimizing the objects of his derision.

Misfires

Mentioned earlier was the possibility for illocutionary text/speech performances to fail in their attempts at derision. Matsuda *et al.*'s (1993) argument presumed that a social or hierarchical structure is enunciated at the moment of a hateful utterance. It is an assumption, then, that the social structure remains constant. It is at this point that an important issue must be raised in relation to Matsuda *et al.*'s argument. In the analysis of hateful speech Matsuda *et al.* seem to refer only to subordination within a social or hierarchical structure. This chapter puts forward the argument that any kind of subordination that relies on language is not only a social subordination but also a linguistic one. The language system is responsible for creating the social system, through which subordination is possible, thus any kind of subordination through language is two-fold, on both the linguistic and the social plane. In order for a hateful utterance to be effective in subordinating its target, a social or language system would have to remain intact and unchanged. However, Matsuda *et al.*'s claim is open to question; as social and language structures are sensitive to temporal shifts and changes, an expression of a potentially injurious illocution is prone to "misfire". It is clear that Matsuda *et al.* take a synchronic worldview of both the language and the social system. Indeed they may be correct in thinking that one can only understand a language system by looking at it in temporal stasis, and many Saussurian linguists would agree. Matsuda *et al.*, within a synchronic paradigm, are then interested more in the *form* that hateful speech can take. Yet it is advanced that a fuller explanation of derisory speech acts can develop from a diachronic analysis – an investigation that also examines *substance* in language.

Linguists who take a diachronic stance provide explanations as to how and why language systems are subject to temporal forces. Issues of "closure" within the work of discourse studies have exemplified the preoccupation with the limits of a linguistic "system" (see Laclau, 1996). Common examples of how the meaning of words can change over time highlight the shifting nature of these "systems". The terms "awful" and "gay" have obviously been subject to re-signification ("awful" at one time denoted one's positive awe or wonder towards an object or action). Similarly, the act of "talking back" shows how those who are the subject of victimization can call into operation the language system and take the opportunity to "fight back". The revaluation of the term "queer" suggests that derisory speech can be turned back to the addressee in a different form. In essence, the re-signified term allows for a reversal of effects, and points to the flexibility of power in terms of speech acts that have an origin and end (in terms of meaning) that remain unfixed and unfixable (Butler, 1997). Parallels can be drawn here between the arbitrariness of the sign – that the signifier and the signified have no solid or relational bond – and the arbitrariness of the derisory speech act – that what is said and the meaning have no necessary bond or consequence. This loosening of the link between act and injury opens up the possibility for counter-speech, as exemplified above. This way of theorizing has certain consequences for the mediation of on-line deviance. With the current paucity of legal remedies to aid the mediation of hate-speech on-line, and the reluctance shown by some on-line communities towards "external" interference (Mackinnon, 1997b), other non-legalistic forms may be required to reconsolidate "inappropriate" behaviour.

Social practices and remedies have to be put into place that ensure the possibility of counter-speech, along with other technical mechanisms such as social ostracism. Examples of counter-speech have been seen in the mediation of "virtual rape". After the failed efforts of technological mediation (e.g., physical ostracism from the community) in the case of Mr Bungle, textual methods were employed which aimed to disempower his actions. These textual performances involved the community "shunning" the assailant and ultimately "shaming" him. These acts, which were textually and socially performative, secured the social ostracism of the offender. Similar instances of vigilante justice have emerged in other cases of sexual harassment on-line. Reid (1999) recounts an instance of "virtual rape" in the Multi-User Domain (MUD) named

JennyMUSH, an environment created for the purpose of counselling women who had suffered off-line sexual abuse. The harasser taunted and verbally abused several of the on-line visitors, while performing acts of sexual violence through text. Given the nature of the environment, the assailant's actions were considered exceptionally harmful. Members of the community were encouraged to textually harass the assailant in an attempt to deliver punishment. Female sexual victimization seems even to have permeated the safe haven of the virtual arena, where perpetrators invade the sanctity of the home and cause unprecedented levels of harm to their victims.

Illocution and harm

The effects of injurious hate-speech off-line have been well documented. Richard Delgado (1993) remarks in *Words that Wound* that immediate mental or emotional distress is the most obvious direct harm caused by a racial insult. Without question, "mere words, whether racial or otherwise, can cause mental, emotional or even physical harm to their target, especially if delivered in front of others or by a person of authority". Delgado is so emphatic on this point that he continues: "the need for legal redress for victims also is underscored by the fact that racial insults are intentional acts" (1993: 94). As already mentioned, humiliation may be an intentional outcome of an injurious illocution. For the purposes of clarity, humiliation is defined as "the deep dysphoric feeling associated with being, or perceiving oneself as being, unjustly degraded, ridiculed, or put down – in particular, one's identity has been demeaned or devalued" (Hartling and Luchetta, 1999: 264). The debilitating effects associated with humiliation, such as social and physical withdrawal, behavioural constriction and isolation, further indicate the harmful nature of some verbal attacks. There are further similarities between the deconstituting effects of injurious illocutions and experiences of disconnection, an associated outcome of humiliation, which can have "profound and negative consequences" on an individual's identity (Hartling and Luchetta, 1999: 261). While it is clear that injurious illocutions can harm individuals, the unintentional effects on the wider community are less well documented. In the context of humiliation and similar emotions such as embarrassment and shame, those who witness the injurious illocution, while escaping the direct harm caused, may become anxious and adopt avoidance behaviour within the community. Even those who deliver the injurious illocution may develop a fear of humiliation and associated emotions (Klein, 1991). In sum, it is believed that certain forms of insults, delivered in a conducive context by an authoritative individual, can not only harm in similar ways to physical acts, but can also have a debilitating effect on the community as a whole.

How these harms manifest within an on-line environment is a key question if forms of on-line injurious speech and textual expressions of violence are to be fully acknowledged. Individuals who use CMC often express themselves through "on-line personae" (Turkle, 1995). The construction of on-line personae and the psychological attachment an individual has to their "virtual self" become important questions when assessing the risk of harm and victimization on-line. At what "self" an injurious illocution is aimed (the on-line persona or the off-line self) might at first seem an important consideration. When Legba was sexually assaulted by Mr Bungle, it was the on-line persona that was victimized and "physically" assaulted through text. However, the psychological effects and harms were experienced by the creator of Legba's persona (Dibble, 1993). It seems clear that any injurious illocution on-line strikes at the identity of the computer user in the off-line world. The anonymity of an on-line persona or its difference from the off-line self that created it are nullified in face of deconstituting and debilitating textual acts. Successful injurious illocutions within a textual environment (those that secure context, reciprocity and subordination) can harm with an effective degree of force to mirror that of off-line successful injurious illocutions. Essentially, the accepted convention of text within the on-line environment leaves individuals (both on-line and off-line personae) susceptible to harm. The permanence and visibility of text within "chat" constantly reminds those who were injured of the act, which gives a certain longevity to injurious text.

If it is accepted that on-line injurious illocutions can harm in similar ways to off-line abusive speech, might textual performances of sexual violence increase the levels of harm experienced? The second type of injurious illocution, which allows for physical violence to be represented in text, may harbour the capacity to harm in ways associated with violence in the off-line world. The re-engineering of physical acts of deviance into textual performances on-line herald a new and unprecedented form of deviance. These acts not only take the form of sexual abuse but also of more general attacks, and combine not only the effects of conventional injurious illocutions but also aspects of the psychological trauma induced by physical abuse. Synchronous forms of on-line communication, especially those characterized by subversive sexual discourses, open themselves up to be used as effective vehicles for injurious speech, where the harm induced is yet to be fully understood or acknowledged.

Forms of redress

Given the non-reporting and non-recording of computer-related crime by the police, our understanding of when and where "it" occurs is very limited. Clearly the prevalence of "serious" injurious text on-line is unknown. While there are organizations who aim to monitor incidents of hate-speech and the like on-line, their efforts seem fruitless due to the non-regulatory nature of the Internet. Further, those who have been victimized on-line may not think it a crime and hence would fail to report such an incident to any authority, even if they knew what authority to report it to in the first instance. Yet this cannot mean that these acts, however prevalent, can be ignored. Even one case of sexual, racial or homophobic abuse on-line, if serious enough in its effects, should be acknowledged in some part of legal redress. Kent Greenwalt (1989), in *Speech, Crime &*

the Uses of Language states that any analysis of the law in regard to abusive speech off-line has to consider the extent to which this language has expressive value. He considers four criteria that might make such expressions criminal:

1 that they might provoke a response of violence;
2 that they may deeply wound those at whom the speech is directed;
3 that such speech causes offence to those that hear it; and
4 that slurs and epithets have a degrading effect on social relationships within any one community.

However, grading each of these criteria on what is and is not acceptable discourse is exceptionally difficult – one cannot reproduce the intonations and other verbal expressions at the time of the incident.

Yet there are some forms of legal redress for abusive acts off-line. In the US, for example, redress may be available under vague disorderly conduct or breach-of-the-peace provisions, where the main source of civil recovery may be the relatively novel tort of intentional infliction of mental or emotional distress. Further, with regard to Greenwalt's first criteria, the "fighting words" doctrine established in *Chaplinsky v New Hampshire* (1942) prohibits someone being called an "offensive name" in a public place, "offensive" being construed by the state court as an expression that "men of common intelligence would understand would be likely to cause an average addressee to fight". In the UK, provision may come under defamation laws or the enactment under of the Public Order Act of 1986 that states "A person who uses threatening, abusive or insulting words or behaviour, or displays any written material which is threatening, abusive or insulting is guilty...if (a) he intends thereby to stir up racial hatred, or (b) having regard to all the circumstances racial hatred is likely to he stirred up thereby". However, the key question is, how applicable are these laws to the on-line setting? If we can identify that on-line injurious speech can be as harmful as off-line abusive speech, then surely these forms of redress should be made applicable. While there are several cases running in the US regarding instances of abusive speech on-line, it seems as if the legal provisions are still vague. Davis makes clear the decision that lies ahead:

> Despite the novelty of..."cyber-actions", courts face the age-old question of deciding whether to develop a new body of jurisprudence to deal with a novel legal problem, or to identify analogous legal precedents that best fit the facts at bar.
>
> (Davis, 2000: 44)

However, it seems unlikely that any current form of legislation could be adapted to deal with acts of the second type of illocution mentioned, those which re-engineer physical violence into textual performances. Recognizing the level of harm induced by such acts seems the first milestone to overcome. Maybe an answer lies in other quasi-legal methods of mediation on-line, where communities have their own mechanisms for redress. The opportunities to "fight back" through counter-speech may serve to prevent and/or mediate certain textual attacks on-line. However, this process of vigilante justice may have similar effects on the community as injurious illocutions themselves; by encouraging community members to taunt and abuse other members, hatred and derisory performances are given a free and legitimate reign, encouraging a lack of trust and interdependence. Without these, a community can become fragmented where members grow ever more anxious over the possibilities of victimization and the eventual demise of their on-line environment. Where the technology that sustains an on-line community is subverted for illicit purposes, such as immobilizing victims, the owners of the technology might develop preventive measures, bypassing legal remedies. Ensuring higher levels of network security, and incorporating automated functions that can identify forms of abusive speech and alert relevant on- or off-line authorities, would further reduce levels of harm and legal involvement.

Conclusion

Prevalence, dispersion and frequency are the unknown factors of abusive speech on-line. Even the taxonomy of injurious textual acts is in a state of constant flux, dependent upon legal, social and political rationalizations. What is known, however, is that most forms of abuse on-line manifest textually. Their force to harm is dependent upon the context of the utterance, a reciprocity between inter-locutors and differing power relations, and that they draw on analogous verbal and physical acts from off-line settings. The notion that "real" and "virtual" phenomena are inexorably connected indicates that these on-line abusive acts affect "actual" lives. The ability for on-line injurious illocutions to convey phys-ical violence in text affords them "extra-performative muscle", where "traditional" forms of violence are re-engineered to function on-line. The individual's reliance upon text on-line to sustain an identity makes it vulnerable to such attacks, resulting in levels of harm that may have psychological repercussions that outweigh the consequences of off-line verbal abuse. In acknowledging these harms, forms of redress must be instituted if basic human rights are to be upheld. Yet, before any regulatory body can develop an appropriate reaction to on-line abusive text, the likelihood and level of harm from differing acts on-line must be delineated. In providing a classification of injurious illocutions on-line, drawing a line between less harmful textual slurs and more damaging acts of textual violence, this chapter acknowledges how harms on-line may vary in severity, and that any form of redress should reflect such difference.

References

Cases
California State v Reliability Research, Inc., 631 F. Supp. 1356 (C.D. Cal. 1986).
Chaplinsky v New Hampshire, No. 225, 315 U.S. 568, (1942).
Cubby v Compuserve, Inc.,776 F. Supp. 135, 138 (S.D.N.Y. 1991).
Stratton Oakmont, Inc. v Prodigy Services Co., No. 94–31063 (N.Y. 1995).

Texts

Althusser, L. (1971) "Ideology and ideological State Apparatuses", in B. Bruster (ed.), *Lenin and Philosophy*, London: Monthly Review Press.

Austin, J.L. (1975) *How to do Things With Words*, Cambridge, Mass.: Harvard University Press.

Baudrillard, J. (1998) *Selected Writings*, Cambridge: Polity.

Becker, P.J., Byers, B. and Jipson, A. (2000) "The Contentious American Debate: The First Amendment and Internet-based Hate Speech", *International Review of Law Computers & Technology*, 14, 1: 33–41.

Butler, J. (1997) *Excitable Speech: A Politics of the Performative*, London: Routledge.

Davis, C.N. (2000) "Personal Jurisdiction in On-line Expression Cases: rejecting Minimum Contacts in Favour of Affirmative Acts", *International Review of Law, Computers and Technology*, 14, 1: 43–54.

Delgado, R. (1993) "Words that Wound: A Tort Action for Racial Insults", in M.J Matsuda *et al.* (eds), *Words That Wound: Critical Race Theory, Assaultive Speech, and the First Amendment*, Boulder, Col.: Westview Press.

Denning, D. (1995) "Crime and Crypto on the Information Superhighway", *Journal of Criminal Justice Education*, 6, 2: 323–36.

Dibbell, J. (1993) "A Rape in Cyberspace; or, How an Evil Clown, a Haitian Trickster Spirit, Two Wizards, and a cast of Dozens Turned a Database into a Society", *The Village Voice*, available at www.levity.com/julian/bungle.html (accessed 1 August 2000).

Goffman, E. (1971) *The Presentation of Self in Everyday Life*, Harmondsworth: Penguin.

Greenwalt, K. (1989) *Speech Crime & The Uses of Language*, New York: Oxford University Press.

Hartling, L.M. and Luchetta, T. (1999) "Humiliation: Assessing the impact of Derision, Degradation, and Debasement", *The Journal of Primary Prevention*, 19, 4: 259–78.

Holland, K. (1995) "Bank Fraud, The Old fashioned Way", *Business Week*, 4, September: 88.

Jameson, F. (1991) *Postmodernism, or, The Cultural Logic of Late Capitalism*, London: Verso.

Kaspersen, H. (1998) "Fraud in Relation to EFT and Telebanking/Teleshopping Systems and Applicability of Criminal Law", in Y. Poullet and G. Vandenberghe, *Telebanking, Teleshopping and the Law*, Dordrecht: Kluwer.

Klein, D.C. (1991) "The Humiliation Dynamic: An Overview", *Journal of Primary Prevention*, 12, 2: 93–121.

Laclau, E. (1996) "Why Do Empty Signifiers Matter to Politics?", in E. Leclau, *Emancipation(s)*, London: Verso.

Lawrence III, C.R. (1993) "If He Hollers Let Him Go: Regulating Racist Speech on Campus", in M.J Matsuda *et al.* (eds), *Words That Wound: Critical Race Theory, Assaultive Speech, and the First Amendment*, Boulder, Col.: Westview Press.

Mackinnon, R.C. (1997a) "Punishing the Persona: Correctional Strategies for the Virtual Offender", in S. Jones (ed.), *Virtual Cultures: Identity and Communication in Cybersociety*, London: Sage.

Mackinnon, R.C. (1997b) "Virtual Rape", *Journal of Computer Mediated Communication*, 2, 4; available at www.ascusc.org/jcmc/vol2/issue4/mackinnon.html (checked 6 August 2000).

Mann, D. and Sutton, M. (1998) "Netcrime: More Change in the Organisation of Thieving", *British Journal of Criminology*, 38, 2: 210–29.

Mann, D. and Tuffin, R. (2000) *Conflict on the Net: a study of racism in Internet newsgroups*, paper presented at the British Society of Criminology Conference, Leicester University.

Markham, A. (1998) *Life On-line: Researching Real Experience in Virtual Space*, California: Sage.

Matsuda, M.J., Lawrence, C.R., Delgado, R. and Crenshaw, K.W. (1993) *Words That Wound: Critical Race Theory, Assaultive Speech, and the First Amendment*, Boulder, Col.: Westview Press.

Miller, D. and Slater, D. (2000) *The Internet: An Ethnographic Approach*, Oxford: Berg.

Neumann, P. (1995) *Computer Related Risks*, Reading, Mass.: Addison-Wesley.

O'Connell, R. (2000) *Through the Looking Glass: a perspective of child sex iconography in cyberspace*, paper presented at the British Society of Criminology Conference, Leicester University.

Reid, E. (1999) "Hierarchy and Power: Social Control in Cyberspace", in P. Kollock and A. Smith (eds), *Communities in Cyberspace*, London: Routledge.

Silver, M., Conte, R., Miceli, M. and Poggi, I. (1986) "Humiliation: Feeling, Social Control and the Construction of Identity", *Journal for the Theory of Social Behaviour*, 16, 3: 269–83.

Sternberg, J. (1998) *It's All in the Timing: Synchronous Versus Asynchronous Computer-Mediated Communication*, paper presented at the New Jersey Communication Association Annual Conference, Montclair, NJ.

Turkle, S. (1995) *Life on Screen: Identity in the Age of the Internet*, London: Weidenfeld and Nicholson.

Whine, M. (2000) "Far Right Extremists on the Net", in D. Thomas and B. Loader (eds), *Cybercrime: Law Enforcement, Security and Surveillance in the Information Age*, London: Routledge.

Williams, M. (2000) "Virtually Criminal: Discourse, Deviance and Anxiety within Virtual Communities", *International Review of Law Computers and Technology*, 14, 1: 95–104.

11 Maintaining order and law on the Internet[1]

David Wall

Introduction

As we come to terms with the Internet, it is now quite clear that it is revolutionizing many aspects of our "social" life. Unfortunately this includes criminal activity (see Chapters 1 and 2). Yet the anarchy that was predicted by those who favoured early regulation[2] has not materialized, and the cyberspace[3] which has been created by the Internet is remarkably ordered considering its sheer size in terms of the large numbers of individuals involved and also the breadth of their involvement (Davies, 1998). So, we either have a case of exaggerated claims, or there is some mechanism that is already operating to create and maintain a sense of order in cyberspace. In fact, it will be suggested later in this chapter that the answer is a combination of both positions. Some claims have clearly been exaggerated, but we can also observe a structure of governance which has emerged to encourage order. But it is with this duality in mind that this chapter will explore the policing[4] of cyberspace, particularly the issue of order maintenance on the Internet. Much of the debate over law and order on the Internet has focused upon the issue of enforcing law and investigating crimes; this emphasis largely ignores one of the primary functions of policing which is the maintenance of order. In fact the terms "order" and "law" have been deliberately reversed in the title and elsewhere, so as to break the conceptual link that has increasingly bound the two concepts since the late 1970s (see further, Fowles, 1993: 116; Wall, 2000). Clearly the policing of the Internet is about more than just simply enforcing the law; rather, it is about regulating the behaviour of Internet users "in the shadow of law" (Wall, 2000).

By engaging the issue at the point where the debate over policing the Internet shifts from legal regulation to the broader issue of governance, the chapter will also seek to establish exactly who is regulating the behaviour of whom (and how) within the power-play that is currently taking place to control cyberspace. It will be argued that the Internet is regulable at a number of different levels because of a number of important factors which shape it. Furthermore, a system of multi-tiered policing has already developed within cyberspace which provides the basis for further developments in the policing of the medium. However, of particular importance is the view that any future developments should include a framework of accountability that would incorporate a series of checks and balances to protect civil liberties against the expression of various political, moral and commercial power interests that are currently vying for control over cyberspace.

The first part of this chapter will revisit briefly some of the points made in Chapter 1 about the problems that can arise in understanding the impact of cybercrimes. The second part will look at regulation and the issue of order and law on the Internet. The third part identifies current models and mechanisms for policing the Internet. The fourth part discusses the future(s) of policing the Internet. The fifth part concludes.

Understanding the impact of cybercrimes

It was established in Chapter 1 that there is broad agreement that cybercrimes exist, but few commentators actually agree as to what they are, and therefore the need exists for a more comprehensive understanding of them. This understanding can be achieved by discerning between different levels, and types, of impact. Thus, the Internet can be seen to have impacted upon human activities in three main ways (Wall, 2000). First, it has acted as a vehicle for the further facilitation of existing criminal activities.[5] Second, it has created new opportunities for existing types of crime; and third, it has facilitated the creation of entirely new types of activity[6] which are largely free of traditional and terrestrial constraints.[7]

Next, instead of making hard and fast classifications that become quickly outdated by techno-social change, four generic groups of offences were identified which are the focus of public concern: trespass, theft, obscenity and violence. Analysis of cybercrimes in terms of these generic areas is arguably more useful than lumping activities, such as fraud, hacking, espionage and theft of intellectual property, under the banner of economic crimes – as was the case, for example, in the EU report on legal aspects of computer-related crime (Seiber, 1998). This is particularly so when some of the acts mentioned do not necessarily involve a financial motive. Each type, or group, for example, demonstrate quite different "modalities of constraint" (Lessig, 1999) which affect their regulability and which render inadequate attempts to aggregate cybercrimes for the purpose of policy formation. In other words, each type of cyberbehaviour requires a different strategic response towards it, and therefore has a different implication for policing.

The four-fold grouping not only demonstrates the contested nature of the general term "cybercrime", and particularly the problems of identifying causality, but it also shifts the focus of enquiry away from media sensitization back to existing knowledge bases in the shape of relevant bodies of law, public debates and also literature. Criminologists can therefore draw upon a range of criminologies to inform research into cybercrimes. So, for example, whilst it will be some time before a comprehensive sociology of cybervictimizations can be researched, because most of the current discussion tends to focus upon the behaviours rather than victim or offender, the literature on white-collar victimization (see, *inter alia*, Sutherland, 1949; Zedner, 1997: 593; Box, 1983: 17; Levi and Pithouse, 2001) provides a steer. It tells us, for example, that we can anticipate that victims of cybercrime will vary in terms of their status, level of victimization and group collectivity, and will range from individuals to corporate bodies to whole societies. Moreover, the (cyber)harms done to them will range from the actual to the felt. In some cases there is no primary victim, as many victims of cybercrimes are secondary, or indirect; for example, as with cyberpiracy or cyberspying/terrorism. In other cases, such as cyberstalking or the theft of cybercash, the victimization is directed towards the individual. Furthermore, like the reporting of white-collar crimes, it is likely that many victims of cybercrime may be unwilling to acknowledge that they have been a victim, or it may take them some time to realize it. Alternatively, where the victimization has been imputed by a third party upon the basis of an ideological, political, moral or commercial assessment of risk, the victim or victim group may simply be unaware that they have been victimized, or even believe that they have not been. This can be the case with the various forms of pornography and hate-speech.

Order and law on the Internet

One of the great misunderstandings about the Internet is that it cannot be regulated and it is therefore lawless, thus it is wrongly assumed that Internet users immediately go on some sort of moral holiday when they enter cyberspace. Such misunderstandings arise from, on the one hand, the trans-jurisdictional and instantaneous characteristics of the Internet, and on the other hand the "flux" in expectations generated by the ongoing debate over the control of cyberspace which has corresponded with the widespread realization of its increased potential for commercial and political exploitation. When combined with media sensitization, these factors combine to (mis)shape public understandings about the Internet.

Initiatives to exercise control over the Internet have tended to come either from the state or the commercial sector, which seek to establish monopoly control over areas which are currently in the public domain of cyberspace. Thus, groups which currently have access to cyberspace are being evaluated, either in terms of their potential threat to established commercial or political interests, or in terms of their potential opposition to new interests. Consequently, we see the labelling of specific groups in terms of their risk, rather than in terms of their benefits.

It is against this political (with a small "p") backdrop that the behaviours of these groups are increasingly being defined, or redefined, as cybercrimes. Such definitions can either be *de jure* cybercrimes through their inclusion within the penal or civil codes, or they can become *de facto* cybercrimes because of the "chilling effect" of moral censure or market pressure that public debate can impose upon individual behaviour. However, whilst the Internet is not without its crime problems, then neither it is a lawless frontier. The Internet is certainly a site of new opportunities (see Chapter 2), and through those opportunities arise not only entrepreneurial but also criminal behaviour. But given the sheer size, user numbers and overall complexity of Internet activity, the Internet is still remarkably ordered. So that we may understand this order we must look at some of the theoretical positions that have been posited with regard to Internet regulation (see Greenleaf, 1998).

Reidenberg (1998), for example, argues that technological architectures of networks automatically generate sets of rules which restrict choice. Johnson and Post (1996) make the counter-argument to Reidenberg, claiming that rule formation occurs through "decentralised, emergent law". The Internet therefore becomes subject to *de facto* rules which result from "the complex interplay of individual decisions" – normative behaviour. These two positions are not dissimilar to the contrast that Bourdieu draws between "field" and "habitus" (Bourdieu, 1977).

Whilst Bourdieu's dichotomy has been much used and abused in criminological and sociological literature over the years, it does usefully signify the strategic direction of discourses. At the risk of over-simplification, technology and/or law can shape the "field", or structural conditions, of cyberspace within which behaviours are expressed. Control over the "field" could therefore be effected either by designing in crime-prevention in order to design out crime, or by increasing levels of security through advanced technological countermeasures. In both cases, crime prevention is primarily achieved by technological means. Alternativeley, the legal compliance model seeks to control the "field" through law. This perspective contrasts with a second perspective, which emphasizes the importance of influencing, normative structures – the "habitus" – by informing individuals and social groupings of the range of choices they have. Here, strategies would either seek to demystify the rhetoric surrounding cybercrime in order to facilitate organizational understanding and learning, or, through open knowledge networks, enlighten users to be more responsible in their patterns of Internet usage.

Bourdieu's dichotomy is a useful mnemonic for illustrating the direction of discourses, but it does not clearly define the nature of the relationship between the two positions. In the debate over the regulation, or regulability, of cyberspace, Lessig (1998, 1999) has provided one of the more coherent linkages which resolves the contradictions between, on the one hand, the "determinist" legal compliance model which assumes that behaviour can be modified simply by changing law, and the "anti-law" school which develops the claims made by Foucault (1978: 144; see also Valier, 2001) that the law itself increasingly comes to operate as a norm rather than as an authority.

Lessig has identified four different "modalities of constraint" which facilitate regulation: architecture, law, social norms and market. First, the law defines desirable and undesirable behaviours and practices. Second, the Internet has a discernible architecture that is constructed of codes and protocols (see, further, Walker *et al.*, 2000). On the one hand, this architecture enables users to increase the scope of the Internet, including creating further opportunities to offend. On the other hand, this same architecture can be used to effect a degree of technical control over users. Third are the "social" norms which individuals tend to carry with them to the Internet from the "terrestrial" world, but which might be reshaped once in cyberspace. Finally, "markets" greatly determine behaviours and overall patterns of usage by creating and destroying opportunities.

Lessig argues that law not only directly affects behaviour by prohibiting conduct, but it also indirectly shapes architecture, norms and markets. In effect, echoing Goodrich's (1998) observation that "law remains an object of passionate attachment". Greenleaf (1998) seeks to further develop Lessig's argument, stating that the secret of effective regulation is therefore to regulate the architecture through law, rather than trying to use law directly to regulate behaviour. While there remains some debate over the extent to which laws can affect architecture, norms and market however, what is perfectly clear is that, although laws do not engender complete compliance, they nevertheless "cast their shadow" over normative behaviour, architectures and markets, and it is under this shadow that policing the Internet will take place (Wall, 2000, see also Manning 1987).

If the "digital realism" suggested by Lessig, Greenleaf and others, whereby the combination of law, architecture, norms and markets upon the Internet results in a regulable environment – even if it is one which Grabosky and Smith (1998: 233) argue is both subject to, and the product of, a series of regulatory dilemmas – then where is the evidence of it?

Who is currently policing cyberspace?

It will be demonstrated in this section that there currently exists evidence to show that the Internet is a regulable environment and that a multi-tiered structure of governance already exists in cyberspace to maintain various types and levels of order (Wall, 1998, 2000). Currently there are five main levels at which policing activity takes place within cyberspace: the Internet users themselves; the Internet Service Providers (ISPs); corporate security organizations; state-funded non-public police organizations, and state-funded public police organizations. At each level the organizations or groups involved will also tend to find an expression in transnational forms (Sheptycki, 1998a; 1998b) because of the global nature of the Internet.

Internet users and user groups

The Internet users and user groups comprise the largest group of individuals to be inducted into policing the Internet. Within any user group there may be a number of sub-groups which have formed around specific issues in order to police websites that offend them. Largely transnational in terms of their membership and operation, these groups tend to be self-appointed and possess neither a broad public mandate nor a statutory basis; consequently they lack any formal accountability for their actions – which may themselves be intrusive or even illegal. However, they would seem to possess a fairly potent force, and a number of visible examples of virtual community policing have already occurred. In addition to the various complaint "hotlines" and the development of software to screen out undesirable communications (Uhlig, 1996a), there are a few recorded "netizen" groups which have attempted to organize Internet users. The Internet Rapid Response Team (IRRT), for example, briefly came to prominence when an e-mail message advertising a collection of child pornography, and which carried a New York address, was received by thousands of Internet users all over the world (Uhlig, 1996a). IRRT's response was to "spam" the New York Police with calls for an immediate investigation. The IRRT was a voluntary group whose philosophy was that "it is up to Internet users as much as anyone else to react quickly when something like this happens" (Uhlig, 1996a). (N.B. The US Federal Trade Commission later formed the IRRT.)

Perhaps the most well known netizen group which actively polices cyberspace is CyberAngels,[8] a 1000-plus group of Internet users who are organized, as their name suggests, along the Guardian Angel model. Divided into "Internet Safety Patrols", they operate in the four main areas of the Internet: Internet Relay Chat (IRC), Usenet, the World Wide Web (WWW), and the net services provided by the largest US ISP, America On-line (AOL).[9] Their function is to actively promote, preserve and protect netiquette, which is "the collection of common rules of polite conduct that govern our use of the Internet".[10] Importantly, they claim the right to question what they encounter, and they argue that they have a civil, legal and human right to bring it to the attention of the proper authorities.[11] Their mission statement says that they are dedicated to fighting crime on the Internet "where there are clear victims and/or at-risk users"; they seek to protect children from on-line criminal abuse; they give support to on-line victims and advise them upon how to seek a remedy; and they seek out materials that will cause harm, fear, distress, inconvenience, offence or concern, "regardless of whether it is criminal or not".[12]

Groups like the IRRT and CyberAngels perform a broad-ranging policing function, but other groups of netizens dedicate themselves to specific types of cyberharm, the most common being child pornography. Phreakers & Hackers (UK) Against Child Porn (PH(UK)ACP),[13] for example, claim not to be vigilantes, but aim to track down offensive sites and interfere with their operation. A similar group is Ethical Hackers Against Porn (EHAP)[14] who, like PH(UK)ACP, "want to stop child exploitation" and claim to work in loose cooperation with government and local officials, even though they admit to "using unconventional means to take down the worst, most unscrupulous criminals known". Of course it is impossible to know whether or not these claims are actually fulfilled.

Among the most interesting alliances that currently exist with regard to the issue of child pornography on the Internet are the coalitions of "mainstream" adult sites who wish to distance themselves from the issue, but who also seek to legitimize their own activities and thus report offending websites. Adult Sites Against Child Pornography (ASACP), for example,[15] claims to have over 700 members and represents more than 300 adult websites.

Internet Service Providers (ISPs)

The ISPs have a rather fluid status which arises from the fact that, although they are physically located in a particular jurisdiction, they tend to function in a transnational way. The moral panic (Cohen, 1972; Chandler, 1996: 229) surrounding the Internet during the mid-1990s over the perceived threat of widespread pornography, and the subsequent threats of legal action (Uhlig, 1996b), have forced ISPs to consider the possibility of controlling some of the activities that are taking place on their servers – most especially the Usenet newsgroups. In August 1996, the UK's then Science and Technology Minister warned that "in the absence of self-regulation, the police will inevitably move to act against service providers as well as the originators of illegal material" (Uhlig, 1996b). This statement was quickly followed by a letter sent to ISPs by the Metropolitan Police Force's Clubs and Vice Unit, warning that they could be liable for any illegal materials that were found to have been disseminated on their servers.[16] Their response in September 1996 was to promote SafetyNet, a mix of self-ratings, classification, user control and public reporting plus law enforcement action (Grossman, 1996; Arthur, 1996). SafetyNet was jointly endorsed by the Metropolitan Police, the Department of Trade and Industry (DTI), the Home Office and the ISPs' own associations; the Internet Service Providers Association and the London Internet Exchange (Uhlig, 1996c). In December 1996, SafetyNet became the Internet Watch Foundation (Tendler, 1996). Since its formation, the standing of the Internet Watch Foundation (IWF) has increased and it has become the quasi-public face of Internet regulation in the UK. One of its functions is to overview the use of the Internet and bring to the attention of ISPs any illegal materials that are reported to its hotline. Between December 1996 and November 1997 the IWF received 781 reports, mostly by e-mail, which covered 4,324 items (mostly on newsgroups). Action was taken with regard to 248 reports, and the great majority, 85 per cent, were related to child pornography, the eradication of which is one of the objectives of the Foundation.[17]

The IWF has a mandate from both the ISPs and the UK government, but it has been argued that the IWF does not command a defined body of public support as its Internet rating system has had very little public discussion.[18] However, it is probably the case that, were the IWF to canvass public opinion over issues such as child pornography, public support would be considerable. Of further concern is the fact that the IWF retains the status of being a private organization with a very public function and, as such, lacks the structures of accountability that are normally associated with organizations with a public function.

Although the legal status of ISPs as publishers is now quite widely acknowledged, their liabilities vary under different bodies of law and have yet to be fully established (see Edwards and Wealde, 2000; Lloyd, 2000; Rowland and Macdonald, 1997). However, cases such as *Godfrey v Demon Internet Ltd.* (1999) and *League Against Racism and anti-Semitism and The Union of French Jewish Students v Yahoo Inc. and Yahoo France* (2000) have had a "chilling" effect upon the ISPs. Consequently, ISPs tend to tread fairly carefully and be responsive to requests for cooperation. Not only are they very wary of their potential legal liabilities, it is probably fair to say that they are fearful of any negative publicity which might arise from their not being seen to act responsibly. Interestingly, the police themselves also appear to be fairly uncertain about their general position with regard to the prosecution of ISPs. Whilst they have continued to warn the ISPs about possible prosecution since 1996, none of the promised prosecutions against Internet Service Providers in the UK has been brought. The general rule of thumb that appears to be adopted across many jurisdictions is that liability tends to arise when the ISP fails to remove offensive material, whether it be obscene or defamatory, provided it has been brought to their attention following a complaint (*Somm*, 1998; *Godfrey v Demon Internet Ltd.*, 1999; Leong, 1998; Epic, 1996: 3).

There is a degree to which the ISPs are organized at a transnational level; examples include the Commercial Internet eXchange,[19] the Pan-European Internet Service Providers' Association (EuroISPA)[20] and the Internet Service Providers' Consortium (mainly USA).[21] However, these organizations tend to be more involved with technical/practical and commercial issues that are germane to ISPs than specifically with the self-policing of ISPs.

Corporate security organizations

Following the mass integration of IT within organizational structures since the early 1990s, and also the growth of e-commerce in the late 1990s, the security departments of corporations and other organizations have increasingly sought to protect their own interests and have therefore become involved in policing the Internet. In the grand scheme of things, the collective impact of this group is fairly minor, but if the popularity of e-commerce grows as predicted then it is anticipated that corporate security organizations will become fairly major players in policing the Internet. A major problem lies in assessing their impact, because their overall visibility is low due to the fact that their primary function is to look after their own "private" interests. Corporate security organizations have a rather odd relationship with the public (i.e., state-funded) police because the public criminal justice system does not offer them the model of criminal justice that they want (Wall, 2000: 161). Consequently the police, on the one hand, resent the loss of criminal intelligence, but on the other hand, police resource managers appear quietly happy not to expend scarce resources on costly investigations.

State-funded, non-public police organizations

The next level of policing involves state-funded, non-public police organizations. This loose collection of bodies are not normally perceived as police, nor are they given the title "police".[22] Their role in policing the Internet either tends to be defined by national Internet infrastructure protection policies, or they themselves are constituted to enforce those plans. National infrastructure protection policies vary, and so therefore do the respective organizations under them. Some governments, such as those of Singapore, China, Korea and Vietnam, have actively sought to control their citizens' use of the Internet, either by forcing users to register with governmental monitoring organizations or by directly controlling Internet traffic coming into their countries through government-controlled ISPs (EPIC, 1996; Caden and Lucas, 1996; Standage, 1996).

Within the European Union, each of the constituent countries have their own Internet infrastructure policies; however, "The Draft Convention on Cybercrime" (European Committee on Crime Problems, 2000), for example, seeks to provide what will effectively become an EU-wide Internet infrastructure protection policy. Until the Convention is signed, each country has its own policy and response. Germany, for example, has set up a regulatory agency, the Internet Content Task Force, and has passed new telecommunications laws requiring ISPs to provide a back door so that security forces can read users' electronic mail if necessary.[23] The Internet Content Task Force also has powers to force German ISPs to block access to certain materials, such as the Dutch site xs4all.[24]

In the United States, the National Infrastructure Protection Center (NIPC) has, since 1998, articulated the national infrastructure protection plan which includes the Internet. The NIPC "brings together representatives from U.S. government agencies, state and local governments, and the private sector in a partnership to protect our nation's critical infrastructures" (NIPC, 1998). Prior to the introduction of the NIPC, a number of state-funded, non-public police organizations became involved in policing the Internet. In part, this was inevitable because the trans-jurisdictional nature of Internet traffic involved federal rather than provincial state agencies which did not fit in with the emerging US strategy towards the Internet. The United States Postal Service, for example, was instrumental in investigating offences of pornography in the case of *United States of America v Robert A. Thomas and Carleen Thomas*, after a computer hacker from Tennessee filed a complaint about the contents of a bulletin board containing obscene materials (Byassee, 1997: 205). The case was subsequently investigated by a United States postal inspector. In another incident the US Securities and Exchange Commission, which was "anxious about the spread of cyber-fraud", brought a case against a publicly-traded company for allegedly conducting a fraud through the Internet. The Commission anticipated that it "will be addressing this kind of conduct on the Internet more frequently" in the coming millennium (Pretzlik, 1996).

In addition to involving state-funded, non-public police organizations, the US government have tried, with varying degrees of success, to introduce legal measures and develop technological devices to regulate cyberspace in order to "protect the interests of U.S. industry" (Reno, 1996). Examples include V-chip technology, which is designed to filter out violence or pornography, and the "Clipper Chip", an "escrowed encryption system" that provides the government with codes to unscramble encrypted files (Akdeniz, 1996: 235–61; Post, 1995: 8; Sterling, 1994; Sussman, 1995: 54). Since the impact of many of these measures is also to curb individual freedom of communication, it is therefore not surprising that much of the debate over Internet regulation has revolved around the First Amendment of the United States Constitution, especially during the legal challenge to the Communications Decency Act 1996.[25]

An interesting example of a hybrid state-funded, non-public police organization in the USA is the Computer Emergency Response Team (CERT), based at Carnegie Mellon University in Pittsburgh.[26] Unlike the UK's IWF, CERT is based within a public institution; it appears, however, to be funded mainly by private sources, but like the IWF it has a public function. CERT exists to combat unauthorized access to the Internet, and its programmers log reported break-ins and carry out initial investigations. Where security breaches are found to be too complicated to deal with in-house, they are farmed out to an unofficial "brains trust" (Adams, 1996)[27] and, where an offence is serious and could lead to prosecution, to the relevant public police organizations.

State-funded public police organizations[28]

The final group of organizations which are involved in policing the Internet are the state-funded public police organizations whose formal status allows them to draw upon the democratic mandate of government. They tend to be organized either locally or nationally, depending upon the jurisdiction. However, whilst they tend to be located within the nation state, they are nevertheless joined by a tier of transnational policing organizations, such as Interpol, whose membership requires such formal status.[29]

In the United Kingdom, the public police is mainly organized locally, but there also exist national police organizations that deal with the collection of intelligence and the investigation of more organized crime. Within the local bodies, several specialist individuals or groups of police officers monitor the Internet (Davies, 1998). For example, a computer crime unit was established by the Metropolitan Police and a smaller, but similar, unit was set up by the Greater Manchester Police. Elsewhere, officers in the West Midlands Police and the Metropolitan Police Force's Clubs and Vice Unit have used the Internet to collect intelligence about offences and offenders relating to the types of crime under their particular responsibility. In recent years, many more police forces have either set up their own police units or have entered into strategic alliances with other police forces to provide or buy in such services.

At a national level, the National Criminal Intelligence Service (NCIS)[30] has taken on the responsibility for providing intelligence on serious offences such as child pornography which cross both force and international boundaries. From April 1998, the investigation of such offences came under the auspices of the National Crime Squad (NCS), a role that was previously held by the various regional crime squads. In April 2001, the NCS's National High Tech Crime Unit became operational. Its function ranges from the broader issue of protecting the critical national infrastructure to specific offences such as Internet fraud and paedophilia.

The future(s) of policing the Internet

The creation of specialist police units, whether local or national, raises an interesting question as to whether or not the public police as a whole should integrate the policing of cyberspace within their "regular" functions (Wall, 1997: 223–9). After all, there exists a strong argument to support the view that, since the state-funded public police forces operate within existing (albeit contested) structures of accountability, especially with regard to due process, then they are the ideal organization to police the Internet. However, the following three factors will weigh heavily upon the minds of police policy-makers when deciding upon the level of public police involvement. The first is the fact that public policing now takes place within a managerial environment that, through increased transparency of process and the publication of performance indicators, has raised the public's expectations of the police. The second is that the resources made available to the police are finite and are likely to remain so for the foreseeable future. Third, the role of the state is also shrinking, as more functions and responsibilities shift from central to local government and the public sector (Crawford, 1997).

The likely consequence of these three pressures for the public police and policymakers, is that the public police will not become directly involved in the general "patrolling" of cyberspace, or for that matter in the actual investigation of most cybercrimes, only the very serious cases. However, the public expectations of the police will mean that they will have an increased gatekeeping function, as they will be the first point of contact for members of the public against whom many of the cybercrimes have been committed. Even taking these consequences into account it is likely that much of the remaining responsibility will be shared between the police and the private sector. At present, for example, the indications are that the most prevalent cybercrimes are small-scale frauds related to the use of credit cards over the Internet, the policing of which is jealously guarded by the banks – only the more serious prosecutable cases are brought to the attention of the police.

This brief discussion of the role of the public police model further illustrates the need to exploit and finesse the structures already discussed. What is not clear at this stage is how the multi-tiered "policing" model could be developed further. Here are some thoughts.

On the one hand, the multi-tiered structure provides for the enforcement of law through state-funded public police organizations and some state-funded non-police organizations. But, for reasons articulated earlier, as the police are called upon to deal with more and more complaints from the public about wrongdoing over the Internet so they will have to develop alliances with the other tiers, with regard to service delivery, training and information resources to deal with this influx of complaints.

On the other hand, the multi-tiered structure also encourages the maintenance of order through Internet users, user groups and ISPs, and to some extent state-funded non-police organizations. In addition to exerting pressures to encourage "conformity" – there is the question as to whose conformity is being encouraged – these lower levels of the model also provide mechanisms by which to resolve the more minor disputes. The problem is that these groups operate upon a self-appointed mandate and lack formal and visible structures of accountability. This is an important factor when considering that it is likely that the bulk of the resolution of (mainly minor) behaviours will remain outside the public police organization.

Consequently, one of the main problems to be overcome will be to introduce structures of accountability which ensure that miscarriages of justice, however minor, do not occur and that basic human rights are respected and maintained. It is at this lower level, as is also the case with the criminal justice process writ large, that most miscarriages of justice take place (McBarnet, 1981). This same point was raised by a 1998 report on the legal aspects of computer-related crime (Seiber, 1998; Walker and Akdeniz, 1998), which also went on to argue that for it to be effective there also needed to be in place an infrastructure of international agreements over the boundaries of acceptable and non-acceptable activities which take due account of fundamental civil liberties.

So, the principle of self-policing that is found within the multi-tiered structure is inherently limited in scope and has a fairly low ceiling of efficacy, after which the various higher levels of policing have to be invoked in order to resolve the situations to which self-regulation fails to resolve, does not apply to, or is not applied (Walker, 1997: 28; Wall, 1997: 222). These policing functions become more coherent if the function of order maintenance is disaggregated from law enforcement. They demonstrate that the pluralistic model of policing the Internet described in this chapter combines elements of both public and private models of policing. It not only reflects the increasing plurality of policing in high modernity at both a national and transnational level (See Sheptycki, 1998a, 1998b), but more specifically it reflects both the organizational bifurcation (Reiner, 1992: 761) and spatial polarization that is also taking place (Johnston, 1993; Jones and Newburn, 1998: 260).

Conclusion

This chapter has demonstrated that cyberspace is not lawless, but it is in fact much more ordered than many commentators would have us believe. Furthermore, the Internet is not only regulable, but there currently exists a complex, if not fairly sophisticated, multi-tiered structure of "policing" governance. The division of tasks within this structure not only bears a resemblance to policing in the terrestrial world, but it also provides a logical basis for developing future systems of Internet governance.

As for the future of crimes on the Internet, it is highly likely that many of the undesirable behaviours that emerge on the Internet will simply work themselves out in a number of different ways; here, Lessig's four "modalities" provide a steer (1999). Some behaviours may simply cease to be popular any more – a passing fad – eradicated by change in the *market*, or by "market reduction"[31] strategies to reduce opportunities for criminal behaviours (see Chapter 2). Or the Internet users and user-groups might develop ways of regulating unwanted behaviour through, for example, the expression of their *social norms* in the form of netiquette. Alternatively, developments in technology might simply eradicate the problem, either by shaping the *architecture* or by deliberate designing in more secure communications, encryption and firewalling. This could be an un-intentional knock-on effect, for example, in much the same way that in our terrestrial world the introduction of steering column locks drastically reduced car theft, crash helmets reduced the theft of motorcycles, and the changeover from (toxic) coal gas to (non-toxic) North Sea gas reduced the incidence of suicide (see Crawford, 1998: 85–7). Finally, new *laws* or *regulations* may prohibit users from various acts; or they will mandate police organizations to intervene; or they will reshape markets, architectures and norms.

At the end of the day we shall still be left with new types of "criminal" behaviour that will continue to challenge our traditional understandings of crimes, deviancy and the anti-social. Our experience to date strongly suggests that we do not need wholly new forms of regulation or policing, but rather we need to adapt, develop and build upon those which already exist. The most important task at hand is not to lose sight of the broader principles of policing and to develop the right balance between maintaining a fair and just state of order, with diversity, whilst also retaining the capability to enforce laws when required.

Notes

1   My thanks go to my colleagues at the University of Leeds, especially Clive Walker and Yaman Akdeniz. The middle section of this chapter is developed from Wall (2000).

2   The argument that arose from the mid-1990s moral panic over pornography fuelled the US Communications Decency Act 1996; much of this Act was later struck down by *ACLU et al. v Reno* (1997). See Chapter 7.

3   Conceptually, cyberspace is a privately controlled (owned) public space, very similar in concept to more physical spaces such as private shopping malls; see Shearing and Stenning (1987); Johnston (1992); Jones and Newburn (1998); Manning (2000).

4   There are various definitions of the term "policing". It is used here in a broad sense to mean the management of behaviour within a space, by a definable group, according to a particular set of definable values. It is from common support for these values that the policing group draws its mandate. For a useful overview of concepts of policing, see Reiner (2000).

5 E-mail, for example, whilst being revolutionary because of its speed and interactive nature, is simply a communication method that is one step beyond the development of the fax.

6 An example of such activity is the creation of software or design of imagery which never actually achieves physical expression.

7 For example, through the disembedding of time and space (Giddens, 1990: 6) which is accelerated by the Internet (Wall, 1997). The debates over the development of cyberspace are causing a reformulation of the debates over modernity; see Escobar (1996: 113).

8 www.cyberangels.org (checked 18 June 2001).

9 www.aol.com (checked 18 June 2001).

10 www.proaxis.com/~safetyed/CYBERANGELS/cyberangels02.html (checked 18 June 2001).

11 www.proaxis.com/~safetyed/CYBERANGELS/cyberangels02.html (checked 18 June 2001).

12 www.proaxis.com/~safetyed/CYBERANGELS/cyberangels02.html (checked 18 June 2001).

13 freespace.virgin.net/pure.kaos/PH(UK)ACP/index.htm (accessed September 1999).

14 www.ehap.org/mission.htm (checked 18 June 2001).

15 www.asacp.org (checked 18 June 2001).

16 See www.cyber-rights.org/documents/themet.htm (checked 18 June 2001).

17 www.Internetwatch.org.uk/stats/stats.html (accessed September 1999, before the relaunch of the Internet Watch Foundation).

18 For a more detailed discussion of the status of the Internet Watch Foundation see Akdeniz www.cyber-rights.org/watchmen-ii.htm (checked 19 June 2001).

19 www.cix.org (checked 21 June 2001).

20 www.euroispa.org (checked 21 June 2001).

21 www.ispc.org (checked 21 June 2001).

22 This implies that the core "police" have a mandate to preserve the peace and enforce the criminal law.

23 See now Teleservices Act 1997.

24 www.xs4all.nl (checked 19 June 2001).

25 *ACLU et al. v Reno*, 117 S. Ct. 2329, 1997. The Act is codified as (47 USC s.223).

26 www.cert.org (checked 19 June 2001).

27 See also www.cert.org/ (checked 19 June 2001).

28 The roles of the various security services are not included here.

29 Europol brings together national police forces from within the EU. See Convention based on Article K.3 of the Treaty on European Union, on the Establishment of a European Police Office (Europol Convention) with Declarations (Cm 3050, 1995).

30 NCIS and the NCS are defined by the Police Act 1997 Pts. I and II respectively.

31 Using intervention strategies to interfere with the operation of a markets in criminal activities – for example, stolen goods – in order to control criminal behaviour. See Sutton (1998).

References

Cases

ACLU et al. v Reno (1997) 117 S. Ct. 2329.

Godfrey v Demon Internet Ltd (1999) 4 All E.R. 342.

League Against Racism and anti-Semitism (LICRA) and The Union of French Jewish Students (UEJF) v Yahoo Inc. and Yahoo France (2000), Interim Court Order, 20 November, The County Court of Paris, No. RG: 00/05308.

Somm (1998), Somm, Felix Bruno, File No: 8340 Ds 465 JS 173158/95, Local Court (Amtsgericht) Munich.

Texts

Adams, J.A. (1996) "Controlling Cyberspace: Applying the Computer Fraud and Abuse Act to the Internet", *Santa Clara Computer and High Technology Law Journal*, 12: 416.

Akdeniz, Y. (1996) "Computer pornography: a comparative study of US and UK obscenity laws and child pornography laws in relation to the Internet", *International Review of Law, Computers and Technology*, 10: 235–61.

Arthur, C. (1996) "New crack-down on child porn on the Internet", *The Independent*, 23 September.

Bourdieu, P. (1977) *Outline of a Theory of Practice*, Cambridge: Cambridge University Press.

Box, S. (1983) *Power, Crime and Mystification*, London: Routledge.

Byassee, W.S. (1997) "Jurisdiction of Cyberspace: applying real world precedent to the virtual community", *Wake Forest Law Review*, 30: 205.

Caden, M.L. and Lucas, S.E. (1996) "Accidents on the Information Superhighway: on-line liability and regulation", *Richmond Journal of Law and Technology*, 2, 1: available at www.richmond.edu/~jolt/v2i1/caden_lucas.html (checked 18 June 2001).

—— (1998) "Regardless of Frontiers: Protecting the Human Right to Freedom of Expression on The Global Internet", Washington: Global Internet Liberty Campaign.

Chandler, A. (1996) "The changing definition and image of hackers in popular discourse", *International Journal of the Sociology of Law*, 24: 229.

Cohen, S. (1972) *Folk Devils and Moral Panics*, London: Paladin.

Crawford, A. (1997) *The Local Governance of Crime*, Oxford: Clarendon Press.

—— (1998) *Crime Prevention and Community Safety*, Harlow: Longmans.

Davies, D.J. (1998) "Criminal Law and the Internet: the investigator's perspective", in C. Walker (ed.), "Crime, Criminal Justice and the Internet", *Criminal Law Review* special edition, London: Sweet and Maxwell.

Edwards, L. and Wealde, C. (eds) (2000) *Law and the Internet: E-Commerce*, Oxford: Hart.

EPIC (1996) "Silencing the Net: The Threat to Freedom of Expression On-line", *Human Rights Watch*, 8, 2 (G); available at www.epic.org/free_speech/intl/hrw_report_5_96 .html (checked 19 June, 2001).

Escobar, A. (1996) "Welcome to Cyberia: Notes on the anthropology of cyberculture", in Z. Saradar and J.R. Ravetz (eds), *Cyberfutures: Culture and Politics on the Information Superhighway*, London: Pluto Press.

European Committee on Crime Problems (2000) "Draft Convention on Cyber-crime", (Draft No. 25 REV.), Committee of Experts on Crime in Cyber-Space, available for download at conventions.coe.int/treaty/EN/projets/cybercrime25.doc (checked 19 June, 2001).

Foucault, M. (1978) *The History of Sexuality, Volume One: An Introduction*, London: Penguin.

Fowles, A.J. (1993) "Order and the Law", in K. Jones, J. Brown and J. Bradshaw, *Issues in Social Policy*, London: Routledge and Kegan Paul.

Giddens, A. (1990) *The consequences of modernity*, London: Polity Press.

Goodrich, P. (1998) "Social Sciences and the Displacement of Law", *Law and Society Review*, 32, 2: 473.

Grabosky, P.N. and Smith, R.G. (1998) *Crime in the Digital Age: Controlling communications and cyberspace illegalities*, New Brunswick, NJ: Transaction Publishers.

Greenleaf, G. (1998) "An endnote on regulating cyberspace: architecture vs law?", *University of New South Wales Law Journal*, 21, 2; available at www.austlii.edu.au/au/other/unswlj/thematic/1998/vol21no2/greenleaf.html (checked 18 June 2001).

Grossman, W. (1996) "A grip on the new", *Electronic Telegraph*, 496: 1 October; available at www.telegraph.co.uk:80/et?ac=005287302314601&rtmo=fwvNoYos&atmo=rrrrrr rq &pg=/et/96/10/1/ecmatt01.html) (checked 18 June 2001).

Johnson, D.R. and Post, D. (1996) "Law and Borders: The Rise of Law in Cyberspace", *Stanford Law Review*, 48: 1367.

Johnston, L. (1992) *The Rebirth of Private Policing*, London: Routledge.

—— (1993) "Privatisation and protection: spatial and sectoral ideologies in British policing and crime prevention", *Modern Law Review*, 56: 771.

Jones, T. and Newburn, T. (1998) *Private Security and Public Policing*, Oxford: Clarendon Press.

Leong, G. (1998) "Computer Child Pornography – the liability of distributors?", in C. Walker (ed.), "Crime, Criminal Justice and the Internet", *Criminal Law Review* special edition, London: Sweet and Maxwell.

Lessig, L. (1998) "The Laws of Cyberspace", paper presented at the Taiwan Net '98 conference, Taipei, March.

—— (1999) "The Law Of The Horse: What Cyberlaw Might Teach", *Harvard Law Review*, 113: 501.

Levi, M. and Pithouse, A. (2001) *White-Collar Crime and its Victims: the Media and Social Construction of Business Fraud*, Oxford: Clarendon.

Lloyd, I.J. (2000) *Information Technology Law*, London: Butterworth.

Manning, P. K. (1987) 'Ironies of Compliance', pp. 293-316 in C. D. Shearing, and P. C. Stenning, (eds) *Private Policing*, Newbury Park, cal: Sage.

—— (2000) 'Policing New Social Spaces', pp. 177-200 in J. E. Sheptycki, (ed) (2000) *Issues in Transnational Policing*, London: Routledge

McBarnet, D. (1981) "Magistrates' Courts and the ideology of justice", *British Journal of Law and Society*, 8: 181.

NIPC (1998) "Mission Statement", National Infrastructure Protection Center, available at www.nipc.gov/about/about.htm (checked 19 June, 2001).

Post, D. (1995) "Encryption vs. The Alligator Clip: The Feds Worry That Encoded Messages Are Immune to Wiretaps", *New Jersey Law Journal*, 23 January.

Pretzlik, C. (1996) "Firm accused of fraud on the Internet", *Daily Telegraph*, 9 November.

Reidenberg, J. (1998) "Lex Informatica", *Texas Law Review*, 76: 553–93.

Reiner, R. (1992) "Policing a Postmodern Society", *Modern Law Review*, 55: 761.

—— (2000) *The Politics of the Police*, 3rd edn, Oxford: Oxford University Press.

Reno, Hon. J. (1996) "Law enforcement in cyberspace", address to the Commonwealth Club of California, San Francisco Hilton Hotel, 14 June.

Rowland, D. and Macdonald, E. (1997) *Information Technology Law*, London: Cavendish.

Seiber, U. (1998) "Legal Aspects of Computer Related Crime in the Information Society, Legal Advisory Board for the Information Market", COMCRIME-Study, prepared for the European Commission, Version 1.0, Vol. 1 – General Report, Brussels: Commission of the European Communities.

Shearing, C. and Stenning, P. (eds) (1987) *Private Policing*, Newbury Park, Cal.: Sage.

Sheptycki, J. (1998a) "Reflections on the Transnationalisation of Policing: the case of the RCMP and Serial Killers", *International Journal of the Sociology of Law*, 26: 17.

—— (1998b) "Policing, Postmodernism and Transnationalism", *British Journal of Criminology*, 38: 485.

Standage, T. (1996) "Web access in a tangle as censors have their say", *Electronic Telegraph*, 475: 10 September; available at www.telegraph.co.uk:80/et?ac=00528730231460&rtmo=3HYABxAM&atmo=rrrrrrrq& pg=/et/96/9/10/ecsing10.html (checked 18 June 2001).

Sterling, B. (1994) *The Hacker Crackdown*, London: Penguin.

Sussman, V. (1995) "Policing Cyberspace", *U.S. News*, 38: 23 January.

Sutherland, E. (1949) *White Collar Crime*, New York: Holt Rinehart & Winston.

Sutton, M. (1998) *Handling stolen goods and theft: A market reduction approach*, HORS 178, London: Home Office.

Tendler, S. (1996) "Public to help police curb Internet porn", *The Times*, 2 December.

Uhlig, R. (1996a) "Hunt is on for Internet dealer in child porn", *Electronic Telegraph*, 518: 23 October; available at www.telegraph.co.uk:80/et?ac=005287302314601&rtmo=0KNJRGXq&atmo=rrrrrrrq&pg=/et/96/10/23/nporn23.html (checked 18 June 2001).

—— (1996b) "'Safety Net' on Internet will catch child porn", *Electronic Telegraph*, 488: 23 September; available at www.telegraph.co.uk:80/et?ac=005287302314601&rtmo=0KNJRGXq&atmo=rrrrrrrq&pg=/et/96/9/23/nint23.html (checked 18 June 2001).

—— (1996c) "Minister's warning over Internet porn", *Electronic Telegraph*, 452: 16 August; available at www.telegraph.co.uk:80/et?ac=005287302314601&rtmo=LS73hKKd&atmo=rrrrrrrq&pg=/et/96/8/16/nporn16.html (checked 18 June 2001).

Valier, C. (2001) "Criminal Detection and the Weight of the Past: Critical Notes on Foucault, Subjectivity and Preventative Control", *Theoretical Criminology*, 5, 4: (forthcoming).

Walker, C.P. (1997) "Cyber-contempt: Fair trials and the Internet", *Year Book of Media and Entertainment Law*, vol. 3, Oxford: Clarendon Press.

Walker, C.P. and Akdeniz, Y. (1998) "The governance of the Internet in Europe with special reference to illegal and harmful content", in C. Walker (ed.), "Crime, Criminal Justice and the Internet", *Criminal Law Review* special edition, London: Sweet and Maxwell.

Walker, C.P., Wall. D.S. and Akdeniz, Y. (2000) "The Internet, Law and Society", in Y. Akdeniz, C.P. Walker and D.S. Wall (eds), *The Internet, Law and Society*, London: Longman.

Wall, D.S. (1997) "Policing the Virtual Community: The Internet, cyber-crimes and the policing of cyberspace", in P. Francis, P. Davies and V. Jupp (eds), *Policing Futures*, London: Macmillan.

—— (1998) "Policing and the Regulation of Cyberspace", in C. Walker (ed.), "Crime, Criminal Justice and the Internet", *Criminal Law Review* special edition, London: Sweet and Maxwell.

—— (2000) "Policing the Internet: maintaining order and law on the cyber-beat", in Y. Akdeniz, C.P. Walker and D.S. Wall (eds), *The Internet, Law and Society*, London: Longman.

Zedner, L. (1997) "Victims", in M. Maguire, R. Morgan and R. Reiner, *The Oxford Handbook of Criminology*, 2nd edn, Oxford: Oxford University Press.

12 Policing "high-tech" crime within the global context

The role of transnational policy networks

Paul Norman[1]

Introduction

In December 1998 the Interior Ministers of the European Union (EU) received the basic elements of the EU's strategy against high-tech crime (Council of the EU, 1998d: IV). The document outlines "Strategic Guidance" for the EU to avoid overlap with the work of other organizations by coordinating work and building upon the efforts of other international bodies. Effectively this sanctions what informally had been occurring for three years between the EU, the G8 countries and, to a lesser extent, the Council of Europe. A number of bodies within these organizations, through overlapping expert group membership, have been operating as policy networks linking the G8 and the EU within the field of action to combat organized crime. This paper will highlight some of the network structures, and how these have affected the development of policies to combat high-tech crime. Arguably, the material presented reinforces the case that a transnational power elite is acting relatively autonomously on a broad range of criminal justice issues in the name of action to counter transnational organized crime. To illustrate this view, the nature of governance within the third pillar will be examined, and how this has changed since the *Treaty on European Union* (TEU) formalized the EU's Justice and Home Affairs (JHA) policy process.

Organizing a system of Justice and Home Affairs governance

The nature of EU governance within the JHA field underwent two fundamental changes in the 1990s. First, ratification of the TEU in November 1993 formalized a relatively incoherent span of policy fora into a hierarchical and more transparent system of governance (Hayes-Renshaw and Wallace, 1997: 94; Bunyan, 1993: 28–31) but fractured by the three "pillars" – the EC treaties and intergovernmental cooperation within JHA and the Common, Foreign and Security policy field. The second, more fundamental change, informs the approach of this paper and can be characterized as a move to selective horizontal policy integration, underpinned by the informal devolution of executive responsibility to a number of key expert or "High Level" groups. This feature has been apparent from an early stage in dealing with cross-pillar drug issues where coordinated action with the EC pillar is required.[2] But the recent cohering of initiatives around the phenomenological theme of organized crime has provided the policy focus for a more fundamental change in the system of governance and distribution of power in the JHA sphere. By examining the issue of hi-tech crime, it will be seen that two key overlapping networks of state actors possessing specialist skills and expertise has been empowered within the transnational context straddling the EU and G8, creating operational and policy frameworks to counter organized crime. In addition, the EU policy community on organized crime is playing a broader role in entrenching a policy acquis to those countries in Europe who are aspirant members of the EU (Norman, 1999). The EU and G8 policy communities are acting together in a way that suggests the development of a transnational network of actors concerned with coordinating an effective response to serious and international crime at the global level, working through international organizations at the policy and operational level.

The genesis of the EU's policy community on organized crime was the initial high-level political initiative at the European Council (Dublin II) in December 1996, which circumvented the third pillar structures in creating a High Level Group on Organized Crime – providing the policy cement for the pillars. The High Level Group was to formulate a coherent and coordinated response to such forms of offending across the EU's pillars. Acting under the Irish Presidency's initiative, the Heads of State were investing the body with *de facto* executive discretion in compiling, coordinating and integrating a gamut of issues around the theme of organized crime. The High Level Group was composed of national experts, and their resultant *Action Plan to Combat Organized Crime* of April 1997 exemplified the new-found willingness to coordinate, in detail, JHA activities with other international fora, and the prospective accession states. However, the European Council's actions, and the subsequent decision of the Council to reformulate the Group, can be regarded as the point of (permanent) departure from the previous decision-making procedures of the third pillar – to a new mode of governance in JHA matters.

To shed light on the importance of this change in JHA governance within the EU, it is necessary to examine the changing nature of the policy process within and outside the EU. The approach seeks to use policy networks analysis to highlight the form of the institutional development within the EU, G8 and the Council of Europe – and their interrelationship in the coordination of policies and action to combat organized crime. The bodies examined are relatively bounded and autonomous, whilst the role that certain key actors have in acting within a number of expert groups appears important. Clearly, a more detailed empirical examination of the agents involved in the respective policy communities would further test the utility of the approach.[3] However, what is presented shows that a comprehensive analysis of the dynamics of the policy networks between the EU and G8 requires cognizance of both infrastructural power and the importance of key agents (Marsh, 1998: 188) to understand the policy impact of such linked networks.

A mode of EU governance in transition

The change in the system of governance within the third pillar can be regarded as a shift from a hierarchical policy machinery to one that creates shortcuts to the policy process where priority action is desired. The need to shortcut the formal policy process stems from the stagnation of the system for negotiating binding legislative instruments within the TEU third pillar regime. The tortuous negotiation of the *Europol Convention*, equalled only by its extended national ratification by each Member State, clearly undermined the credibility of the JHA Council, which itself has a relatively high degree of autonomy from the European Council (Curtin, 1993: 27; O'Keefe, 1995: 895–7). Many of the formal reasons for the delays in negotiating the *Europol Convention* rest upon the unanimity principles enshrined within the TEU, but were manifested in a lack of agreement on the appropriate role of the European Court of Justice, the need for (uniformly high) standards of data protection,[4] the demand for external accountability mechanisms, and ultimately no common view of which way Europol should develop in the future. The *Treaty of Amsterdam* partly addresses this bind by allowing conventions to come into force when half the Member States have completed their national ratification procedures (Article K.6.2.(d)).

Given the stasis of the third pillar policy process, the need to ratchet up work addressing issues of organized crime became paramount by 1996. This was accomplished by the Irish Presidency's push on organized crime issues, subsequently sustained and mediated by the High Level Group on Organized Crime established by the European Council (Dublin II) in December 1996. This expert group was mandated not only to address the (so many) strands of policy essential for the EU to act against serious international and transnational offending, but also any treaty changes it identified as necessary for the efficient functioning of the third pillar. Briefly, the Irish Presidency sought to overcome the JHA Council's inertia by corralling a broad swathe of actions in the field of police, customs and judicial cooperation – separating them from the drugs issue – with the approval of the European Council. This Presidency push sought to "create a High Level Group to draw up a comprehensive Action Plan containing specific recommendations, including realistic timetables for carrying out the work" (High Level Group, 1997: 1). The Group was to complete its work within a relatively short timeframe and report by March/April 1997 in time for any recommended treaty changes to be communicated to the Amsterdam Intergovernmental Conference (High Level Group, 1997: Annex). The resulting Action Plan to Combat Organized Crime was accepted unreservedly by the European Council (Amsterdam) in June 1997. Further, Recommendation 22 was implemented without delay, ensuring that a successor multidisciplinary working party was established to ensure implementation of the Action Plan. The subsequently termed "Multidisciplinary Group (MDG) on Organized Crime" was formed by the addition of "operational law enforcement practitioners [and] prosecutors" to the High Level Group's cohort of "policy-makers at a senior level" (Presidency of the Council of the EU, 1998: 4). The

MDG operates under the auspices of the Presidency and, by the late 1990s, benefited from "eight national experts and practitioners" specifically mandated to further the MDG's work (Council of the EU, 1997: 6).

The MDG on Organized Crime is unhindered by the constraints of working through the elaborate five-tiered hierarchy of the third pillar policy process set up by the TEU, but the formulation of the series of measures outlined in the Action Plan clearly lacked transparency in an area which has been subject to severe critique on this front (Bunyan, 1993: 32–33; European Parliament, 1997: paras N and O). A close reading of the Action Plan and an analysis of the subsequent work of the MDG reinforces the view that the High Level Group was invested with a high degree of autonomy (during its temporary mandate), and that this is sustained (permanently) within the MDG. As Smith highlights, "through establishing a policy community government can depoliticise a policy area and so it is less likely to be politically dangerous" (Smith, 1993: 18), and this appears to be one of the immediate objectives (and successes) of the European Council.

By June 1998 it was clear that the MDG's role was broadening whilst it was coordinating activities with countries and organizations outside the EU, and ensuring the CCEE (Countries of Central and Eastern Europe) are considered in any initiative on organized crime. The first factor was a consideration that the UK was keen to reinforce prior to and during its Presidency in the first half of 1998, and one wholeheartedly supported by the Head of the Policing Organized Crime Unit of the Home Office. The incumbent was during the latter half of 1997 planning the organized crime agenda for the 1998 G8 Summit (Birmingham) and was part of the Presidency troika prior to the UK Presidency. This fortuitous positioning of events, and the presence of an experienced senior official with a clear strategic perspective on the subject (Wrench, 1997), dovetailed neatly with New Labour's political ambition concurrently to play a constructive role within the EU and act as a bridge between the EU and its transatlantic partners (most notably the USA). The importance of the non-EU policy communities in action to combat organized crime is further assessed below, but it is clear that to maximize the ambitions of the new MDG, and the impact of the UK's Presidency, the remit of the body needed to go beyond the strict implementation of the Action Plan.

By June 1998 it was reported to the European Council (Cardiff) that the "MDG has provided a helpful forum for continuing strategic policy development and improving operational cooperation....It has promoted enlargement with key countries and bodies outside the EU...and, at its suggestion, the Council (JHA) has endorsed the approach of G8 recommendations...on organised crime and terrorism...and stated it will draw upon them in pursuing its own work in these areas" (Presidency of the Council of the EU, 1998: 3). The MDG is now an established executive body within the Presidency that is institutionally positioned so that it can seek and get the highest political endorsement (when needed) and call upon the Article 36 Committee to promote pertinent legislative initiatives. Thus the MDG is able to act with relative autonomy, has high *de facto* political authority, and is dynamic enough to adapt to strategic policy development and new demands in EU action to combat organized crime.

G8 and European policy networks

This chapter has so far concentrated upon the development of the system of internal EU governance in the field of action against organized crime. But this focus on the internal JHA policy domain needs to be placed within the broader spectrum of the EU's developing external relations. This embraces EU action within the wider European domain with the Countries of Central and Eastern Europe (CCEE), the Council of Europe, the Transatlantic arenas and G8 (formerly G7-P8). But in attempting to elicit an understanding of the external relations component of JHA governance, it is important to recognize the policy networks that now link the EU to G8 and the Council of Europe. The interlocking of these three groups has been facilitated by the three non-European G8 members (the USA, Japan and Canada) gaining official observer status[5] of the Council of Europe in 1996 (Canadian Department of Foreign Affairs, 1996), further enveloping and reinforcing the possibilities of a G8 international policy community on organized crime acting as a link agency between the two international organizations.[6] The influence of the former G7 in the field of action against money laundering, the control of chemical precursors and in the utilization of mutual evaluation mechanisms has been demonstrated elsewhere (Gilmore, 1997). but recent G8 action to combat organized crime represents a decisive move to a policy domain with a more integrated and deeper field of activity embracing a range of areas including high-tech crime.

To enable an understanding of these organized crime policy networks, first the role of G8 within its Lyon Group will be examined, followed by the developing work of the Council of Europe in this field.

The role of the G8 in the policing of high-tech crime

The G8 Senior Experts Group on Organized Crime, colloquially known as the Lyon Group,[7] is a distinct international policy community concerned with action to combat organized crime. The EU's Transatlantic Dialogue with the USA and Canada clearly reinforces this cooperation as the provisions of the 1996 *New Transatlantic Agenda* and accompanying Action Plan demonstrate (EU–USA, 1995: 7–8; 23–6). The six-monthly EU–US Summits provide the focal point for the appraisal of mutual action in JHA matters, including the "expert level meetings on corruption and money-laundering now under the auspices of the Multidisciplinary Group on Organized Crime" (EU-USA, 1998: 1). However, the Lyon Group's policy outputs, and its success in fulfilling its desire to propagate its work within other international fora, means that it must be regarded as an important part of the machinery of international cooperation against organized crime.

The G8 crime policy domain has been developing for some time, with initial concentration upon political issues such as terrorism and extradition, but later drugs and declarations by Heads of State about global crime problems. The move from rhetoric about crime and globalization to specific action against transnational organized crime emanates from the decision of the 1995 G8 Summit (Halifax) to create the Senior Expert Group on Transnational Organized Crime. Its initially temporary mandate was to develop a wider-ranging but specific set of measures for states to adopt in their action against organized crime, which were presented as *Recommendations to Combat Transnational Organized Crime Efficiently* at the G7-P8 Summit (Lyon) in April 1996. Since this time, G8 has successfully disseminated its policy work across a broad agenda, encompassing action to combat organized crime, project-based [operational] action against international offending (Norman, 1998), as well as high-tech crime.

A number of crucial determinants of this success are important to focus upon in considering the wider EU system of governance in JHA matters. First there is now a close formal association of G8 with the European Union, the Council of Europe and the United Nations. For the EU, both the Presidency of the Council and the President of the Commission now participate in the G8 Summits (cited in Gilmore, 1997: 31). In addition, it has already been noted that all the G8 states are now members or observers of the Council of Europe. Second, the presence of four EU Member States within the G8 was under-pinned by a determination on the part of the UK to forge closer policy links between the G8 and the EU in preparation for its overlapping Presidencies of both G8 and the Council of the EU in 1998. Finally, the composition of the Lyon Group reflects that of the EU's MDG, in that it involves both senior poli-cymakers and practitioners[8] from each state developing policy initiatives and ensuring they can be practically implemented and monitored.

Success in disseminating the work of the Lyon Group has been seen on a number of fronts, but the way that this has been accomplished reinforces the contention that the Lyon Group acts as a distinct international policy commu-nity closely linked via an overlapping membership to the EU's MDG on Organized Crime. For example the Head of Policing Organized Crime Unit of the Home Office leads the UK's Lyon Group delegation. He was consulted on the text published by the Heads of State that announced the creation of the Lyon Group (Wrench, 1997: 39) in Halifax, Nova Scotia. In addition, the offi-cial's concern with hi-tech crime and the promotion of project-based action (Wrench, 1997: 40) were sanctioned in the 40 Recommendations (P8 1996: paras 16 and 28). In preparation for the Presidencies of G8 and the EU, the incumbent gained G8 agreement that hi-tech crime would be a G8 priority for 1997/98 (G8, 1997a: 7), resulting in the establishment of (a number of sub-groups including) Subgroup V dealing with action against high-tech crime.[9] The subgroup met three times in January, June/July and between 10 and 12 December 1997, the latter being the first G8 ministerial meeting and one that endorsed the *Principles and Action Plan to Combat Hi-Tech Crime* (G8, 1997b:

Annex). During the latter half of 1997, whilst the UK formed part of the EU Presidency troika[10] and during the UK's Presidency, "US and Canadian experts were involved in discussions on the subject of high-tech crime...[and] the MDG received reports on the current work by G8 on this subject. Following the G8 agreement on the *Principles and Action Plan to Combat Hi-Tech Crime* the Council (JHA) on 19 March 1998 gave its political endorsement to the approach set out in the 10 Principles on high-tech crime, the 40 Recommendations on organized crime and the 25 Recommendations on terrorism, approved in the framework of the G8" (Presidency of the Council of the EU, 1998: 9). This coincided with receipt of the Commission study on high-tech crime in March 1998 (Seiber, 1998), as requested by the previous High Level Group on Organized Crime. Following recommendations for greater international coordination in the Commission study (Seiber, 1998: 4; 238–9) the G8's work was further considered by the MDG prior to a coordination meeting with the Lyon Group and the Council of Europe (Presidency of the Council of the EU, 1998: 9).

The role of the Council of Europe in the policing of high-tech crime

The Council of Europe established its own Committee of Experts on Crime in Cyber-Space in February 1997, shortly after the Lyon Group's Recommendations raised the issue. The Committee's terms of reference also sought to underline the need for international cooperation (cited in Seiber, 1998: 180). It is noteworthy that the Commission and the Council of the EU, USA, Canada and Japan may send a representative to the Council of Europe's Committee of Experts on Crime in Cyber-Space (European Committee on Crime Problems, 1997: paras 5(d) and (e)). Thus a triumvirate of G8, EU and the Council of Europe had, in little over one year, aligned itself with the G8's initial concern for hi-tech crime – with each forum ensuring that their strategies were coordinated across the organizations and disseminated to its membership.

In trying to elicit mechanisms of this inter-organizational governance in the field of organized crime, it is apparent that the process has been given high-level political endorsement within the revitalized Quadripartite Meetings between the EU and the Council of Europe (Council of Europe, 1995: 8–9). The developing JHA agenda of the Quadripartite Meetings elicit another crucial aspect of the developing formal system of third pillar governance – one that extends into the wider European architecture in order to fulfil the EU's strategic concern to prepare accession states for membership (Norman, 1999). The Quadripartite Meetings are composed of a representative of the Presidency and the Commission from the EU, and the Chair of the Committee of Ministers and the Secretary General for the Council of Europe. At its eighth meeting, in 1996, an Exchange of Letters formalized an expansion of cooperation to all levels and, for the first time, to areas of concern to the EU's third pillar

(EU–Council of Europe, 1996: 1–2). By March 1998, under the UK's Presidency of the EU, this cooperation had deepened to a meeting of the full K4 Committee to discuss "mutual assistance in criminal matters, the fight against corruption, money laundering, hi-tech crime, the sexual exploitation of children, organized crime, the enlargement of the European Union, as well as racism and xenophobia" (EU–Council of Europe, 1998: 3).

Examination of hi-tech crime highlights the parallel tracking of policies within the EU, the G8 and the Council of Europe as increasingly high-level contacts between the EU and the Council of Europe are developed. This dynamic of policy transference from the agenda of one international body to others is also seen in other areas within the broad field of action against organized crime (Norman, 1999).

Conclusion: accountability and policy networks

In outlining the changing nature of governance within the third pillar of the EU and the impact of a range of policy communities, the question arises as to how this affects the accountability of the policy process within the current third pillar. The above has attempted to highlight the presence and form of the networks, their sites of activity and their respective influences. In doing so, this arguably adds to an understanding of the nature of governance in this field – during this period at least – and consequently would inform an analysis of how accountability over this policy domain could be increased. Before addressing this issue it is useful to draw some preliminary conclusions from the material presented above.

It is clear that an analysis centred upon the EU will only partially delineate the system of third pillar governance – the role of the G8 and the Council of Europe highlights the international policy influences in action to combat organized crime in general, and high-tech crime in particular. The extent of the networks' influence (in terms of infrastructural power and agent action) is uncertain at this stage, but it is clear that the policy field of EU police and judicial cooperation in criminal matters is now subject to far greater international influence.

The executive power invested in the MDG on Organized Crime presents those concerned with accountability with fundamental challenges in seeking to oversee its activities and influence the policy process. Unlike the Article 36 Committee (formerly K4) under the *Treaty of Amsterdam*, the MDG has no treaty basis but is a powerful policy community developing policies and deepening operational action to combat organized crime within the EU, the CCEE and beyond. Despite this, there are arguably at least three factors that will progressively ensure that the democratic deficit over EU police and judicial cooperation in criminal matters will not be as severe as that under the TEU regime or the transitional form of governance presented earlier in this chapter. First, the political will to change the image and effectiveness of the third pillar of governance has, since 1997, finally extended to informal consultation with the European Parliament,[11] and to a limited extent with academics[12] and non-governmental organizations.[13] Second, in March 1998 the Council approved measures to qualitatively improve the openness and transparency of proceedings within the third pillar. Whilst this was not as far reaching as the UK Presidency wanted (Council of the EU, 1998a) it has provided the basis for greater transparency and furthered access to Council documents (Council of the EU, 1998c).[14] Finally, the formal requirements of the *Treaty of Amsterdam* have now put into place an obligatory system of consultation with the European Parliament (Art.K.11). The progressive impact of the high-level political will, transparency, openness and the new formal legal obligations raises the prospect of a more open network embracing external non-state influences and enhancing accountability over this policy domain.

Realistically, the influence of the G8 international policy community on organized crime and the Council of Europe cannot be easily brought to account within the broader context of the EU's overriding strategic objectives. These include the importance of the Transatlantic Agenda, the Strategy for Accession and the increasing importance of the EU's External Relations generally in furthering the broad field of justice and home affairs policies.[15] The narrow base of the policy communities requires a more detailed analysis of the policy dynamics of the EU's system of governance in this field, and the international initiatives to coordinate action to meet the challenges of high-tech crime and other policy initiatives to combat organized crime.

Notes

1   A draft version of this paper was presented at the British and Irish Legal Education Technology Association Conference, *Cyberspace 1999: Crime, Criminal Justice and the Internet*, College of Ripon and York, St John at York 29–30 March 1999.
2   In July 1995 a Group of Experts on Drugs was established with a cross-pillar responsibility to coordinate EU drugs work through the Presidency to the European Council. In February 1997 COREPER also created a Horizontal Working Party on Drugs "to coordinate the Union's activities relating to drugs, especially cross-pillar activities" (Council of the EU, 1997: 7).
3   This is the subject of a current research project by the author: "The Organisation and Dynamics of International Police Policy-making and Cooperation in the European Region".
4   The EC Directive does *not* cover the third pillar policy domain.
5   This confers the right to name a permanent observer to the Council of Europe and to participate in ministerial conferences, steering committees, expert committees and (subsidiary) meetings of the Committee of Ministers.
6   Canada has participated in the GMC from its inception and has been keen to participate in a wider range of Council of Europe bodies in the field (Canadian Department of Foreign Affairs, 1996).
7   So-called from the 1996 G7 Summit held at Lyon, where the Heads of State endorsed the Senior Experts Group Recommendations to Combat Transnational Organized Crime Efficiently.
8   The UK's delegation to the Lyon Group initially comprised the Head of the Policing Organized Crime Unit of the Home Office, the Judicial Cooperation Unit, the Foreign and Commonwealth Office, the Association of Chief Police Officers, the National Criminal Intelligence Service and HM Customs and Excise. Later an Immigration Service member was added (Wrench, 1997: 40).

9 For examples of topics discussed, see Seiber (1998: 184).
10 Of past, current and forthcoming Presidencies of the Council of the EU.
11 Including regular briefings to the relevant Committees and early consultation on "most of the measures with a legislative character" (Council of the EU, 1998d: 67).
12 For example the "meeting of leading European Union and other academic and researchers on organized crime...on 18/19 May 1998 in the margins of the MDG" (Presidency of the Council of the EU, 1998: 7).
13 Twenty-eight were held during the UK Presidency.
14 The World Wide Web register of Council documents does not include listings of classified documents, and is not retrospective.
15 Access to Council documents in these areas has consistently been denied. For example, reports of the EU–USA and EU–Canada Summits within the context of the Transatlantic Dialogue have been kept secret on the grounds that references are made to third countries and therefore their release "could be harmful for the EU's relations with these countries". General Secretariat of the Council of the EU, personal correspondence, 20 July 1998.

References

Bunyan, T. (1993) "Trevi, Europol and the European State", in T. Bunyan (ed.), *Statewatching the New Europe: A handbook on the European state*, London: Statewatch.
Canadian Department of Foreign Affairs and International Trade (1996) *Canada and the Council of Europe*, available at www.dfait-maeci.gc.ca/english/geo/europe/EU/counrel.htm (checked 19 June 2001).
Council of Europe (1995) *Cooperation Between the Council of Europe and the European Union (August–December 1995)*, report by the Secretary General to Committee of Ministers, CM(96)41, Strasbourg: Council of Europe, available at www.coe.fr/cm/reports/1996/96cm41.html (checked 19 June 2001).
Council of the EU (1997) *Achievements in the field of Justice and Home Affairs in 1997*, report for the Council to the European Council, 13191/1/97 REV 1 LIMITE JAI 40, Brussels: Council of the EU, available at ue.eu.int/jai/default.asp?lang=en (checked 19 June 2001).
Council of the EU (1998a) *Openness in JHA Business*, note from The Presidency to the K4 Committee, 5146/98 LIMITE JAI 1, Brussels: Council of the EU.
—— (1998b) *Openness and Transparency in the activities of the Council acting in the field of Title VI of the TEU – Draft Council Conclusions*, note from COREPER to the Council, 6407/98 LIMITE JAI 6, Brussels: Council of the EU.
—— (1998c) *Public Register of Council Documents*, I/A Item Note from General Secretariat of the Council to the Permanent Representative Committee (Part 2) / Council, 6423/1/98 REV 1 LIMITE INF 28 API 23 JUR 97, Brussels: Council of the EU.
—— (1998d) *2146th Council Meeting – Justice and Home Affairs – Brussels, 3/4 December 1998*, Press Release 13673/98 (Presse 427), Brussels: Council of the EU.
Curtin, D. (1993) "The Constitutional Structure of the European Union: A Europe of bits and pieces", *Common Market Law Review*, 30, 1: 17–69.
Curtin, D. and Meijers, H. (1995) "The Principle of Open Government in Schengen and the European Union: Democratic regression?", *Common Market Law Review*, 32, 2: 391–422.
European Committee on Crime Problems (1997) *Specific Terms of Reference: Committee of Experts on Crime in Cyber-Space (PC-CY)*, 583rd meeting of the Ministers' Deputies, 4 February 1997, Appendix 13, Strasbourg: Council of Europe, available at www.coe.fr/cm/dec/1997/583/583.a13.html (checked 19 June 2001).

European Parliament (1997) *Report on the Action Plan to Combat Organised Crime*, A4–03333/97, Rapporteur: Cederschiold, Charlotte, Committee on Civil Liberties and Internal Affairs, European Parliament.

EU–Council of Europe (1996)*8th Quadripartite Meeting: European Union/Council of Europe, Strasbourg, 23 October 1996*, General Secretariat of the Council of the EU Press Release 10874/96 (Presse 279), Brussels: Council of the EU.

—— (1998) *11th Quadripartite Meeting: European Union/Council of Europe, Strasbourg, 1 April 1998*, General Secretariat of the Council of the EU Press Release 7290/98 (Presse 93), Brussels: Council of the EU.

EU–USA (1995) *New Transatlantic Agenda and Action Plan*, General Secretariat of the Council of the EU Press Release 12296/95 (Presse 356), Brussels: Council of the EU.

—— (1998) *New Transatlantic Agenda Senior Level Group Report to the EU/US Summit London, 18 May 1998*, Brussels: European Commission.

Gilmore, W.C. (1997) "The G7 and Transnational Drug Trafficking: The Task Force Experience", in P.J. Cullen and W.C. Gilmore (eds), *Crime Sans Frontiers: International and European Legal Approaches*, Hume Papers in Public Policy, 6 (1 and 2), Edinburgh: Edinburgh University Press.

Hayes-Renshaw, F. and Wallace, H. (1997) *The Council of Ministers*, Basingstoke: Macmillan.

High Level Group on Organized Crime (1997) *Action Plan to Combat Organized Crime*, Official Journal of the European Communities, C 251, 1–18, Brussels: European Communities.

McLeay, E. (1998) "Policing policy and policy networks in Britain and New Zealand", in D. Marsh (ed.), *Comparing Policy Networks*, Buckingham: Open University Press.

Marsh, D. (ed.) (1998) *Comparing Policy Networks*, Buckingham: Open University Press.

Norman, P. (1998) "The Terrorist Finance Unit and the Joint Action Group on Organized Crime: New Organizational Models and Investigative Strategies to Counter 'organized crime' in the UK", *Howard Journal of Criminal Justice*, 37, 4: 375–92.

—— (1999) "European Union Police Policy-Making and Co-operation", in F. Carr and A. Massey (eds), *Public Policy in the New Europe: Eurogovernance in Theory and Practice*, Aldershot: Edward Elgar.

O'Keefe, D. (1995) "Recasting the Third Pillar", *Common Market Law Review*, 32, 4: 893–920.

P8 (1996) *Senior Experts Group Recommendations to Combat Transnational Organized Crime Efficiently*, Paris, 12 April, Paris: French Ministry of the Interior; available at utl2.library.utoronto.ca/disk1/www/documents/g7/40pts.htm (checked 19 June 2001).

Presidency of the Council of the EU (1998) *Progress Report on Organized Crime to the Cardiff European Council*, Note from the Presidency to European Council, 7303/3/98 CRIMORG 45 REV 3, Brussels: Council of the EU; available at ue.eu.int/jai/default.asp?lang=en.

Seiber, U. (1998) *Legal Aspects of Computer-Related Crime in the Information Society – COMCRIME-Study – prepared for the European Commission*, Version 1.0, vol. 1 – General Report, Brussels: Commission of the European Communities.

Smith, M.J. (1993) *Pressure, Power and Policy: State autonomy and policy networks in Britain and the United States*, London: Harvester Wheatsheaf.

Wrench, P. (1997) "The G8 and Transnational Organised Crime", in P.J. Cullen and W.C. Gilmore (eds), *Crime Sans Frontiers: International and European Legal Approaches*, Hume Papers in Public Policy, 6 (1 and 2), Edinburgh: Edinburgh University Press.

13 The criminal courts online

Clive Walker[1]

Introduction: Information in, cases out

At the core of the criminal justice process lies an emphasis upon the generation, processing and transmission of information and its networking across agencies. These features render the process particularly appropriate for the utilization of information and communications technologies (ICTs).

> Information enters the system in the form of pleadings and evidence; is processed through various pre-trial, trial, post-trial and appellate operations; and exits the system in the form of orders and judgements, data and opinions.
>
> (Anderson *et al.*, 1993: 1769)

In practice, the application of ICTs to the criminal courts' processes within England and Wales has made relatively slow progress to date. The reasons include cultural, political and financial obstacles (Anderson *et al.*, 1993: 1789; Tata, 2000), but also deeper concerns about the negative impacts of ICTs. "Trial by media" remains an abiding concern for the judiciary, and the Internet is the latest in a long line of forms of communication to engender misgivings (Walker, 1996; 1997–98).

The accentuation of these negative impacts may now be on the decline, and a more positive attitude to ICTs has been explicit since the Lord Chancellor's Department's *Consultation Paper: Resolving and Avoiding Disputes in the Information Age* issued in 1998. The governmental view in England and Wales is that:

> There can be no doubt that we are moving rapidly into the information age, into an era where a rich body of technologies will transform our lives, bringing changes as fundamental as the Industrial Revolution brought to society in the 18th century. No one will be exempt from these changes.

In reality, the use of technologies in courts did not, of course, commence in 1998. This chapter will argue, akin to the views of others about the legal professions (Susskind, 2000), that we are the midst of a progression, ranging from internal, back-office, and inward-looking technological machinery, though inter-agency office technical linkages to court machinery in the public domain and even outward-looking multimedia portals for public access. In line with this range, the Lord Chancellor's Department's *Consultation Paper* sees ICT support for court processes as assisting with multimedia electronic filing and presentation, case management unified between agencies, and litigation support systems (Lord Chancellor's Department, 1998: ch. 4). All of these developments have been encouraged not only because they represent official objectives but also because of the ability of later commercially available software to capture the complexity of court processes (MacMillan, 1998). To some extent, all is happening at once, and so it would be wrong to see the development of ICTs in the courts as occurring in distinct phases. It would also be misleading to depict all criminal justice agencies as having the same needs or moving at the same pace. However, for the purposes of explanation in this chapter, different levels of engagement will be presented.

Back-office, and inward-looking technical machinery

Despite having just disclaimed a strictly chronological impetus, it must be said that the earliest uses of ICTs have been the most enduring and most important. The application of technology at this level advances several official doctrines, especially New Public Management, with its emphasis on performance indicators such as waiting time and unit costs (Raine and Wilson, 1993; 1997). However, the technology involved has so far mainly involved mainframe databases and PC office packages; the Internet has not loomed large. There will follow a brief survey of implementation at different court levels.

The Lord Chancellor's Department has stated its ICT policy towards magistrates' courts as follows:

> The Department is committed to the provision of standard computer services for use in all magistrates' courts. These services will be provided though partnership with the private sector under PFI. The main contract is due to be signed in June 1998. The ICT services will support the efficient operation and performance of magistrates' courts and enable a more effective means of delivering information across the criminal justice system.
>
> (Lord Chancellor's and Officers' Departments, 1998: A para. 50)

To date, the Magistrates' Courts Standards Systems (MASS) has achieved limited interconnectivity. As a result, the influential *Narey Report* (Narey, 1997: chs 2 and 3) continues to expresses concern about delay at this level and recommends electronic data transfer between Crown Prosecution Service (CPS) and police as an important reform. A more extensive LIBRA system was devised at the end of 1998, including preparation of cases, listing, notifications and accounting for fines, as well as information exchange between courts and other criminal justice agencies (Corbett, 1999a).

In the Crown Court and Court of Appeal (Criminal Division), the Court Service has a more developed ICT strategy, maintained by its Information Services Division which is under the control of the IT Sub-Group of the Court Service Management Board (CSMB) (Court Service Information Services Division, 1998: para.1.5.1). The content of the strategy is informed by meetings with the judiciary, through the Judicial Technology Group (JTG) and with other interested parties through the Information Technology and the Courts Committee (ITAC) (Purnell, 1990). Future development is to include "...electronic communication with the professions and the public, with more information being provided both through the Internet and through suitably managed and secure access to Court Service systems" (Court Service Information Services Division, 1998: para.1.1.3). Applying these ideas to specific courts, most attention has been paid to the Crown Court, where the CREST system (an office program for back-room staff) dates from 1991 and has been upgraded as part of the CCS contract (Court Service Information Services Division, 1998; paras.1.1.2, 5.4.1). Future enhancements are being addressed following a Scoping Study conducted by Electronic Data Systems Ltd (the PFI supplier to the Court Service). They include: CDMIS (Central Determinations and Management Information System), which allows for automatic calculations for example in relation to legal aid and costs taxation; programs in relation to jury summoning and management service which will generate jurors' names from the Electoral Roll, produce summonses and records, record attendance and excusals, calculate expenses and maintain management information; and a case management project (CREDO), including the use of terminals in court, improvements to CREST, management information systems and links to external criminal justice agencies. As for the Court of Appeal (Criminal Division), the existing system (CACTUS – Criminal Appeals Case Tracking User System) apparently "meets all the current requirements for case tracking and office support" (Court Service Information Services Division, 1998: para.5.3.1).

After years of underinvestment, the "front-office" full-time judicial staff, but not the 30,000 or so lay magistrates, have been issued with personal computers by the Court Service from 1996 onwards under the JUDITH (Judicial IT Help) project. The mission is to allow access to the judicial communications network known as FELIX, which comprises open and closed conference facilities, a messaging system including the ability to transfer files (Court Service Information Services Division, 1998: paras. 3.2; Mander, 1993; Brooke, 1998). Access to ICTs is meant to confer a number of benefits for the judiciary (Woolf, 1996: ch. 21). It allows the efficient accessing or inputting of data in the courtroom, including the taking of bench-notes from which directions to a jury, a judgement or a sentence can be compiled. A further important task identified for judges is the proactive formulation of case plans and their execution. Even the humble personal laptop computer can facilitate easy access to court documents from home or while on circuit. Litigation support technologies include document indexing, review, search and full text retrieval and document image processing to assist with discovery and trial. The expectation of the Court Service is that "In the immediate future...all staff and all judges will need to have access to a computer to do their work" (Court Service Information Services Division, 1998: para. 1.1.4).

Yet the results so far are mixed. Some insiders relate that the uptake of ICT has been "an immense success", though it is driven by the personal initiative and enthusiasm of individuals from the cohort of higher judiciary and has not received the funding and training necessary to make the same outcome universal (Brooke, 1998). Others paint a less rosy picture. The Lord Chancellor's Department's *Consultation Paper* recognizes two problems:

> The first is that not all judges who want technology have yet been equipped, although plans are in hand to overcome this shortcoming. The second is that many judges will not want to use ICT even if it is available. There is scope here for firmer targets. It could be stipulated that, within five years, every judge in the land is expected to use IT in his or her daily work.
>
> (Lord Chancellor's Department, 1998: ch. 4)

Whether this big stick materializes remains to be seen. It is in any event disappointing to hear that the judiciary may be forced to take up ICT strategies on the government's terms. The channel of communication provided by the Internet could be an important safeguard for judicial independence – allowing the judges to explain themselves to the public without the spin of government or even the self-serving interests of the media interfering with the message.

There is little or no mention of the Internet in the foregoing survey. Naturally, facilities such as e-mail have become an expected part of any office environment, in courthouses as elsewhere. The provision of word processing, e-mail and conferencing facilities has been agreed between the Court Service and the Judicial Technology Group (JTG); it is also planned that a pilot project to evaluate the benefits to the judiciary of using the Internet will be taken forward. This work will form part of the Government Secure Intranet (GSI), which will eventually replace the role of FELIX in providing e-mail and conferencing facilities for all judges (Court Service Information Services Division, 1998: para. 10.1). So, as already related, all judges are to receive computers, and training is to be offered in consultation with the Judicial Studies Board (Brooke, 2000). In addition, computerization of the judges, in conjunction with the passage of the Human Rights Act 1998, has certainly encouraged a demand for access to the Internet in order to obtain legal source material (such as the judgements of the European Court of Human Rights). In this way, an objective for the Internet may be to bolster the knowledge base of lawyers and the ways in which experiences can be shared. The ability to access and store information, as the Judicial Studies Board has begun to do through its website,[2] could have profound implications for the style of judgements, which should become more dependent on reasoning and less on the inherent wisdom, pragmatism and authority of the judge. It is possible that what counts as precedent could also change. Internet technology allied to other forms of ICTs could ensure that most cases from Crown Court upwards could be recorded and reported. But the prospect of a judicial free-for-all in which the most Herculean dispenser of justice can outstrip any colleagues of higher rank or from a more prestigious venue, and in which the choice is between thousands of precedents rather than those officially reported, has set alarm bells ringing. Consequently, the courts have tried to handle the potential flood of unreported and low-level cases by placing strict limits on them (*Roberts Petroleum Ltd v Bernard Kenny Ltd*, 1983; Practice Statement, 1998). In *Michaels and Michaels v Taylor Woodrow Developments* (2000), Mr Justice Laddie expressed his concern that computerized databases of court cases would raise legal costs both through pre-trial research and trial elongation. Whilst the English trial court can and does demand leave to cite an unreported case, this does not avoid the need for research, and so he mused upon a system whereby a decision might be designated, as in the US Federal Rules of Practice Rule 47.6(b), as "Nonprecedential Opinion or Order", though he remarked laconically that this system does depend "on a degree of modesty by the courts which occasionally may not exist" (para. 38). More positively, it has been agreed that electronic databases should be encouraged by a new system of citation and paragraph numbering for judgements (Practice Direction, 2001).

Another form of knowledge-based development through the exchange of information could involve the use of local area networks to create localized guidelines and practices, for example in regard to sentencing. These might be especially relevant to magistrates' courts, wherein the new managerialism has often been an excuse for the stifling rather than the encouragement of local initiative (Raine, 1989: 176).

The ultimate achievement of ICTs would be the replacement of the humanoid judge with some kind of expert-system software which reaches smart decisions in response to the input of sets of data facts. As legal information becomes readily accessible, it is said that the role of the lawyer will become less the demonstrator of legal texts or dispute resolver and more the legal risk assessor and knowledge engineer (Susskind, 1996). There may be at least two flaws to this thesis. One is that the inherent complexity and open texture of many laws means that mere accessibility and knowledge do not, without the training of a lawyer, allow sound interpretation according to legal science. Law in the real world is not about "rule-based, deterministic decisions" but is an interpretative life science which requires weighting and judgement between values based on moral precepts (Anderson *et al.*, 1993: 1771, 1800). Given this normative setting, it seems most unlikely that any Internet-based program could either achieve the subtlety required or avoid undue legal conservatism by always settling in conventional terms. The other doubt is whether the law is, or will ever be, electronically available to the citizen in the street. Such an objective is very difficult to achieve, given the rapidly and constant changing composition of law, especially in a common law, uncodified system.

Inter-agency office linkages

The effective interfacing of ICTs within different legal process agencies represents a major challenge in both civil and criminal justice sectors. Not only are technical difficulties to be overcome, but the ethics of data collection, storage and use should not be ignored (Hebenton and Thomas, 1993). The systems to be linked include not only CREST and MASS but also the Prison Service Local Inmate Database System (LIDS), the Probation Service Case Record and Administration System (CRAMS), the CPS Standard Case Operations (SCOPE) and the police's Police/Home Office Enhanced Names Index (PHOENIX). The Information Technology and the Courts (ITAC) Committee was formed in 1988 from seven constituent bodies – the Bar Council, the Law Society, the Society for Computers and the Law, the Crown Prosecution Service, the Lord Chancellor's Department, the Metropolitan Police and the Serious Fraud Office. The membership has since grown by inclusion of the Home Office (apparently replacing the Lord Chancellor's Department), the Central Computer and Telecommunications Agency (CCTA), the Council of Circuit Judges, the Association of District Judges, the Legal Aid Board and the Justices Clerks Society Information Technology Policy Committee. ITAC recommended in 1990 that a single policy body be established to direct and coordinate the introduction of court technology. The task in regard to the criminal courts has hitherto been entrusted to the Committee for the Co-ordination of the Computerisation of the Criminal Justice System (CCCJS). The CCCJS was formed as a joint initiative between Home Office, Lord Chancellor's Department and Crown Prosecution Service. The first meeting was in 1989, and it comprises Magistrates' and Crown Courts, police, probation, Customs and Excise and DVLC representatives (Corbett, 1998, 1999b). Progress has been disappointing, with imperfect links between agencies and even within agencies (Glidewell Report, 1998: para. 8). Furthermore, its operation is far from comprehensive. For example, the development of police data handling systems, by far the most important in the criminal justice system, has never been within its clear purview and is the province of the distinct Police Information Technology Organisation (PITO), acting now under the authority of the Police Act 1997 Part IV.

The absence of some kind of Criminal Justice Information Technology Organisation (CJITO), as suggested by the Glidewell Report (1998: paras 14, 26) especially one subsuming PITO, means that interagency linkages are under-developed. As a result, a further attempt to redress the situation has been made by the establishment of the project, Integrating Business and Information Systems in the Criminal Justice System (IBIS, 1999). The project draws together the police, prosecution, criminal courts, probation and prisons authorities and reports to a Ministerial Steering Group comprised of representatives from the Home Office, Lord Chancellor's Department, Attorney General's Office and the Treasury. It has the following purposes, progress on which should be secured by 2005: achieving just, effective and efficient processes; meeting the needs of victims, witnesses and jurors; and respecting the rights of defendants

(IBIS, 1999: 7). It is the particular role of IBIS to ensure the development of a strategic plan and to set policies and standards across agencies, but in doing so it faces several inherent difficulties. For instance, IBIS is established as a project rather than an agency. In this way it has no executive powers – it cannot direct but must persuade. Further, a number of important and relevant official agencies deemed outside "the central core" are not within the project (IBIS, 1999: 9). Those cast into the outer darkness include the Serious Fraud Office, the revenue agencies, the Forensic Science Service and a range of authorities, such as the Benefits Agency, which collect data of great value to criminal justice administration.

One might compare the more directed approach in the USA Federal Courts, where the Judicial Conference of the United States represents all Federal judges and controls the Administrative Office of the United States Courts and the Federal Judicial Centre (the principal function of which is judicial training). It is responsible for the Long Range Plan for Automation in the US Courts of 1992 and for administration of the Judiciary Automation Fund which was created by Act in 1990 (28 U.S.C. 612), approving the expenditure of $71.4 million on computerization of the Federal Courts, to be spent in accordance with the annual revisions to the Long Range Plan through the Office of Automation and Technology (OAT) of the Administrative Office of the United States Courts. The Judicial Conference has a Committee on Automation and Technology consisting of fourteen Judges. Likewise, the Technical Information Service of the National Center for State Courts (NCSC) is the principal coordinating body for the use of information technology in State Courts. The National Center for State Courts[3] was founded in 1971 on the advice of Chief Justice Warren E. Burger in order to provide leadership and service to the state courts. Its Court Technology Programs include a Technology Information Service containing information about available software and equipment suppliers.

Court machinery in public use

The initial principal application of ICTs in the public arena of the criminal courts has been in connection with fraud trials. This attention was signalled by the Roskill Report on Fraud Trials in 1986 (Roskill, 1986: paras.6.66, 9.25; Purnell, 1990; Home Office, 1998a). Amongst the reasons are that fraud trials involve complexity both of evidence gathering and presentation, as well as contexts which might be very unfamiliar to the person in the jury box. The digital marshalling and graphic representation of evidence can help enormously. A second, more recent application of ICTs has been in connection with the evidence-giving of litigants, for example, to screen juries or vulnerable witnesses through video-conferencing or other linkages. Typically, prosecutions involving crimes against children, in which video evidence or live links are deployed, are now encouraged by the Youth Justice and Criminal Evidence Act 1999, Part II (Home Office, 1998b; Birch, 2000).

It is almost certain that technology will make a much fuller impact in a much wider range of cases once the recommendations of Lord Justice Auld's Committee on the Review of the Criminal Courts have been implemented. It is widely expected that Lord Justice Auld will follow the precedent in the civil process of the *Woolf Report*, which expresses the belief that ICTs will not only streamline existing systems and processes but will also become "a catalyst for radical change as well" (Woolf, 1996: ch. 21, para.1; Widdison, 1997a; 1997b).

Aside from the development of official policy, the environment in which the courts operate will likewise conduce to the development of court machinery with which the public can engage. In this way, even if, as described previously, not all judges are self-motivated to take up ICTs, there will be pressures from other court users which force them to keep pace. For example, there is an increasing use of ICT by solicitors and barristers (Wall, 2000), with the consequent need for protocols about systems and formats and the possible linkage of courts to professions already envisaged by the Court Service (Court Service Information Services Division, 1998: para.1.1.6). In practical terms, the links will involve electronic communications with courts, the electronic publication of information, and support for lawyers' ICT equipment in court and in court buildings. The application of ICTs to the litigants in court could include the presentation and computer-aided transcription (CAT) in real time of evidence. This allows not only a clear and accurate record which avoids the need for any read-backs or note-taking, but also searching, indexing, linking, annotating and analytical procedures not possible with the printed word. The production of a transcript in this way could, of course, assist with publication via the Internet, a point considered later.

The Court Service has expressed great interest in all of this technology which it sees as having an important role in the "courtroom of the future" (Court Service Information Services Division, 1998: paras.5.4.6, 6.1). The model often cited, drawing together many advanced techniques, is the Courtroom 21 Project, which is a joint project of the William & Mary School of Law (Virginia) and the National Center for State Courts,[4] and is billed as "The World's Most Technologically Advanced Courtroom". It is used for both demonstration purposes and occasionally actual trials. Plans are now well-advanced for a similar project based at the Department of Law at the University of Leeds.

Outward-looking multimedia portals for the public

There are several ways in which the Internet could facilitate engagement between the courts and the public.

Improvements in the quality of the process

Lord Woolf certainly saw this potential of ICTs:

[T]echnology could provide the basis for information systems, available in court building and other public places, to guide the public and court and legal matters....Given the projected level of usage of the World Wide Web, this should be one of the preferred means of delivery of information for the public. Additionally, I am impressed by the idea of using more general community information systems for the delivery of legal guidance.

(Woolf, 1996: ch. 21, para. 9)

The Court Service already has Internet pages[5] with organizational and policy information and a scattering of court judgements. Listing information for the Commercial Court is available on the Internet from other sources.[6] Another current source of information on the Internet is Smith Bernal, the official short-hand-writers, who have made available a wide range of court transcripts since May 1996, though now mainly on a subscription basis.[7] House of Lords' judgements are also available,[8] as are Acts of Parliament.[9] It is proposed that all Court Service-related material will eventually be available on the Court Service site (Court Service Information Services Division, 1998: para.11.2.1). As far as the Lord Chancellor's Department is concerned:

Future plans include providing Daily Lists from other divisions of the High Court, and increasing the number and variety of judgements available on the site. It is also intended to put onto the site a large number of the most commonly used court forms and information leaflets, which would help small businesses, the professions and organisations such as Citizens Advice Bureaux.

(Lord Chancellor's and Officers' Departments, 1998a, A para.105)

However, these grand plans also cause concern, as the Court Service has admitted that "there has been no clear policy for co-ordinating publication of information...and this could lead to more fragmentation and an undue drain on Court Service resources" (Court Service Information Services Division, 1998: para.8.3). Furthermore, much of this initiative is consumerist in nature – the consumers here being the legal professions.

The Court Service does envisage the eventual use of intelligent kiosks to provide members of the public with a simple interface for requesting and providing information. In this way, "Kiosks are expected to support business strategy by improving the quality of service offered to the public and by reducing the level of routine and repetitive work being carried out [by court staff]" (Court Service Information Services Division, 1998: para.11.3.1). Members of the public and lawyers should be able to obtain or file court documents through the Internet which could be utilized for electronic data exchange. All these possibilities are strongly endorsed by the Lord Chancellor's Department's *Consultation Paper* (1998: chs 3 and 5). A practical step has been taken by the Community Legal Service, set up under section 4 of the Access to Justice Act 1999 and with one of its objects being "the provision of general information about the law and legal system and the availability of legal services." Pursuant to this aim, it has established the Just Ask! website,[10] though this is much more a listing of other sites than a new source of information (see Lord Chancellor's Department, 2000).

In these ways, the law could become more available to the "latent legal market" (Susskind, 1996). This will leave private lawyers to cater for the wealthier sector of the legal market, though the implications of opening up in this way may be both palatable and unpalatable:

> [T]he prospect that formal law might become broadly accessible, a part of everyday existence for most people, is quite revolutionary and not without controversy. But that revolution is what information technologies will make possible...Some observers note the increasing encroachment of law on daily life–the "juridification" of the social sphere – with trepidation. Others, however...either assume or applaud it. The debate turns on many things, including fundamentally conflicting visions of what "law" is: Is it a weapon of destruction that threatens to tear the social fabric as its influence spreads, or it is an essential system of support for valued and valuable social relationships?
>
> (Anderson *et al.*, 1993: 1799)

Certainly, such an approach would eventually have radical impact on what constitutes "the court", since in the future:

> The marketplace for virtually all goods and services, including justice, [will be] the network itself, cyberspace. The courts' physical forums [will be] steadily, inexorably disappearing.
>
> (Johnson, 1993: 1751)

By this process, technology can be used to shift radically the nature of the court's persona; it becomes not just a paper-free and networked environment but takes on a virtual existence. Other jurisdictions have already started along this path, including, at various levels, in the USA[11] and also in Singapore.[12]

The denunciatory function of justice – naming and shaming

The advent of a policy of naming and shaming, whether with felons, failing schools or feckless hospital surgeons, can offer yet another facet for Internet use. In the case of the criminal justice system, changes of policy have so far been related to the readier identification of juveniles and young persons found guilty in court. In addition, police forces in a number of US localities have also sought to encourage publicity for certain categories of adult offender, such as those involved with prostitution. These are often relatively low-level offences, which might otherwise escape the attention of newspapers. But the posting of names and photos on the Internet, a record which certainly lasts longer than a newspaper and reaches a much wider audience, may be a further disincentive to transgression. An example of this policy in action is the public notification pages of the police of St Paul, Minnesota,[13] which even includes arrestees, and is billed as a "direct response to the fears, anger and demands expressed by law-abiding men and women". Other conceivable offence types which might be treated in this way include shoplifters and child sex offenders, whose photographs are already circulated amongst police forces and by police forces to vulnerable localities. Fine defaulters are to be exposed in several magistrates' courts areas in England and Wales. Stolen vehicle registers might also benefit from the wider publicity of the Internet, though police education is necessary before many of the opportunities are realized (Hyde, 1999).

Naming and shaming can work for defendants as well as plaintiffs or prosecutors. The low cost and accessibility of the Internet allow individuals and groups to obtain a hearing for their legal points, to an extent which they could not afford in other media outlets and in circumstances where court appearances might not be available. One can expect that persons claiming a miscarriage of justice will make prominent use of the Internet in the future – and in fact they do so already.[14]

The Internet might also be used to produce a public dialogue about sentencing and the degree of naming and shaming. Rather than leaving it to a judge or magistrate to express the limits of tolerance of the community, sentencing levels and priorities might be shaped in this way, just as policing plans are supposed to embody the results of public soundings.

Active public participation in the justice system

The conflict between community involvement in, and professionalization of, the criminal justice system provides the organizing theme for this sub-issue. This conflict has become particularly acute in England and Wales, where trends of specialization, technological sophistication and managerialism have tended to marginalize the role for lay persons within the environment of criminal justice. These trends can be evidenced by diminished lay involvement in the judiciary, for example, through an increase in professional magistrates (Seago *et al.*, 2000). Lay involvement in trial process in the form of the jury also seems to face official hostility. For example, there are also concerns about the efficiency of juries in either-way cases (Home Office, 1995; 1999) and the viability of juries in dealing with complex frauds (Home Office, 1998a) which arise from a tension between efficiency and technical accuracy versus community involvement and the mediation of law through social standards. At the same time, there would be no advantage if professional oligarchies were to be replaced by the "self perpetuation" of particular social strata, especially the middle class who "provide the backbone of the Bench and form its dominant culture" (Raine, 1989: 66). So the Internet could be used to reach out to a wider clientele and, in that way, improve the provision of justice within the system. Thus it would help if the public was more familiar with the local courts and their processes. Becoming a juror or a magistrate might seem less extraordinary or difficult. In regard to the magistracy, a broader knowledge in this way might also avoid that "self perpetuation" of a particular social stratum. Of course, Internet users are at present also predominantly middle class, though there are several government initiatives afoot to ameliorate this social exclusivity (Walker and Akdeniz, 1998). So the immediate impact of Internet recruitment might be to encourage a younger, rather than a more socially diverse, cohort.

There is a more general audience to reach. Part of the characteristic of local justice at Magistrates' Court level is meant to be the accessibility of the local courthouse. This accessibility is diminishing as courthouses are closed, but even if the physical entity becomes more remote, its virtual presence can become more readily accessible, and to a potentially greater audience than the relatively few members of the public who have ever bothered to sit in a public gallery. The two can be linked – the Internet could be used to advertise open days in the physical court buildings and to allow the public to be informed as to past, present and future cases, as well as giving more general information about the nature of the courts and their business.

In summary, the Internet could become the virtual welcome mat for the public. It could provide citizens with an overview of the court, audio clips of welcome and explanations and, above all, an invitation to participate.

Educating the passive wider community

The courts may be the third and least dangerous estate, but they are nevertheless part of the state, and it behoves all democrats to take note of what is being transacted in their name. So, how far can ordinary citizens inform themselves as to the courts and their business and personnel via the Internet? Potentially, the answer is a great deal, but the reality falls far short of that point.

This verdict applies, for example, to the availability of the basic legal materials – the statutes and cases. Lord Woolf complained of the "allegedly excessive costs" levied for permission to reproduce primary legal source materials such as statutes (Woolf, 1996: ch. 21, para.10). Since 1996, the position has significantly improved. Statutes are now increasingly available at the website of the Stationery Office.[15] But the presentation of contemporary individual statutes in this segmented way is of limited value. It makes no link to important factors such as commencement dates, secondary legislation, later amendments or case interpretation. As for case reports, as already noted, House of Lords judgements are online at public websites, as is a scattering of selected cases from other tiers of the court structure. Official concerns about copyright seem to be diminishing, but there is still no completion in sight for an official comprehensive and consolidated statute book, despite plans for its birth set out years ago. Much more ambitious systems exist elsewhere, including the Australasian Legal Information Institute,[16] the emerging UK equivalent, the British and Irish Legal Information Institute, which was established in 2000,[17] and in several US states, such as the People's Law Library of Maryland[18] and the "Access Initiative" of the Supreme Court of Florida.[19]

With these precedents in mind, it is obvious that, in England and Wales too, the Internet could "change the distance between the Court and the public" (Katsh, 1995: 163). An altered stance may in any event become necessary with the passage of the Human Rights Act and the further juridification of political and social life, which means that "the judicial system will serve as a forum for civic discourse about the norms and values that underlie those disputes and will play a significant role in building or reshaping the social, economic, and political institutions involved in them" (Anderson *et al.*, 1993: 1762). In this way, technology and modes of communication can be (re)constitutive of the nature of the institution, including – by encouraging a wider range of evidence and advocacy – becoming relevant at trial (Chesterman, 1997: 143). Admittedly, the Internet might not be the only way of achieving the goal of reaching out to a passive and ignorant public. An alternative is shown by the American-based cable channel, Court TV, which commenced operations in 1991.[20] This tends to give greatest prominence to current reporting of well-publicized cases, especially those being reported on the cable TV side of the operation, and so does not present an entirely balanced picture of life in the courts (Harris, 1993). Yet the prospect of a UK equivalent seems remote. Successive senior members of the judiciary have turned their faces against the televising of court proceedings (Metz, 1996). Nevertheless, the judges have recognized the value of having some channel of communication within their own grasp, and, following cases in which they felt they were misquoted or misrepresented (especially when dealing with sex offenders), they have been advised by the Lord Chancellor's Department to ensure that journalists are provided with a written summary of sentencing remarks in cases likely to attract media interest. The Internet could afford access directly by the public to such information. Indeed, the Internet could provide a third way to the debate about televising or not televising. The technology offers the possibility of real-time transcription which can then be published to a wide audience at low cost: for example, live "webcasts" of proceedings are now available at courts in Florida, Indiana and Ohio (Samborn, 2000). This strategy has several advantages over live broadcasting (assuming livecasting is not utilized). It avoids the perceived intrusiveness and distraction of television. The emphasis is on what is said in court rather than, say, the colour of the defendant's eyes or the shortness of the prosecutor's skirt. The text (or at least the website) could also be linked to wider legal information which could provide explanations of terms and processes in more general terms. The second advantage is cost. Specialist television channels such as Court TV would probably not be viable in the UK, since there is not sufficient volume of cases of interest to the public.

If the courts and judiciary do not manage the public interface with the legal system, then it seems increasingly likely that the litigants and their lawyers will take that step. In fact, a study by the Lord Chancellor's Advisory Committee on Legal Education and Conduct, *Lawyers' Comments to the Media* (1997), found that the police were the principal utilizers of media outlets, outstripping the instances of defence lawyer intervention by a long way. The media can be conceived of as part of the criminal justice system which is meant to be both in public and publicly accountable; the media thus assist with account-giving and the ability of the courts to give an account (Ericson, 1995). But the relationship is at present restricted by the bureaucratic nature of much court work and by the distance of key figures within it, such as judge and jury. The Internet cannot alter these basic circumstances, but it could provide a way both for journalists and for the public as a whole to be afforded greater insights into court work, far more so than the very limited advice on news management in the Lord Chancellor's Department booklet, *The Media: A Guide for Judges* (2000).

An alternative forum for dispute resolution

There is great interest in alternative dispute resolution on the civil side (Lord Chancellor's Department, 2000a, paras.2.11 and 3.4). Almost as strongly in the criminal process, the victim support movement has prompted the questioning of traditional adversarial justice which is seen as often exclusionary from the point of view of the victim. In any event, boundaries between civil and criminal law are breaking down, as illustrated by the Protection from Harassment Act 1997 and the Crime and Disorder Act 1998. Here again, the Internet may provide a possible model which can transcend the simple replication of traditional paper-based processes in a computerized environment. In this way, "the courtroom [becomes] only one component of a much greater dispute resolution system", all served by the same technology (Lederer and Soloman, 1997). A number of private Internet-based ADR systems have been attempted, including the Virtual Magistrate[21] at Villanova University, and iCourthouse.[22]

Breaking down the public–private divide along similar but more authoritative lines, the Court Service or the police could offer standard forms and advice for private mediation. In this way, the Court Service could become multi-layered, with different doors for different purposes. The Lord Chancellor's Department is sympathetic to these ideas on the civil side. But the avoidance of formal courts brings dangers. If courts, especially local courts, are to appreciate and reflect local concerns and outlooks, this almost certainly requires some public expression of the perceived culture of the locality. And there is value in the solemnity of the court setting in terms of truth-giving and truth-finding.

Conclusions

In common with its application in other "political" settings (Walker and Akdeniz, 1998) the Internet has been both underutilized overall and mainly confined to one-way information transfer rather than two-way communication. There is, of course, some benefit in information transfer in this way. Internet technology allows the disembedding of time and space, so that, for example, knowledge which was once the preserve of an exclusive gatekeeping profession such as lawyers can be made more widely available even to those who do not attend courts or law libraries and can be made available instantaneously. The virtual legal community is far less bounded than its physical counterpart and could provide a forum for taking soundings on judicial policies and performance as well as providing more committed and informed lay participants within the process. As was said by the European Court of Human Rights in *Worm v Austria*:

> There is general recognition of the fact that the courts cannot operate in a vacuum. Whilst the courts are the forum for the determination of a person's guilt or innocence on a criminal charge...this does not mean that there can be no prior or contemporaneous discussion of the subject matter of criminal trials elsewhere, be it in specialised journals, in the general press or amongst the public at large...
>
> (*Worm v Austria*, 1997: para. 50)

But this wider perspective tends to be lost in the New Public Management approach largely taken to date. Though the criminal courts have not yet been audited in respect of the application of the Internet, this task has been undertaken in regard to the civil courts. The aims of the Lord Chancellor's Department Consultation Paper, *Resolving and Avoiding Disputes in the Information Age*, appear wide and balanced (Lord Chancellor's Department, 1998: Preface).

So far, the most important benefits we have discussed have been:

- increasing efficiency and so cutting costs;
- improved justice and access to justice;
- better productivity and so reduction in delays;
- greater public confidence in the justice system.

So, alongside the usual concerns for economy, efficiency and effectiveness, there is an apparent concern with justice and access to justice, placing the emphasis on substance rather than process and even reorienting the nature of justice: "We ask is the court a service or a place?" (Lord Chancellor's Department, 1998: Preface). But there is ultimately an overwhelming customer-service orientation, which means that: "In the future, however, there is the possibility that IT will eventually enable legal services to change from being a form of advisory service to a type of information product" (Lord Chancellor's Department, 1998: ch. 2). This runs the danger that the customer is king and will lead to even less being known to the public about court transactions and even less public involvement in the court process. The more the courts are conceived of in terms of being a service at the behest of the private litigant, the more the consumer litigant will question the public aspects of the service. It also leads to the concern that the quality of justice must suffer, as is admitted in the following comment:

> Even if a virtual hearing is less satisfactory than the conventional method, is it not preferable that many more cases could be disposed of, even if at a lesser standard (a Rolls Royce for a few or a Mondeo for many)?
>
> (Lord Chancellor's Department, 1998: ch. 4)

Conversely, the *Consultation Paper* expresses very little concern for the non-consuming but onlooking public. They are hardly recognized in the Paper and are problematic when they do fleetingly make an appearance:

> Future use of digital audio recording in courts opens up the prospect of the live, digitised sound from a hearing being transmitted back to a solicitor's office for study and research. In high profile cases an audio feed might eventually be made available over the Internet, or via a private service running over the Internet. This may also prove possible with video in the longer term, but this would raise even more issues than audio transmissions.
>
> (Lord Chancellor's Department, 1998: ch. 5)

Too often these wider matters are seen as merely "ancillary effects" or issues (Anderson *et al.*, 1993: 1765).

Before complaining about the lack of progress by the courts in taking to the new modes of communication, it is worth entering some caveats. One is to challenge the assumption that ICTs are bound to deliver the expected benefits. Their use in organizational change is unpredictable, as the social contexts into which they are inserted can profoundly impact on the directions of exploitation (Bellamy and Taylor, 1998).

Conversely, their potential to achieve a powerful impact, bringing about the dematerialization of court process, may not be as desirable as the advocates of change may pretend. The saving of the rainforest by the advent of the paperless court file is one thing, but the abolition of "old style, face-to-face hearings", even on appeal or rehearing, is quite another. The point is not simply about how well testimony and real evidence can be effectively tested in a virtual setting, a point raised earlier. Rather, participation and observance are important rights which signify the autonomy of the defendant and the legitimacy of public oversight, as has been recognized under Articles 6 and 10 of the European Convention. Equally, the idea that witnesses and the jury could operate more efficiently if dispersed (presumably to the costless site of their own abodes, as allowed by the Criminal Justice and Public Order Act 1994, section 43), not only raises vulnerabilities in terms of contamination by attention to extraneous evidence, intimidation and the insecurity of communications, but ignores the way in which personal interaction may assist in the verdict-making process. These concerns actually arose in *People of Colorado v Kriho* (2000), in which there were complaints that a juror sought information from the Internet about possible sentences. So, orality remains not just a "ritual" but a central feature of the adversarial process, both in court and in the jury room, and the distanciation or dissolution of the courthouse can be seen to result in the diminution of justice as well as a silencing of civic expression. In addition, the complexities and costs of the new technologies may threaten the equality of arms between prosecution and defence, with the result that the latter may be unable to explore and expose the defects in the former's construction of events. Furthermore, the uncoordinated use of technology may confuse the jury and increase costs and delay (Trammell, 1995). Conversely, linkages between different databases held by criminal justice agencies, as propounded by the interagency CCCJS or IBIS, may easily threaten rights to privacy.

In terms of substantive goals to be achieved in England and Wales, what at first sight appear to be radically empowering policy developments turn out, like many other parts of the "New Labour" reform agenda, to be more about modernization than democratization. This may be true of development of ICT policy in general, and it certainly seems to be true of ICT strategy in the courts, as is reflected by the following, narrowly conceived principles on which the Court Service's overall strategy is based (Court Service Information Services Division, 1998: para.2.1):

The Court Service IT strategy is based on the following principles:
- the IT strategy will be determined by the business strategy, which will take full advantage of IT opportunities;
- all new information systems (IS) services should be provided under a Private Finance Initiative (PFI) contract;
- where possible existing PFI contracts will be used for the provision of such IS services;
- no IS development or technical support work will be undertaken by Court Service staff.

The more specific objectives with respect to the criminal justice system are "...to modernise administrative procedures in the Crown Court and to improve links with all the other agencies involved in the criminal justice system. Improving procedures will result in much-enhanced efficiency and higher quality of service" (Court Service Information Services Division, 1998: para.5.1). Without a single reference to accessibility, democracy, participation or even justice, this is the language of Arthur Anderson, not Thomas Paine. At a time when pressures are often for greater seclusion of the criminal process and certainly for greater technocratization and managerialism, the Internet could counterbalance some of the exclusivity of the process. It is time to move ICTs from the back-office towards public engagement and to achieve change that is even more radical and participatory than Lord Woolf and other commentators have predicted.

Notes

1 Note: The author thanks Professor Horton Rogers, University of Nottingham, and Gill Woolfson of IBIS, for the provision of source materials.
2 www.jsboard.co.uk
3 www.ncsconline.org
4 www.courtroom21.net
5 www.courtservice.gov.uk
6 www.smlawpub.co.uk
7 www.casetrack.com/casetrack_frame.htm
8 www.parliament.the-stationery-office.co.uk/pa/ld199697/ldjudgmt/ldjudgmt.htm
9 www.hmso.gov.uk/acts.htm
10 www.justask.org.uk
11 www.ncsc.dni.us/court/sites/courts.htm;
www.supreme.state.az.us/courthelp;
www.courts.state.co.us/ct-index.htm;
www.uscourts.gov/ttb/oct99ttb/newcases.html
12 www.supcourt.gov.sg/compute/computeindex.htm
13 www.stpaul.gov/police/prostitution.htm
14 See the links at www.leeds.ac.uk/law/hamlyn/1miscarr.htm
15 www.hmso.gov.uk/acts.htm
16 AustLII – www.austlii.edu.au
17 www.bailii.org
18 www.peoples-law.com
19 www.firn.edu/supct or www.flcourts.org
20 www.courttv.com
21 vmag.vcilp.org
22 www.i-courthouse.com

(all checked 20 June 2001).

References

Cases

Michaels and Michaels v Taylor Woodrow Developments (2000) High Court.
People of Colorado v Kriho (2000), 2000 Colo. LEXIS, p. 383.
Roberts Petroleum Ltd v Bernard Kenny Ltd (1983), Appeal Cases, p. 192.
Worm v Austria Appl.no. 22714/93, 1997-V (1998) European Human Rights Law Reports, vol. 25 , p. 454.

Texts

Anderson, R., Borgenson, E., Brest, P. *et al.* (1993) "The impact of information technology on judicial administration: a research agenda for the future", *Southern California Law Review*, 66: 1762.
Bellamy, C. and Taylor, J. (1998) *Governing in the Information Age*, Buckingham: Open University Press.
Birch, D. (2000) "A better deal for vulnerable witnesses", *Criminal Law Review*, 223.
Brooke, Lord Justice H. (1998) "IT and the Courts of England and Wales: the Next Ten Years", 13th BILETA Conference: "The Changing Jurisdiction", Dublin; available at www.bileta.ac.uk/ (checked 20 June 2001).
—— (2000) "IT and the courts on both sides of Hadrian's Wall", *Computers and Law*, 11: 3.

Chesterman, M. (1997) "OJ and the Dingo: how media publicity relating to criminal cases tried by jury is dealt with in Australia and America", *American Journal of Comparative Law*, 45: 109.

Corbett, T. (1998) "The use of electronic paperwork in the justice system", *Justice of the Peace*, 162: 97.

—— (1999a) "Keeping magistrates informed", *Justice of the Peace*, 163: 968.

—— (1999b) "Changes to the criminal justice sector's use of information technology", *Justice of the Peace*, 163: 865.

Court Service Information Services Division (1998) *Information Technology (IT) Strategy*; available at www.courtservice.gov.uk/itstrat.htm (checked 20 June 2001).

Ericson, R.V. (1995) "The news media and accountability in criminal justice", in P.C. Stenning (ed.), *Accountability for Criminal Justice*, Toronto: University of Toronto Press.

Glidewell Report (1998) *Review of the Crown Prosecution Service, Report* (Cm.3960), London: Stationery Office.

Harris, B.A. (1993) "The Appearance of Justice: Court TV, Conventional Television, and Public Understanding of the Criminal Justice System", *Arizona Law Review*, 35: 785.

Hebenton, B. and Thomas, T. (1993) *Criminal Records: state, citizen and the politics of protection*, Aldershot: Avebury.

Home Office (1995) *Mode of Trial* (Cm.2908), London: HMSO.

—— (1998a) *Juries in Serious Fraud Trials*, London: HMSO.

—— (1998b) "Report of the Interdepartmental Working Group on the Treatment of Vulnerable or Intimidated Witnesses in the Criminal Justice System", *Speaking Up for Justice*, London: HMSO.

—— (1999) *Determining mode of trial in either-way cases*, available at www.homeoffice.gov.uk/cpd/pvu/contrial.htm (checked 20 June 2001).

Hyde, S. (1999) "A few coppers change", *Journal of Information, Law and Technology*, 2.

IBIS (Integrating Business and Information Systems in the Criminal Justice System) (1999) *Medium Strategic Plan for Information Systems in the Criminal Justice System*, London: HMSO.

Johnson, P.J. (1993) "Introduction: planning for the next century in the California courts", *Southern California Law Review*, 66: 1751.

Katsh, M.E. (1995) *Law in a Digital World*, Oxford: Oxford University Press.

Lederer, F.I. and Soloman, S.H. (1997) "Courtroom Technology – An Introduction To The Onrushing Future", *Fifth National Court Technology Conference* (CTC5); available at www.ncsc.dni.us/NCSC/TIS/CTC5/103.HTM (checked 20 June 2001).

Lord Chancellor's Advisory Committee on Legal Education and Conduct (1997) *Lawyers' Comments to the Media*, London: Lord Chancellor's Department.

Lord Chancellor's Department (1998) *Consultation Paper: Resolving and Avoiding Disputes in the Information Age*, London: Lord Chancellor's Department.

—— (2000a) *The Media: A Guide for Judges*, London: Lord Chancellor's Department.

—— (2000b) *Civil Justice 2000*, London: Lord Chancellor's Department.

Lord Chancellor's and Officers' Departments (1998a) *Departmental Report* (Cm.3909), London: Stationery Office.

MacMillan, J.E. (1998) "Case management systems in the USA, 1998"; available at www.netjustice.com.au/content/ausconf1.html (checked 20 June 2001).

Mander, M. (1993) "The JUDITH Report", *International Journal of Law and Information Technology*, 1: 249.

Metz, S.A. (1996) "Justice through the eye of a camera: cameras in the courtrooms in the United States, Canada, England and Scotland", *Dickinson Journal of International Law*, 14: 673.

Narey, M. (1997) *Review of delay in the criminal justice system: A Report*, London: Home Office.

Practice Direction (2001) "Judgements: Form and Citation", *The Times*, 16 January.

Practice Statement (Supreme Court: Judgements) (1998) *Weekly Law Reports*, 1: 825.

Purnell, N. (1990) "Technology and the courtroom", *New Law Journal*, 140: 1064.

Raine, J.W. (1989) *Local Justice*, Edinburgh: T & T Clark.

Raine, J. and Wilson, M. (1993) *Managing Criminal Justice*, Hemel Hempstead: Harvester.

—— (1997) "Beyond managerialism in criminal justice", *Howard Journal*, 36: 80.

Roskill, Lord Justice (1986) *Fraud Trials Committee Report*, London: HMSO.

Samborn, H.V. (2000) "Plenty of seats in virtual courtroom", *ABA Journal*, February: 68.

Seago, P., Walker, C. and Wall, D. (2000) "The development of the professional magistracy in England and Wales", *Criminal Law Review*, 631.

Susskind, R. (1996) *The Future of Law: Facing the Challenges of Information Technology*, Oxford: Clarendon Press.

—— (2000) *Transforming the Law*, Oxford: Oxford University Press.

Tata, C. (2000) "Resolute ambivalence", *International Review of Law, Computers and Technology*, 14: 279.

Trammell, G.W. (1995) "Cirque du O.J.", *Court Technology Bulletin*, 7, 4; available at www.ncsconline.org (checked 20 June 2001).

Walker, C. (1996) "Fundamental rights, fair trials and the new audio-visual sector", *Modern Law Review*, 57: 517.

—— (1997–98) "Cybercontempt: fair trials and the internet", *Oxford Yearbook of Media and Entertainment Law*, 3: 1.

Walker, C. and Akdeniz, Y. (1998) "Virtual democracy", *Public Law*, 489.

Wall, D. (2000) "The new electric lawyer and legal practice in the information age", in Y. Akdeniz, C. Walker and D. Wall, *The Internet, Law and Society*, Harlow: Longman.

Widdison, R. (1997a) "Beyond Woolf: the virtual court house", *Web Journal of Current Legal Issues*, 2.

—— (1997b) "Electronic law practice", *Modern Law Review*, 60: 143.

Woolf, Lord H. (1996) *Access to Justice: Final Report*, London: Lord Chancellor's Department.

Index